CRUMBLED SMALL

THE COMMONWEALTH CARIBBEAN
IN WORLD POLITICS

Sir Ronald Sanders

HANSIB

First published in Great Britain in 2005
Hansib Publications Limited
London: PO Box 34621, London E17 4GL
Hertfordshire: Orchard Road, Royston, Hertfordshire SG8 5HA

www.hansib-books.com

ISBN 1 870518 86 1

Design and production by Books of Colour, Hertfordshire

Cover design by Graphic Resolutions, Hertfordshire

To the memory of
William G Demas who lived and died
a committed Caribbean integrationist

ACKNOWLEDGMENTS

I thank many people who have contributed in some way to this book. First, my publisher at Hansib, Arif Ali, who was determined that the book should be published. You are reading it, only because he so firmly believed that its contents should reach a wide audience. Second, Sir Shridath 'Sonny' Ramphal who in 1969, set me on a journey of learning about the Caribbean – an area in which I was born, but about which my education made me quite ignorant. I was assigned the production of several programmes to be broadcast through the Commonwealth Caribbean in the first project undertaken by a nascent Caribbean Broadcasting Union (CBU). The first programme was 'The West Indies Federation'. I went to interview Sir Shridath, then Attorney-General and Minister of State in the Ministry of Foreign Affairs of Guyana. He had been Solicitor-General and Assistant Attorney-General in the West Indian Federal government even though Guyana had opted to stay out of the Federation. He gave me John Mordecai's *The West Indies: The Federal Negotiations*, saying: "Read that first, and come back to talk to me". I still have the book, and the journey of Caribbean inquiry, upon which it launched me, continues. Third, William G Demas, in whose memory I have dedicated this book. I had the great privilege of working closely with him at the Caribbean Development Bank (CDB) in Barbados, and together we traversed the Region during the course of a year. His commitment to the Region was infectious. He raised the desirability of a political union of the Commonwealth Caribbean to the level of a religion, and, by his own unswerving belief, won ardent followers like me. What I learned from him, Sonny Ramphal and Sir Alister McIntyre about the imperatives of a politically unified Caribbean never stops resonating in my mind. Fourth, Dr Peter Lyon, who as Editor of *The Round Table: The Journal of Commonwealth Affairs* saw value in many of the pieces that now make up the whole of this book, and encouraged my writing. Fifth, Dr Anthony Payne and his wife Jill, both of whom advised me on the structure of the book, and, in Jill's case, edited some of it for publication. I have always admired Dr Payne's careful research and his impressive writing on small states and on the Caribbean in particular. Therefore, his advice was all the more cherished. Sixth, Tara-Lisa Persaud who painstakingly proof-read the chapters and supported the idea that the book should be published. Seventh, Rodney Gallagher, whose knowledge of financial services, and sense of fair play informed my thinking on these issues And, last, but not least, Lloyd Searwar, who throughout my adult life not only encouraged me to inquire, and to write on the problems facing the Caribbean, but, also, to help find and implement solutions.

Sir Ronald Sanders

ABBREVIATIONS

ACP	African, Caribbean and Pacific countries
CARICOM	Caribbean Community and Common market
CARIFTA	Caribbean Free Trade Association
CBI	Caribbean Basin Initiative
CDB	Caribbean Development Bank
CDERA	Caribbean Disaster Emergency Relief Association
CFATF	Caribbean Financial Action Task Force
CHA	Caribbean Hotels Association
CHOGM	Commonwealth Heads of Government Meeting
COMECON	Council for Mutual Economic Assistance
CRNM	Caribbean Regional Negotiating Machinery
CSME	Caribbean Single Market and Economy
CTO	Caribbean Tourism Organisation
EDF	European Development Fund
EEC	European Economic Community
EPA	Economic Partnership Agreement
EU	European Union
FATF	Financial Action Task Force
FTAA	Free Trade Area of the Americas
GATT	General Agreement on Tariffs and Trade
GATS	General Agreement on Trade in Services
HTCI	Harmful Tax Competition Initiative
IBRD	International Bank for Reconstruction and Development (World Bank)
IDA	International Development Agency
IMF	International Monetary Fund
NAFTA	North American Free Trade Agreement
OAS	Organisation of American States
ODA	Official Development Assistance
OECS	Organisation of Eastern Caribbean States
OECD	Organisation for Economic Co-operation and Development
OPEC	Organisation of Petroleum Exporting Countries
RSS	Regional Security System
UN	United Nations
WTO	World Trade Organisation
WTTC	World Travel and Tourism Council

CONTENTS

INTRODUCTION

The title of this book, *Crumbled Small: The Commonwealth Caribbean in World Politics* reflects both the small size of the independent states that comprise the Commonwealth Caribbean, and the fact that it is only crumbs from the table of the rich and powerful nations in the world economy that fall to this Region.

The title speaks as well of the 'Commonwealth' Caribbean, i.e. the Caribbean countries that are members of the Commonwealth. They are: Antigua and Barbuda, the Bahamas, Barbados, Belize, Dominica, Grenada, Guyana, Jamaica, St Kitts and Nevis, St Lucia, St Vincent and the Grenadines, and Trinidad and Tobago.[1] The British dependencies, Anguilla, the British Virgin Islands, Cayman Islands, Montserrat, and Turks and Caicos Islands are also part of the coterie of Caribbean small states and, though they are not independent, much of what is said about the Commonwealth Caribbean applies equally to them. They are all small states despite definitional semantics and constitutional niceties.

Many of the Chapters of this book have been published before individually; others have not. Assembling them in a single volume is an attempt to set-out the grave problems that Caribbean small states face in the international community, and to show that their prospects as individual states are far from bright.

The truth is that the small states of the Commonwealth Caribbean are in crisis. There is need for urgent action at the domestic, regional and international levels to spare them from sinking into widespread poverty and becoming client-states of larger nations upon whom they could become economically reliant. However, there is a pretence that things might get worse if they are acknowledged to be bad. Hence, no alarm has been sounded at this crisis by the governments of these countries. The closest statement to an alarm by a Head of Government was made by Said Musa, the Prime Minister of Belize in a 'State of the Nation' address to his people in September 2004 when he said: "The declines in the price of banana, sugar, citrus and shrimps are terms of trade shocks that decrease the growth potential and cause decline in sources of revenue. At the same time, the global instability brought on by terrorism and cross-border crime has been costly and detrimental to the expansion of new service industries… the options available to a small country in the face of a harsh global economic environment are, quite frankly, severely limited".[2]

THE GLOBAL CONTEXT

The Caribbean exists in a global economy in which more than half the population is forced to exist on less than US$2 a day; ten percent of the population enjoy 80 percent of its resources; the terms of trade are dictated by the powerful to the detriment of the weak; and the gap is widening between the few who are rich and ·prosperous and the many who are poor and helpless.

In the international order that has been evolving in the 21st Century, world governance is being increasingly usurped by a handful of powerful governments that impose their will through alliances with vested interests. Policy and rules are made in organisations controlled by the powerful few. As Joseph Stiglitz, the 2001 Nobel Prize winner for Economics, puts it, "We have a system that might be called *global governance without global government,* one in which a few institutions – the World Bank, the IMF, the WTO – and a few players – the finance, commerce and trade ministers, closely linked to certain financial and commercial interests – dominate the scene, but in which many of those affected by their decisions are left almost voiceless."[3] To his list, I would add the G8, the Organisation for Economic Co-operation and Development (OECD) and the Financial Action Task Force (FATF)[4].

In this new order, the United Nations – the only universal world body – can be sidelined by a super-power and its allies. Even the UN Security Council is unable to stem the tide of unilateralist action increasingly being taken by its most powerful member-states. As the invasion of Iraq by the United States and the United Kingdom has proven, the new doctrine of 'pre-emptive attack' can be rapidly enforced to make nonsense of the principles of sovereignty, territorial integrity and self-determination. In September 2004, the Secretary-General of the United Nations, Kofi Annan, described the invasion as "illegal" and "not in conformity with the UN Charter".[5]

This situation is bad enough for large developing countries such as Argentina and Brazil which have been held hostage by the IMF and World Bank from time to time with little room to manoeuvre. It is worse for small states in the Commonwealth Caribbean that are not only subject to the dictates and prescriptions of the IMF and World Bank, but are also threatened by the OECD and the FATF over their financial services which challenge the traditional stranglehold over such services by rich nations. Small states have very limited capacity to resist coercion; they either comply with the demands of these organisations or they face penalties.

The United Nations was created with the promise that the voices of all nations, large and small, would be heard and would participate in a chorus of consensus. It held out the hope that, through reasoned debate and discussion, the world would advance within a framework of agreed rules equally applicable and equally enforced.

The promise has been broken and the hope has been dashed. For decades, the Security Council has been the handmaiden of its five permanent members who each exercise their vetos in what they consider their national interest. The open disregard for the United Nations, including the Security Council, underscores the reality that the rule of law is being discarded in the international community, and replaced by the law of the jungle – the strong subjugate the weak. Talk of reform of the UN Security Council remains only talk, and the veto of the five permanent members is justified by its holders.

In the age of globalisation it appears that governance is the one thing that the powerful governments of the world do not want globalised. Indeed, there are serious proponents of 'justified intervention' in countries, and 'voluntary surrender of sovereignty' by some States. Robert Cooper, a serving British diplomat, actually argues that "when dealing with more old fashioned kinds of states outside the post-modern continent of Europe, we (the rich and powerful states) need to revert to the rougher methods of an earlier era – force, pre-emptive attacks, deception, whatever is necessary to deal with those who still live in the 19th Century world of every state for itself".[6] He also seriously advances the proposition that small states and other developing countries should engage in "a voluntary movement of self-imposition" in which they "open themselves up to the interference of international organisations and foreign states",[7] if they wish to participate in, and benefit from, the international community.

The point is that, through one mechanism or another, the world is being governed by rules and policies made and enforced by a few. As this book goes to press in the last quarter of 2004, this is the world in which the small states of the Commonwealth Caribbean exist. The challenges confronting them in the international economy are massive, and the opportunities open to them are few.

In September 2004, having completed a Financial Sector Appraisal of the member-jurisdictions of the Eastern Caribbean Currency Union (ECCU),[8] the IMF proposed that these very small countries broaden their tax base, reduce their tax concessions and introduce value added tax.[9] These proposals, which will increase both the cost of living and the cost of doing business in these already disadvantaged countries, were made even though the IMF acknowledged that the member-jurisdictions of the ECCU had "pursued expansionary fiscal policies in an effort to generate growth, create employment and maintain living standards".[10]

The IMF prescription for the ECCU jurisdictions was typical of the organisation. It ignored completely the macroeconomic indicators – growth and inflation. In practically all the jurisdictions, these two indicators were solid, and unemployment, for the most part, was relatively low. But, for the IMF, repayment of foreign debt, few tax concessions to the private sector, and low government spending particularly on welfare-type programmes, are key elements in their prescription regardless of what its effect will be on unemployment, health, education and eventually social disruption.

These small states could reject the IMF proposals, but they do so at the risk of being portrayed as reckless, and of being penalised by the IMF, the World Bank and the major powers.

CARIBBEAN CAPACITY AND ITS LIMITS

Within this difficult global environment, the independent Commonwealth Caribbean states are in the unique position of negotiating three sets of major trade arrangements simultaneously. These are (i) Negotiations in the World Trade Organisation (WTO) including under the General Agreement on Trade in Services; (ii) The Free Trade Area of the Americas (FTAA); and (iii) African, Caribbean and Pacific (ACP) countries negotiations with the European

Union (EU) for Economic Partnership Agreements (EPAs). No other region of the world is attempting such complex and tough negotiations all at once. One set of these negotiations would have strained the individual and collective capacity of Commonwealth Caribbean states; three sets have pushed them to their limits.

Central to the Commonwealth Caribbean's argument in each of these three fora has been that, as small economies vulnerable to a wide range of exogenous shocks, they should be given "special and differential treatment" in trade matters. This is not a point that has, so far, been conceded in tangible terms in either the FTAA or WTO negotiations; although the EU has agreed in principle that small economies should be treated differently. It is significant that while paragraph 35 of the WTO's 'Doha Declaration' recognises the economic vulnerability of small economies, it has not provided for a special category for them within the WTO.

CREATION OF SINGLE NEGOTIATING MACHINERY

In 1997, Caribbean Community and Common Market (CARICOM)[11] Heads of Government became seized of the enormity of the external economic negotiations to which they were committed. Therefore, they established the Caribbean Regional Negotiation Machinery (CRNM) as an instrument to pursue these negotiations collectively. Unquestionably, the CRNM has done a good job in very difficult circumstances including insufficient resources. However, with the best will in the world, it is not strong enough to cope with multifaceted negotiations in three arenas. What is more, the constant battle to achieve consensus amongst Governments, which sometimes have different agendas, makes the task of the CRNM even harder. Representatives of many of the smaller states of the Region, those that form the Organisation of Eastern Caribbean States (OECS)[12], often express the view that their interests are not sufficiently well-represented by the CRNM. This has led to some resentment of the CRNM in some quarters.

The CRNM was envisaged as an empowered body, reporting directly to Heads of Government through CARICOM's Prime Ministerial sub-Committee on External Negotiations. It functioned well initially, when it functioned in this way. Indeed, in its early years the Caribbean attracted admiration from other regions of the developing world for its management of regional policy-making in the ACP and WTO negotiations. But the CRNM's success was also its Achilles heel. Some Ministers responsible for Trade, some Ambassadors in Brussels, and even some officials in Capitals, came to regard its 'independence' and access to the Region's political leadership as a threat to their authority. Within three years of its creation, the CRNM, while still notionally reporting to Heads of Government, was required along the way to report to, and take direction from, Trade Ministers. As one academic and former diplomat observed, "When a matter is deemed politically important, the politicians become deeply engaged in order to apprise themselves of developments... Ministers of trade and economic development will not readily overcome the tendency to be involved too early in the negotiation process, notwithstanding the contention of Sir Alister McIntyre, a former CARICOM Secretary-General, that premature Ministerial intervention could complicate the negotiation process. Nor would the Ministers acquiesce readily to a preponderance or burgeoning role of an inter-positioning authority".[13]

Yet, that may be precisely what is needed – not the downgrading of the CRNM as has been done, or its absorption by the CARICOM Secretariat which has been mooted, but the evolution of the CRNM into a more mature executive structure. This was the vision of the West Indian Commission as far back as 1992.[14] Caribbean leaders failed to rise to the challenge then. More than ten years later in 2003, in the Rose Hall Declaration on Regional Governance and Integrated Development issued at the 24th CARICOM Heads of Government Conference at Montego Bay in Jamaica, they brought themselves to accepting "the establishment of a CARICOM Commission or other executive mechanism". They accepted it "in principle", proposed as it was by an expert group of Heads of Government. That group, chaired by the Prime Minister of St Vincent and the Grenadines, Ralph Gonsalves, had been established earlier in the year at a most important Conference initiated by the Prime Minister of Trinidad and Tobago, Patrick Manning, as a 'Consultation on Options for Governance to Deepen the Integration Process'.

Today, the Rose Hall Declaration remains just one more

pronouncement of CARICOM leaders on the way forward; and no progress has been made on the options for governance other than the submission of reports for study. But it is not in the Region's interest to delay action to establish robust machinery for regional decision making, particularly as, in the midst of the already taxing negotiations in three arenas, it faces threats to its economic viability in other areas, such as the banana and sugar industries, the financial services sector and tourism.

THE BANANA INDUSTRY

As this Introduction is being written, Commonwealth Caribbean States that relied heavily on the export of bananas to the European Union (EU) are reeling from the blow to their economies of a binding WTO decision that effectively deprived them of a preferential market in the EU which they had enjoyed under the Lome Convention between African, Caribbean and Pacific (ACP) countries and the EU. The background to this is as follows:

In the late 1980s, "bananas accounted for 69 percent of the export revenue in Dominica, 32 percent of GDP (Gross Domestic Product) and 50 percent of employment; in St Lucia 59 percent of export revenue, 37 percent of GDP and 46 percent of employment; and in St Vincent 42 percent of export revenue, 25 percent of GDP and 54 percent of employment."[15] But, Latin American countries dominated the global market for bananas, accounting for 75 percent of it in 1990. The biggest exporters were: Ecuador, Colombia, Panama, Costa Rica and Honduras. The EU was their largest market after the United States. It is important to note that Commonwealth Caribbean bananas are produced, for the most part, by families on small farms, whereas production in Latin America is done by large trans-national corporations, mostly US-owned, on large plantations where wages are low.

In July 1993, an EU-wide banana import regime gave free entry to ACP bananas and limited the entry of Latin American bananas by quota and tariff. Despite their dominance of the global market and the large size of their production in comparison with the Commonwealth Caribbean, the Latin American countries challenged the EU banana regime in the GATT in 1993 and 1994 and won two panel decisions that the regime was in contravention of the GATT.

The panels also found that preferences given to the imports of ACP bananas into the EU were inconsistent with GATT rules. This created grave uncertainty for the banana industry in the Commonwealth Caribbean. According to the Caribbean Banana Exporters Association, "since 1993 banana exports and earnings from the Windward Islands plummeted by two thirds resulting in an intensification of rural poverty and unemployment".

Both the EU and the ACP countries contested the GATT panel decisions. Nonetheless, the decision signalled that the Caribbean's traditional preferential market in the EU was not safe. The Commonwealth Caribbean countries principally affected were Dominica, St Lucia and St Vincent – three of the smallest states in the Region – although Jamaica, Belize and Grenada were also affected.

A further blow to the banana industry in the Commonwealth Caribbean was delivered in 1997. The biggest producers in the Latin American markets were three US trans-national companies: Chiquita, Dole and Del Monte. Chiquita was a contributor to the US Presidential election campaigns. In 1995, its principals called-in their debts on the administration of Bill Clinton, and the US strongly supported the Latin American countries in their challenge in the World Trade Organisation (WTO) to the EU banana regime. In 1997, a Panel of the WTO found against the banana regime. This launched a dispute that went on for four years between the EU on the one hand, and the US and Latin American counties on the other. In the course of it, another WTO panel decision was handed down in 1999 which found that the EU banana regime discriminated against US marketing companies and Latin American suppliers.

In April 2001, the EU reached agreement with the USA and Ecuador on a two-stage end to the dispute. This provided for an amended quota regime to apply at the end of 2005, and, thereafter, for only a flat rate tariff at a level to be negotiated.

At the beginning of 2004, however, it was clear that, consequent upon the enlargement of the EU, changes would be made to the banana regime which would threaten the viability of Caribbean banana exports still further. A proposal by the EU that there be a 'tariff only' regime for bananas entering their market (i.e. no quota for ACP countries as in the past), will worsen conditions even if an ACP suggestion is accepted to apply a tariff of 275 Euros per ton. In this context, the banana industry is unlikely to survive in any but two or three Commonwealth Caribbean countries, and, even within these countries, only a handful of producers will endure. The economic and social implications of the loss in revenue and the rise in unemployment will, without any doubt, increase poverty, ill-health, the spread of HIV/AIDS, and crime in the Region as a whole.

THE SUGAR INDUSTRY

Sugar, the traditional export of several Commonwealth Caribbean countries to Europe was in no better position. In mid-2004, the European Commission had proposed a reduction of 40 percent in the price paid for Caribbean sugar to be applied over a three-year period beginning in 2005. Caribbean sugar producers claimed they would lose roughly US$90 million annually over the three-year period.[16] A study undertaken by the UK's Department for International Development (DFID) in early 2004 indicated that, if the EU proposals were implemented, only Belize and Guyana in the Commonwealth Caribbean would survive as sugar producers,[17] but even their production and employment would be considerably reduced. If the findings of the study are correct, Jamaica, Trinidad and Tobago, Barbados and St Kitts and Nevis would be forced to abandon sugar production ending the livelihood of well over 300,000 people in Jamaica alone. Guyana has forecast that it will lose US$20 million in revenue between 2005 and 2006, and a further US$37 million in 2007. As a Highly indebted poor Country (HIPC), Guyana can ill-afford these losses. And, the problem of a reduced sugar industry has other severe consequences for Guyana. Not only does the sugar industry employ thousands of people and bring some measure of stability to rural areas, it also largely employs people of East Indian descent. Guyana is already deeply affected by racial divisions between the people of East Indian descent and those of African descent. The loss of jobs to the East Indian community will exacerbate this perennial and crippling problem even more.

Significantly, while the EU proposal arose from a decision by a panel established in late 2003 by the WTO to hear a complaint from Brazil, Australia and Thailand that EU subsidies to its beet sugar producers violate global rules, the EU-proposed reduction in prices paid to its own farmers would be far less than the 40 percent reduction suggested for the Caribbean. EU farmers would also get better compensation; the Caribbean was simply offered the re-allocation of funds already committed to them from the European Development Fund (EDF).

CARICOM Heads of Government, at a meeting in Grenada in July 2004, "noted that the projected loss (of revenue to Caribbean countries) outstrips, by more than 150 percent, the aid that the European Union has committed to regional programmes for the current five-year cycle".[18]

Tellingly, they also "emphasized that the Caribbean sugar exporting countries along with other ACP countries in the Sugar Protocol and the SPS arrangement are major stakeholders in the EU Sugar Regime but have been left out of any serious consideration in the European Commission's proposals".[19] The CARICOM leadership's statement served to underscore the stark reality that, in the international community, the Commonwealth Caribbean states are, increasingly, being marginalised in the decision-making process.

In any event, as Rickey Singh, an experienced and well-informed Caribbean journalist noted: "CARICOM is aware that even in moving together, the Region's sugar producers remain too weak to influence any significant changes in the proposed overhaul by the EU of Europe's sugar industry and purchasing policy."[20]

The observation is frequently made by Caribbean representatives, that their farmers would be forced to grow illicit crops such as marijuana to survive. In turn, this would increase crime in their countries and continue the supply of narcotics to the markets in North America and Europe. Despite this, there has been no plan by developed countries to help Caribbean small states to sell their legitimate agricultural products on the world market.

These developments tend to suggest that Commonwealth Caribbean countries should abandon primary production in agriculture for export, and, instead, develop (a) industries which add value to their primary agricultural production, and (b) service economies concentrating on tourism, information technology and financial services. However, this transition is easier said than done. Adjustment would be a long and painful process during which there would have to be years of unemployment and consequent social and political turmoil. In addition, there would have to be heavy investment in:

education and training; building of modern and cost-efficient telecommunications; and infrastructure to support both the processing of agricultural products and an enlarged tourism sector. It is difficult to see how such investment would be achieved in the small member-countries of the OECS, Belize and Guyana without massive help from developed countries and international financial institutions, and there is no indication that they would be willing to do so; indeed, the opposite is true – the Region is faced with reducing levels of official development assistance and 'graduation' by international financial institutions from eligibility for concessionary loans on the basis that they are 'middle-income' countries.[21] But, in any event, the prospects for the service industries in the Region are not bright.

OFFSHORE FINANCIAL SERVICES

The offshore financial services sector in the Commonwealth Caribbean was in grave danger as this Introduction was being written. The issues surrounding financial services will not be rehearsed here; they are discussed in the Chapter of this book, entitled: 'The Fight Against Fiscal Colonialism: The OECD and Small Jurisdictions'. Suffice to say now that, over the next decade or less, financial services will be meaningful only to the economies of the Bahamas, Barbados, the British Virgin Islands and the Cayman Islands[22]. While these four jurisdictions will lose both revenue and employment from the acute shrinkage of the sector, the costs of regulation and compliance with OECD and FATF requirements for other Caribbean countries will far outstrip the benefits that they could earn. Some portion of the financial services sector in the Bahamas, Barbados, the British Virgin Islands and the Cayman Islands will survive only because they are so well-developed in their particular areas of expertise (the Bahamas and the Cayman Islands in banks, and the BVI in company incorporations and trusts) that erosion cannot eliminate them entirely. In the case of Barbados, its financial services are based on a treaty with Canada, and the Canadian government has expressed itself content with the arrangement. Generally, however, the contribution of financial services will be reduced to the economies of the Commonwealth Caribbean countries now in the business, and the prospect of other Caribbean Countries being able to enter the market on a competitive basis is very remote.

It should be noted that the IMF and World Bank began conducting Financial Sector Appraisal Programmes (FSAPs) of Caribbean and other countries in 2003 using FATF and OECD criteria. In this regard, the IMF and the World Bank are now overseeing the implementation of OECD and FATF requirements. Jurisdictions that fail the IMF/World Bank tests are subject to a number of consequences including the publishing of low ratings.

OECD

In 2000 the OECD published a list of over 40 small jurisdictions which they described as 'tax havens' because they operated offshore financial centres.[23] The OECD threatened these jurisdictions, many of which were in the Caribbean, with sanctions on the basis that their offshore regimes, enjoyed by foreign companies and persons from OECD countries, were depriving OECD member-states of tax revenues, and therefore represented 'Harmful Tax Competition'.

A strong diplomatic demarche by over 40 small jurisdictions, affected by the OECD's 'Harmful Tax Competition Initiative' (HTCI), succeeded in their removal in February 2002, from the previously published 'blacklist' of countries against whom OECD members would apply sanctions. These jurisdictions had to agree in writing that they would 'co-operate' with the OECD in establishing norms and practices that would be implemented and enforced in their territories for the exchange of tax information. In theory, these norms and practices are being developed in the OECD's so-called, 'Global Forum' – a forum for some OECD members and the affected small jurisdictions. In reality, the formulation of these "norms and practices" is done by officials from the OECD and some of its member countries. The formulations are then presented to non-OECD jurisdictions in brief meetings where they find it difficult to successfully argue against any proposals but the most glaringly unacceptable.

The earlier success to decelerate the OECD process came about as a consequence of the high level of governmental involvement against the HTCI. The Prime Minister of Barbados, Owen Arthur, was personally very active, and he was supported in international fora by other Heads of Government. There is no question that the personal involvement of Prime Minister Arthur had a major impact on the OECD and several of the governments of its member-states, including the Commonwealth Secretariat whose Secretary-General, Don McKinnon played an active part in pushing the OECD to soften its position. But, in January 2002, on the eve of announcing its new 'blacklist' of so-called 'un-co-operative jurisdictions', the OECD removed Barbados from its list stating that "Barbados is willing to enter tax information exchange agreements with those OECD member countries with which it currently does not have such arrangements. Barbados has in place established procedures with respect to transparency".[24]

Having lost the personal authority which Prime Minister Arthur had brought to the struggle with the OECD, several Caribbean jurisdictions felt exposed and committed themselves immediately to the OECD process, for fear of being named in the 'blacklist' and attracting sanctions.

Since then, the cause of contesting the OECD's HTCI has not been championed at a sufficiently high level or with the consistency required to worry the OECD. The Organisation has continued to formulate requirements for the exchange of tax information and other matters that will, ultimately, adversely affect Commonwealth Caribbean jurisdictions.

What has saved the Region so far from the OECD's blacklisting and sanctions is that three of the OECD's own members have refused to co-operate with its HTCI. These are Switzerland, Austria and Luxembourg. Furthermore, in January 2003, the EU exempted these three countries as well as Belgium, Liechtenstein, Monaco, Andorra and San Marino from an EU requirement for the exchange of tax information; instead they have been allowed to apply a withholding tax on savings of EU nationals.[25] The day that these countries are cajoled into signing up to tax information exchange with the EU or under the umbrella of the OECD, it is more than likely that every effort will be made to coerce the Commonwealth Caribbean into implementing all OECD requirements, or face sanctions.

TAX HARMONISATION

As matters stand, the issue of the undesirability of tax competition will rear its head again, and it will require strong, well-advised and high-level representation to ensure the Region is not forced to apply taxes to foreign companies at a level that is equivalent to taxes in their native countries. Were the Commonwealth Caribbean to agree to such a concept, they will be in a far worse position than they are today in attracting much needed foreign investment. Already confronted with higher costs because of their remoteness from suppliers of goods required for development, any inability to give tax concessions to foreign investors would make the cost of doing business in the productive sector too high to attract them.

France and Germany are both regarded as zealots within the OECD on the HTCI. They are known to favour very strongly the end of tax competition within the EU, because lower corporate tax rates in Eastern European countries have encouraged firms to migrate from France and Germany. The French Finance Minister has put the matter in bold terms saying that Eastern European countries are "rich enough to cut their taxes" and yet they argue that "they are poor enough to need structural funds that we provide with tax payers' money".[26]

The representative of Germany, at a meeting of the OECD Global Forum in October 2003, expressed similar views to non-OECD countries when he said that without the ability to be able to collect more of the taxes due, and believed deposited in Luxembourg, Germany would not be able to pay contributions to the World Bank, from which developing countries benefited. Antigua and Barbuda responded that "in the absence of revenue from financial services, Caribbean small states would have difficulty in servicing loans from the World Bank".[27]

Should France and Germany succeed in their efforts to implement a system of harmonising tax rates in the EU, it is likely that as investors migrate to regions, such as the Caribbean, the movement would intensify for the imposition of tax rates on foreign investors equal to what they would pay in their native countries. Fortunately, for the Caribbean, there is sufficient resistance to the notion of tax harmonisation in the EU Councils to defer any agreement on tax harmonisation in the foreseeable future. Latvia, Austria and Ireland – each of whom holds key posts in the European Commission – have thrived on low corporate tax rates and are on record as opposing any attempt to make them surrender this advantage. But, Caribbean and other small states should not rely on differences within the EU to preserve their right to set their own tax rates.

FATF AND GLOBAL RULES

The FATF was set-up in 1989 by the G7 member states as a task force charged with the responsibility of looking at problems of money laundering and making a report to its Ministers. It has now become a permanent body, rivalling the OECD.

The objectives of the FATF – to devise means of curbing money laundering by establishing rules, norms and practices – are regarded as unquestionably desirable by Caribbean small states. All of them agreed to subject themselves to evaluations by the FATF to determine whether or not they were in compliance with Forty Recommendations for curbing money laundering that the FATF issued in April 1990. Many of them passed the evaluations successfully; a few didn't. But the few Caribbean small states that did not pass the evaluation successfully were not alone; some FATF member countries were also found wanting.

However, while the FATF produced a blacklist of jurisdictions that they classified as "non-co-operative", including the few in the Caribbean, no FATF member country was listed.

This caused considerable concern in the Caribbean whose governments and authorities felt that a double-standard was being applied, one which required them to change laws, establish strong regulatory and enforcement machinery at the risk of being 'named and shamed', while FATF members were given opportunities to correct their deficiencies quietly. In the course of either conforming with the requirements of the Forty Recommendations, or of appearing on the FATF blacklist, several of the Caribbean jurisdictions lost business, revenue and employment. Nonetheless, they implemented the Forty Recommendations, and the FATF eventually removed all of them from its list of 'non-co-operative jurisdictions'.

As an example of the Region's readiness to co-operate fully with the international community in fighting serious crime, when in October 2001, in the wake of the 9/11 terrorist attacks in the US, the FATF issued Eight Special Recommendations for combating terrorist financing, Caribbean jurisdictions adopted and implemented them swiftly.

In 1996, the Caribbean started its own Caribbean Financial Action Task Force (CFATF) which conducted mutual evaluations of its members not only on the basis of the FATF Forty Recommendations, but also on Nineteen of its own. In other words, the countries of the

Region allocated scarce resources to fighting money laundering even while they were losing revenues.

A further concern of the Caribbean jurisdictions was that they had no part in the formulation of the FATF's Forty Recommendations. The FATF simply imposed them. Caribbean jurisdictions, while supporting the curbing of money laundering, were agitated about the 'one size fits all' approach of the FATF. They pointed out that some of the Forty Recommendations were irrelevant and unnecessarily burdensome to the Region, since it did not have some of the corporate vehicles identified by the FATF as pernicious, and, where they did exist, the extent of their business was so small that it posed no threat whatsoever. The classic example was a recommendation for strong regulation of co-operatives when one of the most vibrant co-operatives in one Caribbean country was a society of eight beekeepers who collectively sold the little honey they gathered in the public market on Saturday mornings.

Despite much agitation by the Caribbean in particular, amongst the FATF-style regional bodies, the FATF decided to ask the IMF and World Bank to carry out the role of policing anti-money laundering regimes. In 2003, the IMF began to conduct Financial Sector Appraisal Programmes (FSAPs), by which they used the FATF's Forty Recommendations as the core criteria for judging effective anti-money laundering regimes. Nonetheless, the FATF maintained the right to continue to revise its Recommendations and to ensure their implementation globally. It is this exclusionary approach of the FATF as well as the belief that rules are being created to force them out of the financial services industry that rankle Caribbean jurisdictions.

Several Caribbean jurisdictions hold the view that the FATF, which has limited membership, ought not to be setting world-wide standards and practices for curbing money laundering. Antigua and Barbuda, the Bahamas and Barbados have all argued in international fora that this task should be the responsibility of an international organisation, since it is concerned with law enforcement both within and across borders and the process should be agreed internationally. However, other Caribbean governments have not pursued this argument actively, and the FATF members have discouraged it. As in the case of the OECD's HTCI, Caribbean governments have not pursued their concerns with the FATF process in a collective and consistent way, nor at a high level.

WTO AND RULES FOR FINANCIAL SERVICES

Another concern is the possibility that OECD and FATF criteria will creep into the rules of the WTO by a process of acquiescence. Should this happen, there would be little point in Caribbean jurisdictions seeking redress in the Dispute Settlement Body (DSB) from measures applied against them by OECD member-states for violation of OECD-formulated rules.

It is often overlooked that cross-border financial services are trade matters, and disputes over them will, increasingly, be arbitrated in the WTO. Antigua and Barbuda had led an initiative in 2003 to raise this issue in the Committee on Financial Services of the WTO. In the first discussion of the issue, Antigua and Barbuda pointed out that "the OECD and the FATF are not international organisations and could not make rules for the world".[28] Both Norway and the US sought to keep the matter off the WTO agenda by stating that "the Committee was not an appropriate place to discuss the issue, since the WTO was not a rule-making body".[29] It is significant that while Norway and the US, two OECD and FATF members, argued against the WTO, a fully international organisation, on the grounds that it is not a 'standard-setting body', they were content that the OECD and the FATF, should make rules even though their membership is limited to a handful of countries.

Commonwealth Caribbean countries should be more active in the WTO in advancing their case in financial services. They should not simply wait to fight rearguard actions as they have had to do with Bananas and Sugar. If financial services sectors in the Region are to survive with tangible benefits for the countries, the issue deserves the active attention of governments at a high level.

TOURISM

Tourism is the Commonwealth Caribbean's largest industry. It provides significant employment, earns foreign exchange to pay for large quantities of imports across many sectors, and provides governments with revenue to finance social services. Of course, its contribution to the economies of some Commonwealth Caribbean countries is greater than in others. For instance, earnings and employment from tourism are far more significant to the Bahamas (47 percent of total employment) and Antigua and Barbuda (71.7

percent of GDP) than it is to Guyana and Dominica. Nonetheless, tourism is important to the Region as a whole.

But, it is also fragile. It is sensitive to conditions both in the Caribbean and in the United States, the United Kingdom and Canada, the principal countries from which tourists to the Region originate. Recession and weak economic growth in the countries from which tourists come, adversely affect Caribbean tourism since amongst the first things that people give-up in periods of economic uncertainty is holidays. The Caribbean has experienced this time and again.

TOURISM AND TERRORISM

Even though the Commonwealth Caribbean has been spared any international terrorist activity in recent times,[30] global terrorism has affected the Region's tourism and is likely to continue to do so if people in the US, Europe and Canada remain concerned about the safety of flying or the likelihood of terrorist attacks on tourism facilities. After the 9/11 atrocities in New York and Washington, tourism arrivals to the Caribbean from the US dropped dramatically. In some markets in the Caribbean, the number of US tourists has not yet attained the levels before 9/11.

Over the next few years, security against terrorism will undoubtedly become part of the criteria by which US and European agencies judge the suitability of the Commonwealth Caribbean as tourist destinations for their people. Since the 9/11 terrorist atrocities in New York and Washington, the cost of implementing US requirements for port security in the Caribbean has become high, and it will become even higher as more demands are made for better security. The Prime Minister of St Kitts and Nevis, Denzil Douglas, explained the burden as follows: "The explicit cost of increasing the level of security at our airports and harbours, and of putting regulations in place to combat terrorist financing and money laundering, also increase the huge burden that small islands states must now bear. Of course, it can be argued that all countries – large and small – must incur such costs, but these costs include a huge fixed component that does not vary with the size of the country so that the burden borne by small states is grossly disproportionate to size and population".[31]

Nonetheless, Caribbean countries should address the possibility of a terrorist attack in the Region with seriousness. The US government certainly does; in early 2004, the Federal Bureau of Investigation (FBI) established an office in Trinidad to address terrorism specifically. The United Kingdom is also concerned, and in March 2004 at a meeting in Jamaica, the UK government agreed to help CARICOM governments establish machinery for intelligence sharing, border security and maritime co-operation.[32] Three months later, in London, CARICOM governments welcomed an offer from the British Government to organise a meeting between officials of the UK, CARICOM, Canada, US, France and Netherlands to discuss ways to improve maritime co-operation.[33] These were good beginnings in getting expert help for the Region, but they need to be deepened and moved forward quickly.

Every nightmare scenario should be considered and a blueprint for action devised by a Regional group supported by anti-terrorism experts from Canada, the United States, the United Kingdom and other EU countries. The blueprint should include preventative measures such as intelligence gathering and improved border controls. Additionally, other measures should be included in the plan including: higher levels of un-intrusive security at tourism facilities, education of the local population about terrorism through mass media programmes, emergency hospital arrangements encompassing the provision of medical assistance from neighbouring Caribbean States. However, a crucial dimension to any plan of action must be co-operation with agencies of the US, Canada and the UK for a rapid response to any incident, and a command structure at both national and regional levels that would go into operation for all aspects of dealing with a terror attack should there be such an occurrence in one country, or indeed in several countries simultaneously.

Any act of international terrorism in the Region, particularly if it is directed at tourists, is likely to have an adverse effect on tourism to the area as a whole. It is precisely because the Caribbean is regarded as 'safe' and not an area of terrorist interest that its tourism industry was not as badly affected as other regions of the world after 9/11 and the terror attacks on hotel resort facilities in Bali and Kenya in 2002. But, should any terror attack occur, the Caribbean will have to be seen to be able to cope efficiently and adequately if its tourism industry is to avoid serious harm.

IMPORTANCE OF CO-OPERATION AGREEMENTS WITH LARGER COUNTRIES

Co-operation arrangements with agencies of the US, the UK and Canada, particularly if such co-operation allows for the presence of military and other personnel acting with some authority in the Caribbean, will have to be carefully worked out. The autonomy of Caribbean governments will have to be preserved, while acknowledging the limitations of Caribbean capacity, and the necessity for skilled and experienced assistance. But, such co-operation arrangements are necessary and vital and they should not be delayed or ignored.

It is noteworthy that, as this Introduction was being written, Grenada was devastated by Hurricane Ivan on 7 September 2004. The devastation was so comprehensive that 9/7 is certain to become as important a date for Grenada as 9/11 is for the United States. Over 90 percent of the buildings on the island were decimated. Government could not function; telecommunication and electricity services were destroyed; and in the first two days lawlessness prevailed as looters set on shops and homes. The destruction of the prison also resulted in the escape of at least half of the prison population.

Both the Caribbean Disaster Response Agency (CDERA) and the small Regional Security System (RSS)[34] responded immediately to the plight of the Grenadian people, but they were adversely affected by the inability of other countries, which had also been damaged by the same hurricane, to join in providing emergency help. For example, while Barbados responded by sending in military personnel and construction teams, particularly for telecommunications and other utilities, and Antigua and Barbuda despatched police and military personnel, Jamaica, which suffered the effects of the hurricane, three days after Grenada, was unable to send help, and usually the Jamaican military contingent is the biggest amongst the groups that give assistance to the smaller Caribbean territories. Damage was also done in Barbados, St Vincent and the Grenadines, St Lucia and Tobago. The Cayman Islands were as devastated as Grenada. The multiple battering of several islands hampered the capacity of the RSS to respond quickly to Grenada's predicament. Armed bandits robbed vessels that were taking relief supplies to Grenada,[35] and CDERA and the RSS were forced to suspend relief operations temporarily until the problem could be hastily addressed through the assistance of Trinidad and Tobago whose government provided 200 of its troops to restore law and order.

What this situation revealed was the weakness of the RSS to cope with a major security issue in the absence of assistance from military forces of larger Commonwealth Caribbean countries such as Jamaica and Trinidad. This weakness was tacitly acknowledged by CARICOM leaders who met in Trinidad on 15 September 2004 to consider the Grenada situation after the passage of Hurricane Ivan. They "sanctioned the staging of an early meeting among Regional Security Chiefs to address 'clear lines of military and security command', and a Co-operation Agreement between the RSS and non-RSS States with respect to co-ordinating security in Grenada".[36] At that meeting which was held in Trinidad nine days later, the Heads of six regional defence forces said they would recommend to Heads of Government that there should be "a more co-ordinated relief effort, a unified command structure and a legal framework for the deployment of troops".[37]

The absence of a unified command structure and a legal framework may have contributed to the abuse of authority by some members of the security forces in Grenada in the weeks following the passage of Hurricane Ivan. It was reported that "some members of the security forces were removing food hampers from the relief supply centre and giving them to young women in exchange for sex".[38]

It was the presence of a British military ship, HMS Richmond, which saved Grenada from an even worse fate. According to CDERA, it had been working with the HMS Richmond from the start of the hurricane season and between them they had established arrangements for dealing with an emergency. CDERA said the HMS Richmond "had sailed through stormy weather to ensure it was in Grenada's harbour immediately after the hurricane".[39] The crew of HMS Richmond rescued the Prime Minister, Dr Keith Mitchell, whose home had been flattened and gathered Ministers of the Government to help put a command structure in place. In addition to giving urgent medical assistance to people, they also "performed critical initial evaluation which guided the Regional Response Mechanism and paved the way for (the) arrival of emergency personnel".[40]

The limitations placed on the actions of the crew of HMS Richmond were pronounced in the Cayman Islands where looting also took place in the wake of Hurricane Ivan. While the crew could render assistance, they had to go ashore unarmed and could not participate in law enforcement. The Chief Executive of Cable and Wireless in Cayman, Timothy Adam, wrote an open letter on 15 September which he distributed to the media. In the letter, Adam declared, "Grand Cayman urgently needs military intervention to restore and preserve law and order. This needs to happen today". While the Cayman government did not join Adam in his plea, the case he made for intervention from the UK and the US emphasised the weakness of local security forces in a major catastrophe and the importance of a carefully designed co-operation programme with other countries that could deliver much-needed assistance without surrendering autonomy. Adam described a situation in which the local police were only just maintaining order.[41]

These events, including the crucial role played by HMS Richmond, especially in Grenada, underscore the importance of integrated national and regional plans, supported by the international community, to deal with catastrophes, including a terrorist act, or more than one simultaneously, in the Region.

TOURISM AND HURRICANES

2004 saw one of the most active hurricane seasons in the Caribbean with Hurricanes Charley, Frances, Ivan and Jeanne creating havoc in the Bahamas, Cuba, the Dominican Republic, Haiti, Jamaica, Grenada, the Cayman Islands, St Vincent, St Lucia and Tobago. Ivan's devastation of Grenada and the Cayman Islands, including all the tourism plant, again portrayed vividly the harm that hurricanes do to tourism.

Between 1995 and 2000, dreadful hurricanes had severely affected tourism to a number of countries, amongst them Antigua and Barbuda which, up to 2002, had not achieved the level of stay-over tourists that it had in 1994. Hurricane Ivan has crippled Grenada and Cayman's tourism industry for at least two years, and, even then, only if the hotel plant and other tourism infrastructure are re-built quickly. In Antigua and Barbuda, despite re-construction by hotels with government assistance and considerable government investment, through borrowings, to rebuild infrastructure after Hurricane Luis in September 1995, it was two years before tourists returned to Antigua in significant numbers.

A further problem is that insurance companies hiked premiums in the Caribbean Region after an increase in both the intensity and number of hurricanes hitting the area repeatedly since 1995. The cost of insurance has sky-rocketed to the point where hotel owners in some countries have taken the decision not to insure their properties, preferring to rely either on hope, or on savings that could help them rebuild; others have continued paying high premiums at the expense of improving their services, or expanding and refurbishing properties. After Hurricane Ivan's passage in September 2004, preliminary reports put insured losses in the Cayman Islands alone at close to US$2 billion, and one rating agency suggested that it "may be too much for three local Cayman firms".[42] As one economist pointed out, "Disaster insurance is extensive in the United States; it is less commonplace in developing countries and rudimentary at best in the Caribbean".[43]

What is needed is at least a Regional Disaster Fund to which contributions can be made by both Governments and the private sector for post-disaster financing. But, it would be preferable and more beneficial for the Caribbean if the IMF and World Bank would provide such a facility for which Antigua and Barbuda called after Hurricane Luis in 1995. Both institutions now have lending facilities for emergency assistance after natural disasters, but their rules on access to the facility and their slow response time in disbursing funds are unhelpful to countries which need urgent response to rebuild.

It should be acknowledged that the Caribbean Development Bank (CDB) had agreed, in the wake of Hurricane Ivan, to provide emergency loans of up to US$500,000 at concessional rates. The regional bank also invited affected countries to apply for loans for rehabilitation projects. But, given the scale of the damage done to countries running into hundreds of millions of dollars, the CDB's limited resources, while invaluable, were a drop in the bucket.

Trinidad and Tobago, which is an oil and gas producer, also responded swiftly to the plight of the several Caribbean countries battered by hurricanes in 2004. Conscious that CARICOM countries represented its second biggest export market and that its own economy could be hurt from reduced sales to countries affected by the hurricanes, the Trinidad and Tobago government put up US$5 million to help countries rebuild. Grenada and Jamaica were offered US$1.6 million each, Bahamas and Cuba US$500,000 each and St Vincent and the Grenadines US$600,000. But, while this was a generous gesture by the Trinidad and Tobago government, its help could not

31

match the scale of assistance that the affected countries required. As Prime Minister Manning put it, at the 59th Session of the United Nations General Assembly in September 2004, "We have committed ourselves through direct financial and other levels of assistance. But what Grenada and Haiti require is well beyond the Region's capacity to deliver. I urge the wider international community and donor agencies to respond adequately and to play their part."[44]

In the light of experience, there clearly is a need in the Region for the governments and tourism private sector organisations to formulate plans nationally and regionally for managing hurricanes better. Such plans should include: bolstering considerably the resources of CEDERA and the RSS, improved building standards for all tourism plant, secure accommodation for tourists during hurricanes, means of evacuating tourists quickly, a Regional facility for insuring hotels, a disaster Fund supported by the international community for rebuilding infrastructure, and an international public relations strategy.

It should be noted that the State of Florida in the United States gets more hurricanes than individual Commonwealth Caribbean states, yet it recovers more quickly and tourists return there within weeks. Of course, Florida has considerably more financial and other resources on which to call than any Commonwealth Caribbean state, but it also has machinery for implementing established plans to overcome the damaging effects of a hurricane.

CRIME AND TOURISM

Increasingly higher rates of crime, particularly those directed at tourists are impacting on visitors to the Region and their governments who are responsible for advising them of the safety of tourist destinations. This entire situation negatively affects new investment in the tourism sector and employment opportunities.

One study has suggested that, "rising unemployment and other economic woes have brought a rash of muggings and drug-related violence to some formerly calm destinations in the Region".[45]

Whatever the cause of increased crime against tourists, the problem was viewed sufficiently seriously by the governments of the United Kingdom and Canada that they issued travel advisories in 2004 warning their nationals about crime in the Caribbean.

There is an obvious need to tackle this problem, but, of course, it can not be tackled in isolation from the causes of crime in each Commonwealth Caribbean country individually and the Region as a whole. Suffice to say in this Introduction that increasing crime against tourists has become an issue for Caribbean tourism, and it has to be considered as part of a comprehensive plan for preserving the Region's place as a desirable tourism destination.

In the Chapter entitled, 'Crime in the Caribbean: An Overwhelming Phenomenon', I focus on the implications of increasing crime in the region. I argue that crime is overwhelming the Caribbean, and Commonwealth Caribbean countries in particular require significant help from the international community to curtail its escalation. The problem is already huge, especially as it comes at a time when the revenues of governments from trade (including services) are declining while expenditures are increasing. The requirement for additional allocation of scarce resources to fight crime is simply beyond the budgets of many countries.

A crucial area of assistance to small Caribbean states would be in the curtailment of the smuggling of small arms by drug traffickers and other criminal elements. The spread of small arms internationally is now a bigger problem than Weapons of Mass Destruction (WMD). At least with WMD, the countries involved are known, a UN agency exists and works in the monitoring of such weapons, and international treaties are enforced. In this matter, Commonwealth Caribbean governments should mount a campaign in every fora available to them, including the UN, the OAS, the Commonwealth, to alert the international community to the real dangers they face from this problem, and to mobilise action against the spread of small arms. However, Caribbean governments also have to address the fact that the biggest sources of illegal weapons used by criminal elements are the armouries of the Police and Military in their own countries.

TOURISM AND THE WTO

The World Trade Organisation has become an important forum for tourism issues. Within the Committees of the WTO, definitions are being agreed, binding commitments are being sought and given, and procedures and practices are being established. These already form the basis for identifying and settling disputes. They affect the Commonwealth Caribbean now and they will do so well into the future. But, these issues are not addressed in a consistent and meaningful way by Commonwealth Caribbean countries in the WTO. Indeed, only three of these states, Barbados, Jamaica and Trinidad and Tobago have resident missions at the WTO in Geneva.

For instance, while many Commonwealth Caribbean countries have sought to preserve aspects of their tourism market for nationals, they have not reserved them in the commitments made to the WTO under the General Agreement on Trade in Services (GATS). These include: travel agents and tour operator services, the construction of hotels below a certain size, certain types of restaurants and tourist guide services. Reserving the less costly end of the tourism sector for locals will in no way deny foreign investment at the high-cost end of the industry which is sorely needed.

There are four sub-sectors of Tourism and Travel Related Services, and the US has requested that Caribbean countries fully liberalise them. If this is done, the areas that Commonwealth Caribbean countries are trying to preserve for nationals will be eroded completely. Beyond these specific concerns, there are many other fundamental issues related to tourism in the WTO that are not being addressed; one of them is as basic as the definition of tourism. This is a matter that the Caribbean as a whole has to agree if the Region is to push for a change in the definition of tourism that would be more advantageous.[46]

The point is that tourism is, in part, a trade matter, and trade matters will be defined, disputed and resolved in the WTO. Therefore, Commonwealth Caribbean countries have to be more active in the WTO committees than they are. In a real sense, diplomatic representation at the WTO has become extremely important for Caribbean interests in trade, both in goods and services, and they ought to have adequate missions that work collectively to safeguard and promote their interests.

'LEAKAGE' FROM THE TOURISM INDUSTRY

Commonwealth Caribbean countries already experience a high rate of 'leakage' from tourism because of (i) the large number of imports required to sustain the industry; (ii) the significant amount of money that is spent in the major tourism markets on advertising, promotion and public relations; and (iii) dividends paid to the large number of foreign owners of hotels. In reality, too, much of the money earned by Caribbean tourism never reaches the Region. Tour operators in the principal tourism markets negotiate reduced rates for hotels and other services in the Caribbean and the bulk of the money paid by tourists for holidays remain in the tour operators' country of origin. It is also well-known that, where Caribbean hotels have representatives in the principal markets, only a portion of the monies paid by tourists, either directly or through a tour operator, is sent to the Caribbean.

Given the necessity for increased expenditure to attract tourists, the higher costs for security, the continuing leakage from tourism earnings, and the stagnant contribution of tourism to the economies of some Commonwealth Caribbean states, there should be no assumption that tourism will remain a life line for the Region. Indeed, it is significant that in the seven member countries of the OECS, "there has been little new investment in their hotel and accommodation sector during the last decade, as well as a reduction in tour operator generated business".[47] In 2001, just over two-thirds of all tourist arrivals to the Commonwealth Caribbean were to only three countries: the Bahamas, Barbados and Jamaica.[48]

The response to declining levels of tourism to the Caribbean, particularly after 9/11, was driven by hotel owners, not by governments. Generally, the response was to reduce the costs of hotel accommodation, offer tour operators cheaper deals and push governments into inducing airlines, such as American and British Airways, to continue flights by giving them financial support. If anything, this response, rooted as it was in addressing a grave problem with a short-term solution, served only to reduce still further the revenues earned from tourism.

Despite many inter-governmental meetings and encounters between Governments and Caribbean tourism organisations, there has not been a comprehensive and agreed approach to the problems of Caribbean tourism. The industry remains one of fierce competition between Commonwealth Caribbean countries. Furthermore, the Region's tourism organisations, the Caribbean Tourism Organisation (CTO) – an inter-governmental grouping, and the Caribbean Hotel Association (CHA) representing the private sector, are deeply divided.

However, the CHA is proactive. In 2004, it commissioned a study by the World Travel and Tourism Council entitled, 'The Caribbean: The Impact of Tourism and Travel on Jobs and the Economy'. The study projected that over the next ten years, travel and tourism will create directly and indirectly 3.2 million jobs in the Caribbean as a whole, and will contribute US$58.5 million to Regional GDP.

The CHA has also adopted an aggressive stance in the EU and has been pushing the EU to recognise the importance of tourism in the proposed Economic Partnership Agreements between the EU and Caribbean countries. However, governments ought not to leave the field to the CHA alone, for while public and private sector interests converge in many areas, they also diverge. In this regard, governments, the CTO and the CHA should be working together on an agreed agenda that advances tourism in all of the three arenas in which the Caribbean is now involved in trade negotiations.

UNSPOKEN AGENDA?

The problems faced by Commonwealth Caribbean countries are not restricted to the unfriendly international environment in which they exist. There are many domestic issues as well, not least of which is whether these small states individually have the capacity to be viable as independent States, i.e. to satisfy the needs of their people for the preservation of law and order, social and economic progress, security and defence from foreign intruders including drug traffickers, terrorists, and other criminal elements, provision of social services such as education and health, and the advancement of their interests and values in the international community.

The question of the individual capacity of Commonwealth Caribbean countries to be viable as states is raised constantly in the international community. Yet, it is the same countries and agencies that deny Caribbean small states the special and differential treatment in trade and economic matters that would help them to be viable. In the words of a leading US academic, Francis Fukuyama, "Strengthening these states through various forms of nation-building is a task that has become vital to international security but it is one that few developed countries have mastered".[49]

Many of the Region's domestic issues are linked to the burdens placed on Caribbean small states by the international community, and the failure to recognise that, in order to maintain political and social stability, these states require an agreed programme of economic and financial assistance. It is unlikely, however, that the major developed countries (the US, and the EU) will readily agree to such a programme. Their main interest in the Caribbean surrounds money laundering, drug-trafficking, security including terrorism and migration of people. This situation raises the cynical suspicion that perhaps there may be an unspoken agenda to do the minimum to support these small states in the expectation that they will be compelled to do as Robert Cooper proposed, i.e. to engage in "a voluntary movement of self-imposition" in which they "open themselves up to the interference of international organisations and foreign states", so that they could participate in, and benefit from, the international community.

Commonwealth Caribbean states ought not to be daunted by this. Instead, they should use the US/EU concerns about drug trafficking, money laundering and security to argue their own case for special and differential treatment in trade and economic matters, and for assistance in security matters that do not compromise their national autonomy. To do so, they will need to invest in a strong diplomatic service capable of advancing their interests in international agencies and major world capitals. As I argue in the Chapter on 'The Relevance and Function of Diplomacy in the Foreign Policy of Small States', diplomacy is the only real foreign policy tool available to small states, and it should be strong and effective.

Of course, a more deeply integrated Commonwealth Caribbean in the form of a Federation or even a strong Confederation that would allow countries such as Jamaica to participate in some aspects of common arrangements without being part of a full federal arrangement, remains the ideal for the Commonwealth Caribbean in world politics. But, there is little hope of this happening in the foreseeable future.

For the present, hope has to be placed in the creation and evolution of the Caribbean Single Market and Economy (CSME) within CARICOM that is scheduled to begin in 2005. The deadline will most probably not be met since, in the last quarter of 2004, many of the CARICOM member states had not taken the required actions for CSME readiness. Barbados, Jamaica and Trinidad and Tobago may be able to make a start to which others would join.

But, even if the CSME comes into being on a staggered basis, a question posed by the Prime Minister of St Vincent and the Grenadines has a compelling resonance: "Does not the single economy require the creation of an appropriate supra-national entity to which there ought to be a transfer of a measure of sovereignty, in its pooling, similar, though not necessarily identical, to that of fashioning the European Union?".[50]

GREATER REGIONAL CO-OPERATION NECESSARY

This Introduction has dealt with some of the external difficulties confronting the small states of the Commonwealth Caribbean. The picture appears gloomy, and it is. The reality is that smallness is powerlessness, and, for the most part, these small states have achieved gains in the international community only when they have acted in unison.

As this Introduction is being written, Commonwealth Caribbean small states are facing a crisis. It may be less of a crisis in Trinidad and Tobago whose oil and gas resources, and the financial reserves the government has built-up, place it in a more advantageous position than others. The Bahamas and Barbados may also be better off because they have steadily moved their economies into the services sector. But, all three, like the others, remain vulnerable for the reasons already set-out here.

Governments have to face-up to the crisis, state it boldly to their people and the international community, and act resolutely to overcome it in the only way that is sensible – and that is to make their small countries bigger through arrangements of joint governance that are so patently necessary to make them more viable. The alternative is to let the culture of smallness perpetuate itself, and for hardship to eventually force them either into a new form of colonialism with larger countries, or to pawn their people's future with the IMF and the World Bank. This is the compelling conclusion of this study of the challenges facing the small states of the Commonwealth Caribbean – states, that in the words of a former British Foreign Secretary are "crumbled small"[51], and have to cope with the reality of their smallness in world politics.

Sir Ronald Sanders
September 2004

NOTES & REFERENCES

1   Along with Haiti, Surinam and the British colony, Monsterrat, these states form the Caribbean Community and Common Market (CARICOM).

2   Musa, Said; Prime Minister of Belize, 'State of the Nation' address, September 2004.

3   Stiglitz, Joseph; *Globalization and its Discontents*, Allen Lane, The Penguin Press, USA, 2002.

4   The OECD and FATF are both organisations created by a handful of rich and powerful nations. Membership of these organisations is limited to these countries, but they both make rules and set standards that they seek to impose internationally either through the IMF and World Bank or by coercive economic measures.

5   The UN Secretary-General made the statement in an interview with the BBC Television World Service on 16 September 2004, see Internet website: http://news.bbc.co.uk/2/hi/middle_east/3661134.stm

6   Cooper, Robert: 'The Post Modern State', *Re-Ordering the World: The long-term implications of 11 September*, Mark Leonard (ed), The Foreign Policy Centre, London, 2002, p. 16.

7   *Ibid.*

8   The members of the ECCU are: Anguilla, Antigua and Barbuda, the British Virgin Islands, Dominica, Grenada, St Kitts and Nevis, St Lucia, St Vincent and the Grenadines, Montserrat.

9   IMF Country Report No. 04/299, September 2004.

10 *Ibid.*

11 Membership of CARICOM is described in Note 1.

12 The Organisation of Eastern Caribbean States (OECS) consists of Antigua and Barbuda, Dominica, Grenada, St Kitts and Nevis, St Lucia, St Vincent and the Grenadines and Montserrat. Other non-independent countries are Associate members; these are: Anguilla, The British Virgin Islands.

13 Grant, Cedric: 'Democracy and Governance in the Caribbean', Fourth Lecture in the Distinguished Lecture Series Sponsored by CARICOM to commemorate its Thirtieth Anniversary, 7 May 2003, St Vincent.

14 *Time for Action: Report of the West Indian Commission*, The Press – University of the West Indies, Jamaica, 1993.

15 Sutton, Paul: 'The Banana Regime of the European Union, the Caribbean and the World Trade Organisation'.

16 Communiqué of the 25th Conference of Heads of Government of the Caribbean Community and Common Market (CARICOM), in Grenada, July 2004.

17 UK officials indicated to ACP representatives at a meeting in London on 27 August 2004 that the DFID report was 'not a policy statement of the UK Government; they were simply independent consultants' views'.

18 *Op. Cit,* note 16.

19 *Ibid.*

20 Singh, Rickey: 'Our Caribbean: When sugar is not sweet', *The Daily Nation*, Barbados, 23 July 2004.

21 Guyana is an exception. It is classified as a 'Highly Indebted Poor Country' (HIPC) and therefore qualifies for debt relief and concessionary loans.

22 Cayman Islands is a British Colony.

23 See, *Towards Global Tax Co-operation: Report to the 2000 Ministerial Council Meeting and recommendations to the Committee on Fiscal Affairs: Progress in identifying and eliminating harmful tax practices*; OECD, Paris, 2000.

24 Internet website of the OECD: www.oecd.org

25 See, letter of 27 January 2003 from Sir Ronald Sanders, Antigua and Barbuda's Chief Negotiator on International Financial Services to Mr Donald Johnston, Secretary-General of the OECD on the absence of a level playing field on website: www.antigua-barbuda.com under 'Latest news'.

26 Parker, George: 'Sarkozy fires parting shot at low-tax Eastern Europe', *Financial Times*, 10 September 2004.

27 See, Second intervention by Sir Ronald Sanders, at OECD Global Forum, Ottawa, 15 October 2003, www.antigua-barbuda.com under 'Latest news'.

28 See, World Trade Organisation document: S/FIN/M/42 of 12 November 2003, Committee on Trade in Financial Services, Report of the Meeting held on 6 October 2003. The Author was the representative of Antigua and Barbuda.

29 *Ibid.*

30 There was one major domestic terrorist incident in Trinidad in July 1990 when an extremist Black Muslim group, the Jamaat al Muslimeen, tried to overthrow the government headed by A.N.R. Robinson. They held the Prime Minister and other members of Parliament hostage for five days while looting took place in Port of Spain, the country's Capital. They surrendered to the Police, but the group has remained active and is a source of concern. Earlier, in 1976, a bomb was placed on a Cuban passenger aircraft, CU 455, in Barbados by a Cuban exile living in Miami. All the passengers died as the plane blew-up after leaving Barbados.

31 Douglas, Denzil Prime Minister of St Kitts and Nevis at the Opening of a Meeting of Commonwealth Finance Ministers in Basseterre, St Kitts, 29 September 2004.

32 Communiqué issued at the meeting of members of the CARICOM Ministerial sub-committee for resource mobilisation for crime and security and a United Kingdom Senior level team on security co-operation, 3 March 2004, Kingston, Jamaica.

33 Communiqué of the Fourth UK/Caribbean Ministerial Forum held in London, 10-12 May 2004.

34 Membership of the RSS is Barbados and the OECS countries only.

35 Singh, Rickey: 'Pirates: Bandits preying on boats bringing aid to Grenada', *The Barbados Advocate*, 11 September 2004.

36 See, 'CARICOM leaders recommend grant aid for Grenada', Press Release 144/2004 from the CARICOM Secretariat, 17 September 2004.

37 Reported in *The Trinidad and Tobago Express Newspaper* of 25 September 2004. The six military heads came from Antigua and Barbuda, The Bahamas, Barbados, Guyana , Trinidad and Tobago and St Kitts and Nevis.

38 Noel, Leroy; 'Food for sex rampant in Grenada', Caribbean Net News, 27 September 2004; www.caribbeannetnews.com/2004/09/27/rampant.htm

39 'HMS Richmond crew, British Government come in for high praise', *The Barbados Advocate*, 11 September 2004.

40 *Ibid.*

41 Adam, Timothy, Chief Executive Cable & Wireless (Cayman Islands) Ltd, 'Send US forces to restore order', *Weekend Nation*, Barbados, 17 September 2004.

42 Rivera, Nelson; senior financial analyst at A M Best, in 'Caribbean insurers hardest hit by Ivan' in *The Barbados Advocate*, 18 September 2004.

43 Rambarran, Jwala: 'Caribbean Region weathering the storm: Managing natural disaster risk', *The Barbados Advocate Business Monday*, 13 September 2004.

44 Manning, Patrick; Prime Minister of Trinidad and Tobago, Address to the 59th Session of the United Nations General Assembly in New York, 24 September 2004.

45 Griffin, Dr Clifford, 'Analysis and Recommendations Re: Harassment of and crime committed by and against tourists in the Caribbean' (undated).

46 For a full discussion of the tourism issues for the Caribbean in the WTO, see: Dunlop, Adam: 'Tourism service negotiation issues: Implications for CARIFORUM", prepared for the Caribbean Regional Negotiating Machinery (CRNM), July 2003.

47 Background Paper prepared for Policy Workshop on Caribbean Tourism, sponsored by the Foreign and Commonwealth Office, London, 6-7 November 2003.

48 *Ibid.*

49 Fukuyama, Francis, *State Building: Governance and World Order in the Twenty-First Century*, Profile Books, London, 2004.

50 Gonsalves, Ralph, Prime Minister of St Vincent and the Grenadines, Address to the 24th Annual Conference of the Insurance Association of the Caribbean, St Thomas, USVI, 6 June 2004.

51 Lord Rosebery, British Foreign Secretary, Speech in Adelaide, 1884, cited by Peter Lyon in 'Small States and the left-overs of Empire' in *The Round Table*. London, April 1984.

CHAPTER ONE

The Emergence of Caribbean Small States

The central issue of this study is the vulnerability of Caribbean small states to intervention and to restriction of their decision-making capacity. But to understand the extent of their vulnerability in the international system it is necessary at the outset to identify the economic and political climate into which they emerged and in which they operate as independent entities.

DEFINITIONS

STATEHOOD

The use of the term 'small state' immediately raises questions of definition. Pre-eminent among these questions are: what is a state, and are the Caribbean territories to be regarded as states in the international system? A basic observation, which is universally admitted, is that statehood has never been authoritatively defined in an international decision or instrument. This has led to much debate on what is a state[1]. However, the definition usually cited, and widely accepted in international relations practice, is set out in the 1933 Montevideo Convention on the Rights and Duties of States. Article I of the convention provides that:

> The state as a person of international law should possess the following qualifications: (a) a permanent population; (b) a defined territory; (c) government; and (d) capacity to enter relations with other states.[2]

First written as part of MA thesis, 'Caribbean Small States in the International System: Their Problems and Prospects', University of Sussex, August 1989.

Admittedly, the provisions set out in the Montevideo Declaration are not sufficient to explain statehood, but the idea which they convey is that 'there are two essential elements to Statehood: the existence of a separate territorial community with its own system of government, and the independence of that territorial community from all others'.[3] In this context, it can be concluded that the small Caribbean territories in this study are states since they have defined territories, permanent populations, governments which have coercive power to enforce laws within their territories, the capacity to enter relations with other states by virtue of their independence from Britain by acts of the British Parliament, and their recognition as independent states by a large majority of other states in the world. These are 'the characteristics which are shared by the states which play a regular and full part in international life'.[4]

SMALL STATES

Having established that the Caribbean territories are states, we come now to the categorisation of them as 'small states'. How does one determine what constitutes a small state? Are the relevant factors limited territory, small population, lack of military capability and economic weakness? And even if these are the relevant factors in deciding which states are small, is there some determinate line in land area, population size, military establishment, or economic development that allows one to distinguish between small states and others? These are issues that have been grappled with by several scholars in trying to reach a solution to the problem of defining a small state.[5] For the most part these studies are distinguished by their agreement that smallness is a comparative and not an absolute term, and that there are great difficulties associated with defining it. One study points out that 'there are no special rules of international law governing the nature, status or relations of small states and still less binding principles defining what is meant by such a term'.[6] There is also little value in trying to construct an analytical framework with which to attempt to define a small state, for, as David Vital points out, 'the varieties of condition and behaviour of states is very great and the number of states very small. It is therefore hard to decide where to look for regularities and out of what material to construct the analytical schemata'.[7]

Nonetheless, a conception of a small state has evolved in recent years and is now in common usage in the United Nations and other international organisations. This conception is based mainly on the size of the state's population, although other factors are taken into account. Among them are: the size of its territory, the level of its economic development and the depth of its vulnerability to the external environment in economic, military and cultural terms. Thus, if a state has considerable territory as Guyana does (215,000 sq kms) but a population of less than a million (in Guyana's case in the 1980s 807,000), and the other considerations apply, it would be considered small. By the same token, if the state has limited territory as in Singapore (620 sq kms) but a population of more than a million (in Singapore's case in the same period 2.6 million) and is relatively well developed, it would not be considered small.

This conception of a small state began to evolve as a result of a study undertaken in 1969 by the United Nations Institute for Training and Research (UNITAR).[8] The UNITAR study used population as a key indicator of smallness and fixed an upper limit of around one million. Subsequent studies, particularly one undertaken at the request of Commonwealth Heads of Government following the 1983 invasion by the United States of the Caribbean island of Grenada, adopted the UNITAR population criterion of one million or less. However, the Commonwealth study concluded that certain states with populations larger then one million but with common problems and regular regional interaction with small states should also be considered. On this basis they included the Caribbean state of Jamaica (population over two million) and the Pacific state of Papua New Guinea (population over three million), 'since they share many characteristics and also maintain integral links with all small states in their region'.[9]

By these measurements, there were in the late 1980s 46 small sovereign states in the world: 13 in Africa and the Indian Ocean, 13 in Latin America and the Caribbean, eight in Europe and the Mediterranean, three in the Middle East, and nine in the Pacific. Significantly, of these 46 states, 35 had populations of less than half-a-million, and 29 of under 200,000. The 12 small states in the Caribbean on which this study will focus had populations at that time ranging from 47,000 (St Kitts and Nevis) to 2.3 million (Jamaica). The table below provides a profile of each Caribbean small state.

TABLE 1

Country	Pop. '000	Area '000 sq km	GNP per capita	Pop. Density per sq km
Antigua & Barbuda	82	440	211	186
Bahamas	241	13, 935	2, 488	17
Barbados	254	430	1,358	591
Belize*	175	22,963	219	8
Dominica	80	751	115	107
Grenada	100	344	134	291
Guyana*	807	215,000	310	4
St Kitts & Nevis	47	269	80	175
St Lucia	143	616	196	232
St Vincent & Grenadines	112	389	121	288
Trinidad & Tobago	1,217	5,128	5,130	237
Jamaica	2,351	10,991	2,256	214

*Belize and Guyana are mainland territories

Source: *Basic Statistical Data*, Commonwealth Secretariat, London, May 1989.

CARIBBEAN SMALL STATES

All of the 12 independent Caribbean small states are former colonies of Britain. These states emerged into the international system over a twenty-one year period between 1962 and 1983.[10] A common feature is their narrow resource base and (with the exception of Guyana and Belize) relatively high population density. For the most part, their economic structures are undiversified, but in any case they would not benefit from economies of scale. Industrialisation is constrained by the small size of domestic markets, difficulties in penetrating foreign markets and inadequate supplies of local raw material for processing industries. The prevailing feature of their economies is their relative openness. Three commodity groups have long accounted for nearly all the exports of the region with Britain being the main market for sugar, bananas and citrus. Guyana and Jamaica also produce bauxite, but prices are unstable. Trinidad and Tobago produces oil, but its reserves are dwindling. The region is also susceptible to natural disasters and during the 1980s three hurricanes devastated production in five states. Caribbean small states are, therefore, economically weak. In their interaction with other states and actors in the international system, they not only lack economic muscle but are vulnerable to the superior economic strength of all around them. Their size vindicates the assertion made in 1884 by Lord Roseberry that 'empires, and especially great empires, when they crumble at all, are apt to crumble exceedingly small'.[11]

These states were among the remnants of the British Empire, and their emergence as independent states in the international system followed upon the failure of experiments by the British government to avoid granting them independence individually. The experiments took two forms: a Federation, which lasted from 1958 until it collapsed in bitter recrimination among its units in 1962, and 'Associated Statehood' – a kind of halfway house to independence in which the states concerned enjoyed full internal self-government but their external affairs and defence remained under the control of the British government.

On immediate examination, these states fall neatly into the category of states used to explain dependency theory. Their small populations, small domestic markets, limited range of natural resources (in a few cases, only beaches), limited access to capital markets, heavy dependence on aid, and narrow range of local skills correspond to those characteristics which lead dependency theorists to categorise them as being subject to external dominance, particularly by capitalist countries. They are also extremely weak in military terms. Moreover, they are geographically located in close proximity to the United States which, ever since the enunciation of the Monroe Doctrine in 1823, has regarded the Caribbean area as vital to its security. This geographical closeness to the United States and the economic and military weakness of Caribbean small states severely restrain the policy choices open to the latter, as we shall see in Chapters Two and Three.

In the eyes of the dependency theorists, the factors just described render these states mere superstructures incapable of 'bringing any real economic independence to the area'.[12] If one were to extend this argument – as the dependency theorists do – to suggest that without economic independence a state cannot claim to be politically independent, then the obvious conclusion one would reach is that the independence of Caribbean small states is a formal notion with no real effectiveness. But there are many critics of dependency theory as it is applied to the Caribbean. One early contributor to the development of dependency literature in the area now argues that, while 'dependency theory provides a useful descriptive analysis of under-development in former colonies... (it) omitted the next logical step – the development of an operational model of economic development.'[13] It is not the purpose of this study to add to the debate on the adequacy or inadequacy of dependency theory as a framework for analysing the condition of Caribbean small states. At this juncture, however, it does nevertheless acknowledge the seductiveness of the assertion, explicit in dependency theory, that there are obvious structural constraints on the policy options open to Caribbean small states in the international system; constraints which affect their autonomy. By autonomy, I mean their capacity to decide on, and manage, their affairs as they see fit.

But to appreciate fully the constraints on the operation of Caribbean small states in the international system, it is necessary to understand their domestic condition. And it is to this that we now turn.

THE NATIONAL ENVIRONMENT

This section draws on the work on security issues by Barry Buzan who differentiates between weak states and weak powers. He defines a state's power as 'the range and size of resources and capabilities it commands.'[14] By this definition, Caribbean small states are obviously weak powers in relation to the rest of the world as we have seen from examining their economic resources, and as we shall note again when we look at their military capacity later in this chapter. But, at this point, we are concerned with whether Caribbean small states can be said to be weak or strong states as distinct from weak or strong powers. This discussion is germane to determining whether their weakness 'invites the intervention of other states'.[15]

Buzan measures a state's weakness or strength in terms of what he calls its 'sociopolitical cohesion'.[16] He renders an understanding of what he means by sociopolitical cohesion by presenting a list of nine kinds of conditions, any one of which would lead to a query of whether a state is strong. These are:

1. High levels of political violence (Kampuchea, South Africa, Ethiopia)
2. Major recent changes in the structure of political institutions (Iran, Ethiopia, Spain, Portugal)
3. Conspicuous use of force by the state in domestic political life (Afghanistan, Turkey, South Korea)
4. A conspicuous role for political police in the everyday lives of citizens (Soviet Union, Romania, Poland)
5. Major political conflict over what ideology will be used to organise the state (Peru, El Salvador)
6. Lack of coherent national identity, or the presence of contending national identities within the state (Nigeria, Ethiopia, South Africa)
7. Lack of a clear and observed hierarchy of political authority (Chad, Lebanon)
8. A high degree of state control over the media (Nicaragua, Soviet Union, China)
9. A proportionately small urban middle class (Zaire, Bangladesh).[17]

Of Buzan's conditions, only one applies to the Caribbean small states, and even then to only four of them. This relates to a 'lack of coherent identity or the presence of contending national identities within the state'. In Guyana and Trinidad and Tobago, the population is divided between people of African descent and Indian descent. This division led the Prime Minister of Trinidad and Tobago, Dr Eric Williams, to write of his country at independence: 'two races have been freed, but a society has not been formed'.[18] In Antigua and Barbuda, prior to independence the Barbudans wanted to secede from Antigua; and in St Kitts-Nevis, the Nevisians have also showed secessionist leanings. Undoubtedly, there remains within these societies some groups who would cling to an identity that is parochial (in the case of Barbuda and Nevis) or racial (in the case of Guyana and Trinidad and Tobago), but it is significant that, since the independence of these countries, these issues have retreated from national political discourse in each of the states concerned. But of greater significance is that, while racial animosity did exist in Guyana and Trinidad and Tobago, and there was some sentiment of grievance on the part of the Nevisians and Barbudans, there was never any question of a lack of identification with the state as a whole. Thus, a geographer, having spent years studying societies in Caribbean small states and comparing them with the United States, concludes:

West Indians have learned through experience how to deal with many distinctions, invidious or otherwise. In the smaller islands especially, propinquity and the need for local collaboration demand intimacy even among people who see themselves as racially different. A socio-racial continuum makes West Indians seem highly sophisticated by contrast with Americans, white or black, who are cut off from the other race.[19]

On the basis of Buzan's model, therefore, it is possible for us to conclude that Caribbean small states, while being weak powers, are strong states.

In determining the security environment of a state, Buzan also lays considerable stress on the legitimacy of political power and ideology within a state. Note should be taken here that prior to 1979, when the Caribbean small states experienced their first coup d'etat, Grenada would have been regarded as a weak state. For it experienced a 'conspicuous use of force' by the then Prime Minister, Eric Gairy, who utilised special squads of armed ruffians to 'buttress his position'.[20] There was also a high level of political violence, including an incident in which the then leader of the opposition, Maurice Bishop, was beaten and his party's entire leadership imprisoned.[21] In addition, there was a 'high degree of state control over the media'. On 13 March 1979, Bishop and his followers seized power in a bloodless and popular coup. However, over the following four years, there were obvious manifestations of a weak state. The new government imprisoned over a hundred so-called counter-revolutionaries including journalists, took control of the media, and suppressed debate on the ideology which should be used to organise the state.[22] It should be noted that since 1983 a greater degree of national consensus has developed in the state. Political parties have operated in freedom, general elections have been held and a government has been chosen. The press has also operated without state restriction.

But the condition of Grenada before the 1979 coup, and afterwards, is not a recurrent phenomenon in the Caribbean. In the contemporary

Caribbean scene, with the exception of Guyana where widespread allegations of rigged elections have long been made within and outside the country,[23] Caribbean small states 'represent the only area in the Third World where politics based on free elections, multiple parties, and liberal-democratic freedoms are still predominant'.[24]

THE MILITARY DIMENSION

As already indicated, part of the weakness of Caribbean small states, as powers, is the fact that they have no military capability of any significance. At the end of the 1980s they owned not a single combat aircraft and no warship of even frigate class. Hence, they have no air force and no navy, save for a few recently acquired and under-manned coast guard vessels. In the case of Belize, which at independence from Britain inherited a territorial dispute with Guatemala, British troops continued to provide security. Guyana, Jamaica and Trinidad and Tobago are the three Caribbean territories with modest armies. Of the three, Guyana's is the largest in per capita terms, and it was developed because that country also inherited a territorial dispute at independence – Venezuela lays claim to a large slice of Guyana. But, in Latin American terms, Guyana's army is marginal.

The seven smallest islands are part of a Regional Security System (RSS) which was developed in the late 1980s. In most of the countries, this consists of nothing more than a handful of specially-trained policemen and a fledgling coast guard service. Of these seven islands, Barbados has the largest standing defence force. Grenada had a relatively large army up to the invasion in 1983 by forces of the United States. This army was disbanded immediately after the invasion.

But while the Caribbean small states pose no military threat to others, they also have no capacity to defend themselves from superior military forces. And such forces need not come from larger states, as we shall see when we discuss intervention in Chapter Three.

THE ECONOMIC DIMENSION

Sufficient has already been said about the economic circumstances of Caribbean small states to demonstrate that they are highly vulnerable to the international environment, and that each, by itself, has little economic capacity to advance its interests in the international system. At this juncture account should be taken of one very striking feature which is a clear result of a problem of small populations. It costs the large financial institutions, such as the World Bank and the International Development Agency (IDA), the same amount of money and man-hours to service a loan for one hundred million dollars as it does for one of a million dollars; consequently they tend to favour large loans. This caused the Prime Minister of St Vincent and the Grenadines, James Mitchell, to lament to his fellow Heads of Government in 1986 that

> Many financial institutions find it impractical to offer loans below a fixed floor level – usually around US$25 million. None of us can singly handle a loan of this magnitude for any infrastructure project in one year.[25]

Restricted from access to soft loans from the international development agencies and unable to afford the high interest rates of commercial loans, Caribbean small states have often found themselves in an economic quandary. This situation led Mitchell to describe the severe limitation on the policy actions open to Caribbean small states in the following stark terms:

> Economic realities now are clearly telling us that we will not mobilise the resources to fulfil our people's demands on a continuing basis as we are now structured… Each of our economies is still largely mono-culturally oriented – sugar, bananas, cocoa, tourism. Within this framework we will simply be unable to make the structural adjustment to our economies required to enable us to recover from natural or economic shocks over an extended period. Our economies, no matter what we do, in the face of unfavourable external realities will continue to stagnate relative to our population growth at home, and the state of progress in the rest of the world.[26]

COSTS OF ADMINISTRATION

One final point remains to be made about the national environment and this concerns the costs of administration, including the costs of participation in the international system. The tax base of small populations severely limits the revenue available to governments. In turn, the lack of sufficient revenue contributes to the decline of effective administration, and is felt most particularly in external relations. For when governments are faced with the choice of spending resources on domestic or external concerns, they invariably choose the domestic ones. The reasons for this are obvious: the survival of the elite who make up the government depends upon the support they are able to muster in the national context. What is more, even if national interest is not defined in the narrow terms of the survival of the elite, but is broadened to cover the vital interest of the state, expenditure for provision of services in the national context is still more justifiable than such expenditure on international relations. This problem is not unique to small states, but it is more chronic for them since their resources are so limited that they frequently have to make the decision to neglect their external interests in favour of satisfying their domestic demands.

In any event, no Caribbean small state is as involved in the international system as larger states. There are some international institutions, for instance, in which many of them have no resident representation and in whose work they participate only at the level of general conferences. Among these are the International Labour Organisation, the World Health Organisation, the Universal Postal Union and the International Telecommunications Union. But it is at the level of bilateral representation that the limited participation of Caribbean small states is more marked. All of them have resident representation in London, Washington and Ottawa. But even by the end of the 1980s, only four of them – Barbados, Guyana, Jamaica and Trinidad and Tobago – had resident missions elsewhere, and even then their representation was limited.

The high costs of participation in international affairs, through maintaining resident missions, caused a public servant to remark that none of the missions of six of the small Caribbean states have 'anything near the capacity in their diplomatic establishments to come to terms, for example, with the intricacies of the American Congress – so increasingly influential in the decision-making of the US government'.[27] In addition, the length of international conferences and the cost of maintaining delegations at them has proved to be prohibitive for Caribbean small states. Thus, beyond a token presence, many of them have been unable to participate in international meetings, even when matters of great importance to them have been under discussion.

The situation is not different for the Foreign Ministries themselves in the majority of small Caribbean states. These are little short of nominal institutions: they are understaffed, deficient in trained and able personnel, and incapable of dealing with the range of issues (and reams of documents from international organisations) with which a Foreign Ministry is beleaguered. And while conditions are somewhat better in the larger of the small Caribbean states, the general observation made here remains valid. Obviously, this has grave implications for policy formulation. For, in the absence of adequate information, governments either formulate no policy or they depend upon unreliable information for such policy information. By unreliable information, I mean information from the international press which may not be accurate; and information from representatives of other governments which may be misleading.

In short, against this background it can be seen beyond doubt that the economic and political climate in which small Caribbean states operate severely limits their capabilities as actors in the international system.

NOTES & REFERENCES

1   See Fred Halliday, 'State and Society in International Relations: A Second Agenda', *Millennium*, Vol. 16, No. 2, 1987, pp. 215-229; see also Ian Forbes, 'The International Relations Discourse and Halliday's Second Agenda', Hidemi Suganami, 'Halliday's Two Concepts of State', and Fred Halliday, 'States, Disclosure, Classes: A Rejoinder to Suganami, Forbes and Palan', *Millennium*, Vol. 17, No. 1, 1988, pp. 61-66, 71-76 and 77-80 respectively.

2   *League of Nations Treaty Series*, 165, p. 19.

3   James Crawford, 'Islands as Sovereign Nations', *International and Comparative Law Quarterly*, Vol. 38, April 1989, p. 281.

4   Alan James, *Sovereign Statehood: The Basis of International Society*, George Allen & Unwin, London, 1986, p. 13.

5   See Burton Benedict (ed), *Problems of Smaller Territories*, The Athlone Press, London, 1967; August Schou and Arne Brundtland (eds), *Small States in International Relations*, John Wiley & Sons, New York, 1971; and Peter Selwyn (ed), *Development Policy in Small Countries*, Croom Helm, London, 1975.

6   Sheila Harden (ed), *Small is Dangerous*, Frances Pinter, London, 1985, p.51.

7   David Vital, 'The Analysis of Small Power Politics', in Schou and Brundtland (eds), *Small States in International Relations*, p. 18.

8   Unitar Series No. 3, New York, 1969. The study was done by Jacques Rapoport.

9   Report of a Commonwealth Consultative Group, *Vulnerability: Small States in the Global Society*, Commonwealth Secretariat, London, 1985, p. 9.

10 Jamaica and Trinidad and Tobago became independent in 1962; Barbados and Guyana in 1966; The Bahamas in 1973; Grenada in 1974; Dominica in 1978; St Lucia and St Vincent in 1979; Antigua and Barbuda, and Belize in 1981; and St Kitts-Nevis in 1983.

11 Lord Roseberry, Adelaide, 1884, cited by Peter Lyon, 'Small States and the Left-Overs of Empire', *The Round Table*, Special Edition, 75th Anniversary Issue, 1985, p. 48.

12 Clive Y. Thomas, *The Poor and the Powerless: Economic Policy and Change in the Caribbean*, Latin America Bureau, London, 1988, p. 72.

13 Courtney Blackman, Speech to the Students of Chancellor Hall, University of the West Indies, *Caribbean Monthly Bulletin*, Vol. 14, 1980, p. 45.

14 Barry Buzan, 'Peoples, States and Fear', in Edward E. Azar and Chung-In Moon (eds), *National Security in the Third World: The Management of Internal and External Conflicts*, Edward Elgar, Hants, 1988, p. 18.

15 *Ibid.*, p. 28.

16 *Ibid.*

17 *Ibid.*, pp. 20-21.

18 Eric Williams, *History of the People of Trinidad and Tobago*, André Deutsch, London, 1964, p. 278.

19 David Lowenthal, *West Indian Societies*, Oxford University Press, 1972, p.320.

20 Anthony Payne *et al*, *Grenada: Revolution and Invasion*, Croom Helm, London, 1984, p. 8.

21 *Ibid.*, p. 13.

22 See, in addition to Payne *et al*, *Grenada*, Hugh O'Shaughnessy, *Grenada: Revolution, Invasion and Aftermath*, Hamish Hamilton, London, 1984.

23 See Tony Thorndike, 'Guyana', *The Latin American and Caribbean Review*, Eighth Edition, World of Information, Essex, 1986, pp. 87-88.

24 Carl Stone, 'A Political Profile of the Caribbean', in Sidney W. Mintz and Sally Price (eds), *Caribbean Contours*, Johns Hopkins University Press, Baltimore, 1985, p. 13.

25 J. F. Mitchell, 'Thoughts on OECS Political Union', a paper presented to the Heads of Government of the OECS, Tortola, 13 October 1986, mimeo.
26 *Ibid*.
27 Vaughan Lewis, 'Closer Political Union', *Caribbean Affairs*, Vol.1, No. 3, July-September 1988, pp. 159-173.

CHAPTER TWO

Problems in the International System

This chapter focuses on the problems of Caribbean small states in the international system. But, before we begin this discussion, we need to consider what is meant by the term 'international system' for the purposes of this study. K.J. Holsti defines an international system as 'any collection of independent political entities – tribes, city-states, nations or empires – which interact with considerable frequency and according to regularised processes'.[1] This is the definition adopted here, for it highlights the facet of the international system with which this study is primarily concerned, namely the interaction between states. Further, the definition is broad enough to take account of the various forms of interaction between states, including political, economic and military – all of which will be considered in this study.

The development of the system dates back to the 17th Century and owes much to the enforcement by European states of their concept of an international society of juridically sovereign states. The emergence of states such as the United States, China and Japan into the international system did not alter the nature of the system or the rules by which it worked, for all three adopted the original European standards in international trade, diplomacy and legal relations.[2]

By the end of the Second World War when, it is arguable, the *modern* international system came into being, the essential basis of the system was still intact i.e. a pattern of interaction between juridically sovereign states. However, the War made an impact upon the system in two important ways: first, the United States and the Soviet Union, both possessing nuclear weapons and each espousing an ideology in direct confrontation with the other, emerged as the world's super-powers; and second, the colonial peoples embarked

---

First written as part of MA thesis, 'Caribbean Small States in the International System: Their Problems and Prospects', University of Sussex, August 1989.

upon a season of independence movements that was to see a Europe, exhausted by war, release into political independence colony after colony in Africa, Asia, the Caribbean and the Pacific. When these states entered the international system after centuries of domination and exploitation by one European power or another a new international system in which the European states were a small minority was created. But it was a system in which the numerous newly independent states were at a severe disadvantage in comparison with the two super-powers – the United States and the Soviet Union – and with Europe in terms of economic strength, social welfare and military capability.

This situation was strengthened by other developments such as the evolution of a post-war economic order created by Western states at the Bretton Woods Conference in 1944. As Javed Ansari has observed:

This international economic system had made possible the unquestioned leadership of the USA, on the one hand, and the spectacular economic recovery of Europe and Japan on the other.[3]

The economic order was founded on the corner stones of the International Monetary Fund (IMF) and the International Bank for Reconstruction and Development (the World Bank) in which the Western powers enjoyed weighted voting. The third foundation stone of the order was the General Agreement on Tariffs and Trade (GATT) which was firmly committed to an organisational ideology of a liberal trading system, seen by Third World states, including the small ones, as inimical to their aspirations; particularly, their aspirations for expanded trade on a basis which discriminates in their favour so that they could catch up in the development process, and which corrects the inequities they suffer.

Of course, in the decades since the Second World War, the international system has undergone great change. Even by the end of the 1980s it was no longer dominated by the United States and the Soviet Union. While the preponderance of nuclear weapons remained mainly in the control of those two states, other countries – France, Britain and China – had developed their own nuclear arsenals, and military power had become a zero-sum game which, as Olaf Palme observed, 'could destroy neutrals as well as belligerents, the South as well as the North'.[4] The system had changed in other ways too.

First, the United States was no longer the leading economic power in the Western World; the European Community, which planned to bring a single internal market into effect in 1992, and Japan commanded as important a place in the management of the economic system.[5] Secondly, economic decline in the USSR precipitated in the late 1980s what Fred Halliday called a 'diplomatic accord' between the United States and the Soviet Union, and this led to a rapprochement on a number of issues including attempts by them to end 'regional' conflicts in the Third World.[6] Thirdly, beginning in 1964 with the establishment of the United Nations Conference on Trade and Development (UNCTAD), the newly independent Third World states launched an institutional challenge to the management of the international economic system by the Western developed countries. Their objective was 'to increase their access to the management and thus to the rewards of the international economic system'.[7] But their efforts in the early 1970s in the United Nations (UN) to persuade Western developed states to accept their plans for a New International Economic Order (NIEO) failed, and Third World countries remain excluded from management of the economic system.

INDEPENDENCE OF CARIBBEAN SMALL STATES

Since the 1960s, over 30 small states have become independent states in the formal sense, enjoying a presumption of equality with larger states in the international system. The way was cleared for their independence and subsequent admission to membership of the UN by several factors. First, in the late 1960s and into the 1970s, Britain, whose colonies made up the majority of small states, fared badly economically.

In 1969, Denis Healey, then Secretary of State for Defence, declared that the seal had been set for 'Britain's transformation from a world power to a European power'.[8] By 1977, the British economy had so badly declined that the government was forced to seek assistance from the IMF and accept its conditionality. Thus, the British government was more than ready to be spared the burden of the defence and economic upkeep of the leftovers of its empire – small states scattered mostly in the Caribbean Sea and the Pacific Ocean.

The Minister of State in the Foreign and Commonwealth Office at the time, Ted Rowlands, admits that he 'made a modest contribution in four and a half years to the creation of a series of small states' by actively encouraging colonies into independence.[9] Part of the process was to deny them economic assistance which Britain could ill afford. Thus, in 1978 when the Deputy Premier of Antigua and Barbuda, Lester Bird, justified his government's decision to seek independence, he did so on the basis that

Avenues will be opened for membership of institutions like the Inter American Development Bank, providing us the opportunity for direct financing of development projects; we will be able to reap benefits from the World Bank and the specialised agencies of the United Nations such as UNESCO, UNDP and FAO.[10]

Secondly, in the late 1950s, the developing states in the UN – fresh themselves from the experience of colonialism – demanded independence for all colonial peoples and countries. In 1960, the UN adopted Resolution 1514 in which it was declared that 'questions of territorial size, geographical isolation and limited resources should in no way' delay the granting of independence to colonies.[11] Thus, the UN set the rules for independence. Small states, whether they were economically viable or not, whether they had the capacity to defend themselves or not, whether they could be effectively independent of other states or not, were to be accepted into the international system, and into the UN itself.

However, admission was one thing; achieving changes in the international system – and in the UN's own structure – was quite another. Third World states have long had a majority in the General Assembly, but while General Assembly decisions of the UN, in certain circumstances, can have the effect of establishing binding rules, they are not normally binding on member states, and can only achieve implementation if the larger states support them. Thus, in those cases where large states have supported Third World initiatives, rules and norms have been established in the international system. An example of this is the resolution, already discussed, which urged the granting of independence for colonial peoples. This resolution had the support of both the United States and the Soviet Union. However, other attempts by the Third World majority to alter the international system failed dismally as and when at least one of the super powers opposed them. A good example of this is the Third World's attempts to push for a New International Economic Order (NIEO) in the UN General Assembly following the disarray of developed countries in the wake of an oil crisis in 1973 when the Organisation of Petroleum Exporting Countries (OPEC) not only raised prices but imposed an embargo against supplying oil to certain Western nations including the United States. At the Sixth Special Session of the UN in 1974, which the United States boycotted, Third World countries secured the adoption by consensus of two documents: 'The Declaration on the Establishment of a New International Economic Order' and a 'Programme of Action on the Establishment of a New Economic Order'. The declaration sought:

> The establishment of a new international economic order based on equity, sovereignty, equality, interdependence, common interest and co-operation among all States, irrespective of their economic and social systems which shall correct inequalities and redress existing injustices, make it possible to eliminate the widening gap between the developed and the developing countries and ensure steadily accelerating economic and social development and peace and justice for present and future generations.[12]

Later that same year, the twenty-ninth session of the UN General Assembly, by majority vote, also adopted the 'Charter of the Economic Rights and Duties of States'. The Charter sought to establish that:

> Every State has and shall freely exercise full permanent sovereignty, including possession, use and disposal, over all its wealth, natural resources and economic activities.[13]

It is significant that six industrialised countries opposed the Charter and ten other countries abstained showing that they did not support it. Among the states which opposed the Charter were the United States, Britain and West Germany. Japan, France and Canada were among those which abstained.[14] In the end, none of these three attempts by Third World states to affect change in the international economic structure came to anything. As two analysts observed:

The fact still remains that the balance of power has not undergone any lasting, fundamental change, and that the Third World is, in the present state of affairs, incapable of imposing on the industrialised countries any effective implementation of the majority of its demands.[15]

The important general point here is that while small states, like many other Third World countries, have joined the international system as juridically sovereign states, they have done so at its margins, with little power to change its fundamental rules and little capacity to derive benefits from it. However, there are some specific features of Caribbean small states in the international system which need additionally to be considered.

THE GEO-POLITICAL SETTING

An important aspect of the decolonisation experience of the Caribbean small states was the fact they suddenly found themselves linked to Latin America in international organisations as part of the same regional grouping. But a history of political separation, and connections to rival metropoles in Europe, had divided the two groups of countries. The realisation that they could only function on the international scene as members of the same group was traumatic on both sides, and although they both have always shared common problems – not least problems of security – only a few of them on each side have tried to build a modus vivendi which could be mutually beneficial.

However, such bilateral relations as exist between individual Caribbean and Latin American states have tended to be based on what each Latin American state perceives as its own interest. Venezuela, for instance, has diplomatic relations with every independent Caribbean small state, including Guyana with which it has a border dispute. This has been attributed to the fact that the important commercial and industrial centres of Venezuela face the

Caribbean sea where outlets are of prime significance for the export of oil.[16] Mexico has also shown an interest in the Caribbean small states, and this is linked to its own territorial claim to part of Belize. Mexico's interest has traditionally been to forestall Guatemala from pressing its claim for all of Belizean territory.[17] And Argentina, in the wake of the 1982 war with Britain over the Falklands/Malvinas, has actively pursued relations with the Caribbean small states – all of which had condemned Argentina in the United Nations in 1982 for initiating the use of force in the conflict with Britain.

Individual bilateral relations apart, the two groups rival each other for offices allocated to Latin America and the Caribbean within international organisations. This rivalry has not been helped by the fact that many of the countries in Latin America and the Caribbean have similar resources which each has developed independently and is marketing competitively. They also compete with each other for aid and investment. But of far greater significance is that there are few direct links between the two groups in trade, and air transport links exist only between the Caribbean and Venezuela and Brazil. With the exception of Belize and Guyana, all the Caribbean small states became relatively early members of the Organisation of American States (OAS).[18] This organisation groups together the countries of Latin America, Canada the Caribbean and the United States of America, but, apart from meetings of the Organisation itself, it has not promoted wider contact between Latin America and the Caribbean. At one time it was felt that the Latin American states were 'not overjoyed at the prospect of commingling with "black" states'.[19] Thus, a study of the relationship between Latin American and Caribbean countries concluded:

> It would seem then, that there are basic and very significant differences between Latin America and the Caribbean in ethnic, cultural, political and institutional terms, and in size; and that these differences along with the lack of adequate contact and exchange between the two groups of countries present real difficulties in the way of pursuing collaborative relationships.[20]

In short, the small Caribbean states and the larger Latin American territories share very little more than the same geographical region of the world, and their relationship is not mutually supportive. This lack of co-operation between the two groups contributes to the inability of the Caribbean small states to safeguard themselves from domination by the strongest power in the hemisphere – the United States of America.

RELATIONS WITH THE UNITED STATES

The relationship between the United States and the Caribbean is one which restrains the freedom of action of small Caribbean states both in their domestic and international affairs. In a real sense, the dominance of the United States in the hemisphere and the readiness of successive US administrations to coerce the governments of small Caribbean states, as well as to intervene directly in their territories, deprives them of the choice of maintaining close relations with countries regarded as enemies by the United States. This situation also constrains their freedom of action in terms of the ideology which they pursue domestically and the positions which they adopt internationally.

The underpinnings of the US attitude to Caribbean small states is the doctrine declared by US President James Monroe in 1823 to the effect that no power should extend its political system into Latin America and the Caribbean because the US would regard this as 'endangering our peace and happiness'.[21] The so-called 'Corollary' to the Monroe Doctrine, pronounced by President Theodore Roosevelt in 1904, more firmly established the US view that it has 'the right to intervene in the countries of the Western hemisphere when it considered it necessary to forestall intervention by non-American powers'.[22] As Gordon Connell-Smith has remarked:

> This came to mean that the United States would not permit the countries of (the region) to enter into international relationships outside the hemisphere which could threaten (US) security.[23]

US administrations have another reason for wanting to ensure that no governments come to office which would be friendly toward what they consider to be their enemies. Forty-four per cent of all foreign cargo tonnage and 45 per cent of the crude oil imported into the United States transit the sea lanes that pass through the Caribbean.[24] Thus, as Lloyd Searwar puts it, 'despite their small size the Caribbean states are thrust into the front ranks of US defence objectives'.[25]

But, apart from US security concerns in the area, Caribbean small states are locked into an economically dependent relationship with the United States. At the end of the Second World War, when the United States emerged as the strongest single economic power in the world, it gradually began to replace Britain's economic influence in the Caribbean small states. And, while the strength of the United States as an economic power in the world has waned somewhat, its dominant economic position in the Caribbean has increased. Throughout the 1970s and 1980s US investment and aid in, as well as its trade with, Caribbean small states was bigger than any other single country. What is more, its influence over financial institutions such as the World Bank and the IMF gives it additional economic weight in the reckoning of Caribbean small states.

The measure of US influence over the Caribbean small states in the international system can be taken by the extent of the relations they had with communist countries. At the end of the 1980s, of the twelve small states, seven had diplomatic relations with the People's Republic of China, and most of them established these relations only after the United States did so. Only five had relations with Cuba, and only three with the Soviet Union.

A further dimension of the US-Caribbean relationship is that the United States is the most favoured destination for Caribbean emigrants. The US and Canada are the only two countries which still allow immigration from the Caribbean, but Canada's policy has tended to be the more restrictive. This emigration is as important to the governments of Caribbean small states as it is to the people, for it acts as a safety valve against the demands of growing populations.[26] Note should be taken, however, that the US has become keen to 'regulate migration' from the Caribbean 'because large groups of immigrants are increasingly a source of local anxieties' in many American states.[27]

THE REGIONAL ENVIRONMENT

Caribbean small states have operated an economic integration grouping for over thirty years. The Caribbean Free Trade Association (CARIFTA) was created in 1968 and it was deepened in 1973 to become the Caribbean Community and Common Market

(CARICOM). What was significant about the creation, and deepening, of the integration process is that they were both principally motivated by external considerations. In the case of six of the countries which were then not independent, their concern in 1968 was to be free of Britain. They perceived their only hope of gaining independence as lying in a strong economic relationship amongst themselves and other Caribbean states. In the case of the two mainland territories, Belize and Guyana, both of which had stayed out of the West Indies Federation, their governments believed that they would benefit from the support of Caribbean integration partners in their territorial disputes with Guatemala and Venezuela. Jamaica, Trinidad and Tobago and Barbados were the only three countries which saw the economic integration process in domestic terms. Their industries were better developed than the others and the increased market provided a greater opportunity. As Irene Hawkins observed:

> Jamaica and Trinidad and Tobago, and to a lesser extent Barbados, were unloading their industrial products in the markets of the small agricultural Leeward and Windward Islands. They in turn sold very little to these three countries, for the simple reason that they produced practically nothing but a handful of agricultural products which the big three mostly grew themselves.[28]

This realisation, and the subsequent protests which arose, was overshadowed by external events. In 1972, the British government acceded to membership of the European Economic Community (EEC). This immediately raised alarms in the Caribbean over the future of their agricultural products exported to Britain under Commonwealth agreements. The issue was further complicated by a decision of the enlarged EEC to negotiate 'individually' with independent Caribbean countries on an economic arrangement which would include aid and trade. No formal participation was envisaged for the non-independent countries. However, in the Caribbean, it was felt strongly that for the preservation of the existing trade benefits with Britain, a common approach – and, if possible, a common single relationship with the enlarged EEC covering all the members of the Caribbean integration movement – was absolutely essential.[29] One analyst noted:

This was one of the reasons that led to the transformation of the existing integration scheme (CARIFTA) into a more closely integrated grouping, the new Caribbean Community and Common Market (CARICOM), a grouping better equipped to ensure the deepening process within the movement and also to represent the movement as one solid bloc, with an international legal capacity and a treaty making capacity vis-à-vis the outside world and the EEC particularly.[30]

The joint negotiations by the Caribbean with the EEC were of considerable benefit to individual Caribbean countries, resulting in institutionalised arrangements on trade and aid, particularly recognition of the principle of non-reciprocity of trade access which the Caribbean demanded. It is to be noted, however, that the Caribbean small states did not seek to repeat this joint negotiating exercise when the United States proposed a Caribbean Basin Initiative (CBI) in 1981 to allow certain products from the Caribbean duty-free access to the US market. As a result, Grenada and Guyana – both with socialist governments at the time – were excluded from benefits.[31] Similarly, when the Canadian government also proposed CARIBCAN, a preferential trade agreement for the Caribbean, the governments sought no negotiations and Canada unilaterally decided what the arrangement should be.

It is also significant that the governments of the Caribbean small states have not worked out common arrangements for dealing with transnational corporations (TNCs). Indeed, in this regard, the tendency has been to compete with each other for foreign investment. Consequently, foreign companies have been able to play one country off against the other, frequently getting over-generous tax holidays and other incentives. In the years since its establishment, CARICOM has suffered many strains. Its most difficult period was 1975-1980 when personal relations between a few heads of government deteriorated and no conference was held by them, even though an annual conference is a requirement of the CARICOM treaty. It was also a difficult period economically. High oil costs following OPEC's price increase in 1973, and recession in the Western countries to which, as we have seen, the economies of the Caribbean are linked, took a grievous toll. Intra-Caribbean trade, which had reached a high point in 1973, rapidly declined and by 1988 had still not returned to its apex, though after 1986 there was a steady improvement.[32]

Politically, this period also tested the durability of the integration movement as some countries – Guyana, Grenada, Jamaica and, for a time, St Lucia – adopted resolute socialist positions, while other governments remained right-wing. Although the CARICOM treaty called on its member-states 'to co-ordinate' their foreign policies, each pursued its own course, and voting on issues in the UN General Assembly often reflected a division in Caribbean ranks.

After 1982, with the death of a number of heads of government, the removal of the Marxist government in Grenada and the change from a socialist government in Jamaica, CARICOM Heads of Government Conferences resumed on an annual basis, and, as has been noted, intra-Caribbean trade improved. There had also been a reversal of the ideological divergence of governments and a willingness once again to deepen the integration process. This was evidenced by the fact that, between 1986 and 1989, the governments decided to remove all barriers to intra-Caribbean trade, to set up a common external tariff by January 1991 and to enter joint production and joint marketing programmes by January 1990.[33] As Vaughan Lewis says, this may have been due to the fact that:

> The countries have now reached the end of the line of unilateral, extra-regional initiatives. These now seem to be largely unproductive, and to have the consequences of always turning their initiators back to the region for support.[34]

THE WIDER INTERNATIONAL CONTEXT

Four further observations should be noted about Caribbean small states for they distinguish their operations in the international system and are relevant to their capacity, or lack of it, to resist intervention in their affairs.

First, these states command 12 votes in the UN system i.e., in the UN General Assembly and in the general conferences of all the UN agencies such as UNESCO, ILO, WHO, etc. These votes are important to larger and more powerful states which, for one reason or another, wish to defeat resolutions which do not suit them, or to support resolutions which they consider to be in their interests. The Caribbean small states also command ten votes in the OAS. This voting power in the OAS – half of the voting strength of the Organisation – is important to larger powers, particularly the United States, Britain and Argentina. It is significant that, throughout the hostile relations between Britain and Argentina over the Falklands/Malvinas, both countries lobbied Caribbean small states for their support in the UN and OAS.

Secondly, of the 12 Caribbean small states only four – Guyana, Jamaica, Barbados and Trinidad and Tobago – have attempted on any sustained basis to widen their international participation to embrace Third World organisations concerned with alerting the international system to achieve greater benefits for developing countries, although it should be noted that under the Marxist government of Maurice Bishop, between 1979 and 1983, Grenada was also active in Third World groupings such as the Non-Aligned Movement (NAM) and the Group of 77 (G77). In the G77 and the NAM, Guyana and Jamaica were particularly active in the early 1970s in the promotion of the NIEO. However, it is difficult for small countries to be genuinely non-aligned, particularly when they live under the shadow of the United States which has traditionally regarded NAM with deep suspicion.

Since the US invasion of Grenada in 1983, those Caribbean small states which are members of the NAM and the G77 have dropped their profile, and the others have not bothered to join.[35] In any event solidarity in the G77, evident in the late 1960s and early 1970s, has now virtually disappeared.[36] From the mid 1970s, the approach of the leading Western industrialised countries towards the developing countries has been designed to divide the G77, applying different policies to different sub-groups of the G77.[37] A resurgence of bilateralism placed some Third World countries – Caribbean small states included – in a situation of greater dependency on major developed countries. It also led to a widening gap in the levels of development among the developing countries themselves, and thus created a situation in which agreement between them for changes in the international economic environment became difficult. A series of vertical linkages on a regional basis, offering trade and tariff preferences to some regions, served to further weaken their solidarity. Among the vertical linkages were EEC agreements with African, Caribbean and Pacific (ACP) countries on aid and trade, US adoption of the Caribbean Basin Initiative giving Caribbean and Central American countries preferential access to the US market for certain goods, introduction of CARIBCAN also giving some Caribbean products special access to the Canadian market, and special trade agreements between Japan and certain countries in Asia. As is obvious, Caribbean small states were beneficiaries of most of these vertical agreements. Many of them, therefore, saw no need to become embroiled in Third World battles with the industrialised countries.

Thirdly, membership of the Commonwealth and the African, Caribbean and Pacific (ACP) group gave Caribbean small states a wider diplomatic reach than they would otherwise have had. The Commonwealth is particularly valuable to them, because the biennial summit conference places their heads of government directly in contact with the Prime Ministers of Canada and Britain, who also participate in meetings of NATO and the OECD. Further, the Commonwealth summit gives them access to other influential Third World leaders. With regard to the ACP, membership considerably strengthens their bargaining position with the EEC on trade and aid matters. The cohesion of the ACP has been valuable to all the Caribbean small states, for they have derived preferential – even though limited – access to the EEC market, as well as aid, under the various Lomé Conventions. Note should be taken, however, that the aid and trade benefits secured by the ACP have not been as extensive as the countries would like. According to some analysts, the EEC has not provided better terms of trade and it has sought to impose conditions on its aid, including the right to approve the economic strategies of aid recipients. As one writer put it, the EEC-ACP pacts 'are geared toward perpetuating or updating dependence by the ACP countries'.[38]

Fourthly, little contact took place between Caribbean small states and the Soviet Union and other communist countries including Cuba. As mentioned earlier, five Caribbean small states had diplomatic relations with Cuba and only four with the Soviet Union. This is not to suggest that Cuba and the Soviet Union were not interested in the Caribbean. Left-wing parties in the Caribbean small states often

70

attended conferences in Moscow and Havana, and these parties sent supporters for training in a variety of disciplines to the Soviet Union and Cuba. But, as one writer suggested, 'neither country would or could sustain any overt military action in the region'.[39] What is more, the most vociferous opposition parties in Caribbean small states have tended to be the left-wing groups, and governing parties have accordingly adopted the US stance of attacking communism as evil. Therefore, there is a general feeling of mistrust at the level of governments between Caribbean small states and communist states.

CONCLUSION

We can now conclude that Caribbean small states, by virtue of structural constraints, have generally been firmly locked in the camp of the Western industrialised states, particularly the United States. Their dependency on these countries has been increased by the special preferences in aid and trade which have been accorded to them by the United States, Canada and the EEC. Their links to other Third World states are weak except through the Commonwealth and the ACP, and they had virtually no relationship with communist countries, except one of mutual suspicion. As a consequence, the autonomy of Caribbean small states – the ability to make decisions and follow them through by independent action – is severely restricted. Whether, and for how long, they can continue to operate in the international system as sovereign entities is, and remains, an open question.

NOTES & REFERENCES

1   K.J. Holsti, *International Politics: A Framework for Analysis*, Prentice Hall, London, 1974, p. 29.
2   See Hedley Bull, 'A Universal International Society', in Hedley Bull and Adam Watson (eds), *The Expansion of International Society*, Clarendon Press, Oxford, 1984, pp. 117-126.
3   Javed A. Ansari, *The Political Economy of International Economic Organisation*, Harvester Wheatsheaf, Sussex, 1986, p. 188.
4   Report of the Independent Commission on Disarmament and Security Issues under the Chairmanship of Olaf Palme, *Common Security: A Programme for Disarmament*, Pan Books, London, 1982, p. x.
5   Joan Edelman Spero, *The Politics of International Economic Relations*, George Allen & Unwin, London, 1985, p. 30.
6   Fred Halliday, *Cold War, Third World: An Essay on Soviet-American Relations*, Hutchinson-Radius, London, 1989, p. 163.
7   Spero, *Politics of International Economic Relations*, p. 28.
8   Cited by Paul Kennedy, *The Realities Behind Diplomacy: Background Influences on British External Policy 1865 – 1980*, Fontana Press, London, 1981, p. 376.
9   Edward Rowlands, 'What overall can the Commonwealth do for its small states?', Report of the Annual Conference of the Royal Commonwealth Society, *The Small States and the Commonwealth*, 19 June 1984, London, mimeo.
10 Lester Bird, *A Declaration for Development*, Statement to the Antigua Labour Party Convention, 7 September 1978, St. John's, Antigua.
11 See paragraph 17 of UN Resolution 1514 adopted by the General Assembly on 14 December 1960.
12 United Nations General Assembly, Sixth Special Session, Official Records, A/RES/3201 (S-VI), 9 May 1974.
13 United Nations General Assembly, Twenty Ninth Session, Official Records, GA/SUP. 31, A/3281.
14 Phillippe Braillard and Mohammad-Reza Djalili, *The Third World and International Relations*, Frances Pinter, London, 1986, p. 171.
15 *Ibid.*, p. 173.
16 See Demetrio Boesner, 'The Policy of Venezuela towards the Caribbean', in L.F. Manigat (ed), *The Caribbean Yearbook of International Relations 1975*, A.W. Sijthoff, Leyden, 1976.
17 See Vaughan Lewis, 'Commonwealth Caribbean Relations with Hemispheric Middle Powers', in Anthony Payne and Paul Sutton (eds), *Dependency Under Challenge: The Political Economy of the Commonwealth Caribbean*, Manchester University Press, Manchester, 1984, pp. 238-258.
18 Belize and Guyana were initially precluded from joining the OAS by virtue of their border disputes with two existing members – Guatemala and Venezuela respectively.
19 Tad Szulc (ed), *The United States and the Caribbean*, Prentice Hall, New Jersey, 1971, p. 208.
20 D.O. Mills and V.A. Lewis, 'Caribbean/Latin American Relations: A Study prepared for the Economic Commission for Latin America (Subregional Office for the Caribbean) and the Caribbean Community Secretariat', CEPAL/CARIB 82/16, 2 November 1982, p. 7.
21 Cited by D.P. O'Connell, *International Law*, Vol. 1, Stevens and Sons, London, 1970, p. 307.

22 Gordon Connell-Smith, 'The Grenada Invasion in Historical Perspective: From Monroe to Reagan', *Third World Quarterly*, Vol. 6, No. 2, April 1984, p. 433.
23 *Ibid.*
24 See Abraham F Lowenthal, 'The US, Central America, and the Caribbean', in John D. Martz (ed), *United States Policy in Latin America: A Quarter Century of Crisis and Challenge, 1961-1986*, University of Nebraska Press, Lincoln, 1988, p. 272.
25 Lloyd Searwar, *Peace, Development and Security in the Caribbean Basin: Perspectives to the Year 2000*, Report of a Conference held in Jamaica, 22-25 March, 1987, Canadian Institute for International Peace and Security, Ottawa, p. 7.
26 See Dawn Marshall, 'The International Politics of Caribbean Migration', in Richard Millett and W. Marvin Will (eds), *The Restless Caribbean: Changing Patterns of International Relations*, Praeger Publishers, New York, 1979, pp. 42-50.
27 See Lowenthal, 'The US, Central America, and the Caribbean', p. 273.
28 Irene Hawkins, *The Changing Face of the Caribbean*, Cedar Press, Barbados, 1976, p. 229.
29 See *From CARIFTA to CARICOM*, Commonwealth Caribbean Regional Secretariat, Guyana, 1972.
30 Hans-Joerg Geiser, 'The Lomé Convention and Caribbean Integration: A First Assessment', *Revista/Review InterAmericana*, Vol. 6, No. 1, Spring 1976.
31 Grenada was allowed benefits under the CBI after the US invasion in 1983, and in 1989 Guyana was allowed benefits after its government reversed its socialist policies, including divesting nationalised industries and permitting unrestricted foreign investment.
32 See CARICOM Secretariat Press Release 49/1989, 'Intra-CARICOM trade sees further advance in 1988', Georgetown, Guyana.
33 See 'Grand Anse Declaration and Work Programme for the Advancement of the Integration Movement', Press Release 63/1989, CARICOM Secretariat, Georgetown, Guyana.
34 Vaughan A Lewis, 'Some Perspectives on Caribbean Community Integration', *Caribbean Affairs*, Vol. 1, No. 1, 1988, pp. 85-100.
35 Of the 12 Caribbean small states, only five were members of NAM by the end of the 1980s. These were The Bahamas, Barbados, Guyana, Jamaica and Trinidad and Tobago. See Sally Morphet, 'The Non-Aligned Movement and the Foreign Ministers Meeting at Nicosia', *International Relations*, Vol. 9, No. 5, May 1989, pp. 404-405.
36 See Chakravarthi Raghavan, 'UNCTAD and the Group of 77 at Twenty-one: Hope or Uncertainty?', *Third World Affairs 1985*, Third World Foundation, London, pp. 54-63.
37 See Carol Geldart and Peter Lyon, 'The Group of 77: A Perspective View', *International Affairs*, 1981, p. 96.
38 S.K.B. Asante, 'The Lomé Convention: Towards Perpetuation of Dependence or Promotion of Interdependence', *Third World Quarterly*, Vol. 3, No. 4, 1981, p. 672.
39 Gary Lewis, 'Prospects for a Regional Security System in the Eastern Caribbean', *The Round Table*, No. 298, April 1986, p. 672.

CHAPTER THREE

Sovereignty and Intervention

In the previous chapter, I tried to establish that Caribbean small states are strong states but weak powers in economic and military terms. Further, I suggested that as a consequence of being weak powers they are vulnerable to intervention and, indeed, to severe constraints on their decision-making capacity. This chapter is concerned with identifying some of the ways in which these states have suffered intervention and deprivation of their decision-making capacity since 1962 when the first two of them became independent states in the international system. We begin with a discussion of their status as sovereign states.

THE ISSUE OF SOVEREIGNTY AND INTERVENTION

Sovereignty has two aspects: internal and external. There is internal sovereignty in the sense that the state is the supreme law-making authority within its defined territory and has the coercive power to enforce its laws. There is also external sovereignty in the sense that the state is independent of all other entities and speaks and acts for itself internationally. It is external sovereignty with which this chapter is concerned.

The literature on sovereignty has as many definitions as there are analysts, and there are those who argue that sovereignty has become such a 'flawed, outmoded and inadequate concept' that it should be 'demoted'.[1] Undoubtedly, states no longer have the absolute quality of sovereignty which they enjoyed in the 18th and 19th Centuries. The emergence of TNCs, membership of international organisations,

First written as part of MA thesis, 'Caribbean Small States in the International System: Their Problems and Prospects', University of Sussex, August 1989.

international legal agreements – all these have helped to erode the status of sovereignty by constraining states from independent action in many areas. Measured in those terms, there is more than a little appeal in J. G. Starke's argument that 'in a practical sense, sovereignty is largely a matter of degree'.[2]

But, however much sovereignty may have lost its quality of absoluteness, and however intense the process of interdependence in the world may have become, the possession of sovereignty is of great importance to small states. For it is their status as 'sovereign' states – independent of higher authority – that gives them access to the international system. Article 2 (1) of the UN Charter specifically states that 'the organisation is based on the principle of the sovereign equality of all it members'. And, as J.D.B. Miller points out:

When we say a state is sovereign, this is a separate statement from saying that it is politically or economically viable. It is merely to say that this state, however poor and ineffective, is accepted as a state by others, and consequently can claim the privileges, opportunities and the diplomatic equality which those others have.[3]

The access to the international system which small states achieve by virtue of being sovereign is extremely important since it gives them a vote in international organisations with which, to an admittedly limited degree, they can bargain with larger states. It also gives them access to the international system should they have need to bring larger states to book for acts of intervention. And, as indicated earlier, while they cannot change the structure of the international system, unless supported by larger states including the super powers, they can participate in the elaboration of certain rules which benefit them. Moreover, sovereignty allows them to enter agreements with other states and international organisations, such as the World Bank, for financial assistance.

There is a further reason why sovereignty is vitally important to small states: it is the very possession of sovereignty that protects a small state from extinction. For, as J.D.B. Miller again argues, 'other states wish to see the principle of sovereignty respected'.[4] In this connection, the fact that so many states have a vested interest in preserving the principle of sovereignty acts as a deterrent to large states which might wish to absorb small ones. An example of the importance attached by states to sovereignty can be gleaned from the statement of Commonwealth Heads of Government authorising a study of the security needs of small states. They made it clear that the study should be 'consonant with the right to sovereignty and territorial integrity that they (small states) share with all nations'.[5]

This brings us to the issue of intervention. And here it should be made clear that the involvement of State A in the affairs of State B by invitation of the legitimate authority of State B cannot be regarded as intervention. Indeed, if State B has voluntarily imposed limitations on its own sovereignty, it can be argued that it has, in fact, exercised its sovereign rights. And the consequences which flow from the exercise of such rights can be accepted as legitimate. As Hedley Bull put it:

> A state's freedom to invite other states to undertake tasks within its sphere of jurisdiction is, indeed, an aspect of its sovereignty; and any suggestion that there could not be assistance of this kind by one state to another on the basis of consent would be generally regarded as intolerable.[6]

The problem of intervention arises where State A seeks to coerce State B into taking action, or not taking action, against the will of State B. Further, intervention could be said to have occurred if State A uses force, or other coercive measures, against State B to bring about a result which might not otherwise have occurred, and which is designed to benefit State A. This kind of action is a restriction of the capacity of State B to exercise rights to which it is entitled as a sovereign state.

But, if uninvited intervention is a limitation on the capacity of a state to exercise its sovereign rights, it is still pertinent to ask: intervention by whom? And here there may well be a new dimension introduced by the problems faced by small states. Until now, the discussion of intervention has referred only to interference in one state by another state. Indeed, in international law[7] in the UN Charter and in UN resolutions, references to the actors in intervention have been limited to states. For example, Article 2 (4) of the UN Charter declares:

All members shall refrain in their international relations from the threat or use of force against the territorial integrity or political independence of any state, or in any manner inconsistent with the Purposes of the United Nations.

Further, in Resolution 2131 (XX) adopted in 1965 by the UN General Assembly, it was stated that:

No state has the right to intervene, directly or indirectly, for any reason whatever, in the internal or external affairs of any other state. Consequently, armed intervention and all other forms of interference or attempted threats against the personality of the state or against its political, economic or cultural elements are condemned.[8]

Of great significance, as well, is the fact that this resolution, while limiting itself to actions by states, did not limit intervention to armed force. It said:

No state may use or encourage the use of economic, political or any other type of measure to coerce another state in order to obtain from it the subordination of the exercise of its sovereign rights or to secure from it advantages of any kind.[9]

The experience of small states, however, has highlighted the reality that interference – a *de facto* intervention – can derive from actors other than states. This has been clear for some time on the economic front with, for example, the leverage exercised by TNCs over even the middle-sized states,[10] but new realities are emerging in the security area where, up to quite recently, intervention was essentially a threat from other states. Now, entities far less powerful than states can pose real security threats to very small states, and even intervene militarily to seize governmental control against the wishes of all or most of the population.

The experience in 1988 of The Maldive Islands is instructive. There an attempt was made, without overt or covert involvement by any state, to topple the government by a military incursion mounted from outside and executed with the aid of mercenaries. This was clearly not intervention in the traditional sense. It was, however, a practical demonstration of the vulnerability of small states to intervention from groups other than states. And it raised the question of whether there ought not to be a reappraisal of the concept of intervention itself at least in the context of sovereignty, particularly as those who have studied the security needs of small states argue that fifty determined men could take over most small states.[11]

In the light of the foregoing discussion, when the term 'intervention' is used subsequently in this study it is intended to cover actions by states alone. Those acts by private groups such as mercenaries, TNCs and drug traffickers which erode the sovereign authority of states will be described as restrictions on their autonomy.

INCIDENTS IN CARIBBEAN SMALL STATES

Since their independence from Britain, the state which has intervened most in Caribbean small states is the United States. In the period after the Second World War, when the United States started to see global relations through an East-West prism, American administrations became obsessively concerned with stopping communist movements in Latin America and the Caribbean. Each communist group in these countries was seen by the Americans as a Soviet foothold in their backyard. This obsessive concern has remained a dominant extension of the Monroe Doctrine and the Roosevelt 'Corollary', referred to earlier, by which the US has tried to legitimise its position that it has the right to intervene in the countries of Latin America and the Caribbean. However, it is worth noting that the International Court of Justice has rejected the United States' idea of its right to intervene in another state. When in the mid 1980s Nicaragua took the United States to the Court on charges of intervention, the Court found:

> The United States authorities have on some occasions clearly stated their grounds for intervening in the affairs of a foreign state for reasons connected with, for example, the domestic policies of that country, its ideology, the level of its armaments, or the direction

79

of its foreign policy. But these were statements of international policy, and not an assertion of rules or existing international law... The Court therefore finds that no such general right of intervention, in support of an opposition within another state, exists in international law.[12]

This did not stop continued intervention by the United States in Nicaragua, particularly in support of the opposition forces.

In any event, the US has repeatedly intervened overtly and covertly in Latin American and Caribbean countries to end communist movements and stamp US hegemony on the area. These interventions have been well documented,[13] so here we can simply note that in Guatemala in 1954 a covert military operation removed the left-leaning government; in British Guiana (now Guyana) in the period 1961-64 US involvement helped to delay independence and remove a Marxist government; in the Dominican Republic in 1965 US troops landed to prevent what Washington feared might become a communist takeover; and in 1983 the US invaded Grenada, ostensibly at the invitation of the Governor-General of the country, but in a campaign which, it has been suggested, was designed to overthrow the Marxist government and was planned and rehearsed at least two years before in an exercise code-named 'Operation Amber'.[14]

An indication of US covert intervention in the affairs of Caribbean small states came in 1972 when Barbados, Guyana, Jamaica (then under the socialist government of Michael Manley) and Trinidad and Tobago established diplomatic relations with Cuba effectively breaking the Latin American diplomatic embargo on Cuba. Conscious that they would each suffer the wrath of the United States if they established relations with Cuba individually, they did so collectively. The United States took action against these states; action which intensified after the latter allowed Cuba to use their airports, in 1975, as transit points for the movement of Cuban troops into Angola to support the Marxist government there against rebel forces backed by the United States. The nature of US action was not officially disclosed, nor was the US named specifically as taking action against the states involved, but the Second Meeting of Foreign Ministers of the Caribbean small states noted in a communiqué in March 1976 that 'there was evidence of a campaign of planned, sustained hostility from some circles against some member states particularly Guyana and Jamaica'. That same year, the Fifth Conference of Heads of Government of Non-Aligned Countries in Colombo stated in its communiqué that it had examined:

> In particular, the situation of certain Non-Aligned countries in the area (Latin America) that are targets of pressure, coercion and intimidation. The Conference especially took note of the statements by the Prime Ministers of Guyana, Jamaica and Barbados concerning attempts to 'destabilise' their governments.

Note should be taken that, in the late 1960s and early 1970s, the independent Caribbean small states – then only four in number – enjoyed greater flexibility in terms of the hegemonic control of the United States than they did in the late 1970s and the 1980s. In the former period, the US was still reeling from the effects of the costly war it had fought in Vietnam, and its economy had gone into the doldrums. Its confidence as both a military and economic power was shaken. Moreover, OPEC had demonstrated US vulnerability to oil supplies from the Third World. In 1972 'the United States used oil for 46 percent of its energy and imported almost one third of that required oil'.[15]

By 1976, the US had recovered from Vietnam and had set arrangements in train to reduce its vulnerability to oil supplies. Thus, the American administration could turn its attention to developments in the Caribbean where the governments of Guyana and Jamaica were pursuing socialist economic strategies domestically and non-aligned policies internationally. The US began to reassert its hegemony over the area. As Michael Manley notes, his foreign policy as Prime Minister of Jamaica 'was not likely to please the US establishment. In due course they were to make known the extent of their displeasure'.[16] Handed a prescription for economic reform by the IMF which he could not accept and faced with large-scale violence allegedly supported by the American CIA, Manley lost power to the US-linked opposition party led by Edward Seaga.[17] Significantly, the first overseas visitor received by the US President, Ronald Reagan, in 1981 was Edward Seaga.[18] One year later Jamaica broke off diplomatic relations with Cuba.

Having settled Jamaica firmly back into the US camp, the US administration then concentrated its attention on the Marxist government in Grenada which had taken power in a coup d'etat, albeit bloodless and popular, in 1979. That country too was 'restored' to US suzerainty by the 1983 invasion. Since then socialism has virtually disappeared from the discourse of Caribbean small states. Only Guyana attended the 1988 Non-Aligned Heads of Government Conference and, again except in Guyana, leftist political parties were quickly reduced to pressure groups calling for a change on specific issues rather than demanding overall structural change. Strikingly, even Michael Manley, who was re-elected to office in 1989, publicly espoused the virtues of the capitalist system and said that his government 'intends to foster the best relations with our great neighbours to the North.'[19] The earlier destabilisation of his government, together with the invasion of Grenada by the US, in effect caused Manley and other Caribbean leaders to set limits on their national autonomy in relation to activities of which the US might approve. Even Guyana began to withdraw from its previous socialist position. In short, as Colin Clarke observed, 'as President Reagan started his second term, it was clear that US hegemony in the Caribbean had been substantially restored.'[20]

An analysis of the extent of US intervention in Caribbean small states would be incomplete without taking account of the great impact on them of their proximity to the US. The flow of US tourists with their high-spending capacity and the dominance of US media in the region have led Caribbean peoples to adopt US standards and apply US values in their own way of life. In the majority of Caribbean small states US television is received on over ten channels twenty-four hours a day. A report on television in the Caribbean small states noted that the programming on US television, broadcast in the Caribbean,

Is specifically created for its primary audience. As a result, the material is strongly ethnocentric, reflecting values and standards of American society... [Further] while US television programmes allow Caribbean viewers to learn about the United States and the world, viewers learn very little about themselves and their own culture.[21]

Since many Caribbean small states have no national newspapers, and the broadcast media in all of them do not have the resources to compete with US television, knowledge creation and opinion formation in Caribbean societies about international events are being fashioned by American television broadcasters. This has serious implications for foreign policy decision making by governments which may find it difficult to gain the support of their own people for policies which do not conform with US opinion. In this connection, the results of a survey conducted in secondary schools on the impact of new media technology in Jamaica are instructive. Seventy-five percent of the students surveyed could not name the leaders of neighbouring Caribbean states, yet 89 percent named the President of the United States.[22]

THREATS TO TERRITORIAL INTEGRITY

The problem of drug trafficking exemplifies the security dilemma which Caribbean states face in relation to the United States. At their annual conference in July 1989 the heads of government of Caribbean small states, recognising their military weakness in dealing with drug traffickers in their region, and obviously unwilling to give the United States freedom to operate in their territorial waters, decided to propose the creation of a UN force 'which would provide assistance in particular situations requiring intelligence and interdiction capabilities beyond the resources of individual states'.[23]

Caribbean small states lack the financial resources to respond adequately to problems of drug trafficking. Experts suggest that the trade in illicit drugs is now bigger than world trade in arms or oil and some have put a figure on it of US$500 billion annually. Since the early 1980s, a substantial portion of that trade has originated in three South American countries – Peru, Bolivia and Colombia – which produce virtually all the trafficked cocaine.[24] Three quarters of the US drug market, worth in excess of US$100 billion annually, is fed by the production of Latin American countries, and Caribbean small states are being used as transit points for shipments.[25] Against the background of these figures, the total expenditure of the government of Antigua and Barbuda – one of the better-off small Caribbean islands – is US$99 million for the financial year 1988-89, and its expenditure on the police and military is expected to be US$6.2 million.[26] Of the US$6.2 million, less than a third, or US$2 million, would be allocated specifically for combating the illegal traffic in drugs. By the same token, the Bahamas allocates 13 percent of its national budget to interdiction of drug traffickers, yet it has succeeded in closing down only 'certain drug corridors'.[27]

Policing the waters of Caribbean states is a major problem. The many coves and bays that characterise the topography of the Caribbean countries lend themselves to drug traffickers whose light aircraft drop shipments into the sea where they are uplifted by fast boats which return to land undetected. Such coast guard services as exist are hopelessly under-equipped and under-funded. As an example, of the six smallest Caribbean states, Antigua and Barbuda is better able to police its waters since it possesses a Cutter and two Boston whalers – gifts from the United States. However, to be manned effectively the fleet requires a total of fifty persons; in 1989 it had a strength of only twenty-two.[28]

What this situation indicates is the way in which criminal elements are able to make incursions into the territory of Caribbean small states at will and with no fear of interdiction. The effects are considerable at the domestic and international levels. Domestically, local helpers have been recruited and are paid with cocaine. Those who do not become addicts themselves sell the drug to others. Thus, as one publication in Antigua noted:

Drug dealing and drug abuse have descended upon Antigua with the same force and devastation of the biblical plague of locusts. In their wake, the purveyors of this evil have left a trail of young people reduced to begging and incapable of productive activity.[29]

The large sums of money which drug traffickers are able to dispense has also led to corruption of officials, including police and the military – and, in one case, the Chief Minister of a British dependency.[30] And while such corruption has not been limited to small states,[31] its impact has been greater, given the smaller numbers of people that require to be corrupted in order to control the law enforcement system.

But while Caribbean small states have been faced with incursions into their territory by drug traffickers, they have been confronted with similar incursions from agents of the United States in pursuit of such traffickers. The US coast guard has pursued boats suspected of carrying illicit drugs into the territorial waters of Caribbean states, and sought to arrest the occupants in accordance with US law. Further, US agencies have set up covert operations in Caribbean territories without the permission of the governments, and they have then sought to remove persons arrested by such operations to the United States without extradition orders by the court. In July 1988, at a meeting of the Heads of Government of the Caribbean states, the Prime Minister of the Bahamas accused the United States of 'gunboat diplomacy', and the governments took the extraordinary step of writing a joint letter to the US President protesting at US attempts to impose 'extra-territorial jurisdiction' on Caribbean states.[32]

VULNERABILITY TO FOREIGN COMPANIES

Sufficient has already been said about the economic circumstances of Caribbean small states to make it clear that they are vulnerable to coercion from larger powers and TNCs upon whom they are dependent for aid and investment. The asymmetry in the bargaining capacity between these small states and larger states on the one hand, and the small states and TNCs on the other, leads to the setting of conditions which undermine the autonomy of the states concerned. Among the conditions set by large states are: the right to 'dialogue' on the economic policies of the small states and insistence on economic strategies favoured by the donor state. With regard to TNCs, it should be noted that foreign companies do not have to be very large to coerce small states. The Group of Commonwealth Experts which considered the vulnerability of small states in 1985 observed:

In terms of bargaining power, negotiating skills and access to relevant information, small states are usually seriously disadvantaged in dealing with these firms. Their economic strength tends to give the corporations considerable political influence which in some instances they have used in order to wrest special concessions, for example, favourable adjustment in tax regulations... Mini-states can find themselves at a similar disadvantage when dealing with smaller businesses, and they face problems of a different kind when the foreign investor is a group or individual whose motives are predatory rather than genuinely commercial.[33]

VULNERABILITY TO MERCENARIES

The military weakness of Caribbean small states also makes them extremely vulnerable to attacks by mercenaries intent on assuming control of a country against the wishes of the majority of the people. I have already referred to the case of The Maldive Islands in 1988. A mercenary invasion of another small island, The Seychelles, in 1981 further illustrates how vulnerable small states are to mercenary attack. So concerned was the President of the Maldives about his country's vulnerability that he announced his intention

To submit a proposal to the United Nations that a mechanism should be devised which would result in a quick response from the UN or any other organisations in the event of the security of a small state being threatened.[34]

While no Caribbean small state has yet experienced an actual mercenary invasion, there have been two widely known attempts. In December 1978 a plot was hatched to overthrow the government of Barbados through the use of South African mercenaries.[35] And, in April 1981, a group of mercenaries, gathered in North America, put in motion a plan to seize control of Dominica. The plan was uncovered by the US Federal Bureau of Investigation and quickly brought to an end.[36] Further, in January 1989 when a group of Colombian drug traffickers were held in the British Virgin Islands, they were removed to a high security prison in Britain immediately after their conviction because British officials feared that a mercenary attack may have been organised by Colombian drug barons to free their men.[37]

Mercenary attack on Caribbean small states always remains a real possibility for, as the former Commonwealth Secretary-General, Shridath Ramphal, has observed, 'it only takes twelve men in a boat to put some of those governments out of business'.[38]

CONCLUSION

Again, to sum up briefly, Caribbean small states, by virtue of their economic and military weakness, are subject to intervention, restrictions of their autonomy and violations of their territorial integrity. In their present arrangements as separate states, it appears unlikely that they will ever be able to develop the capacity to resist these undesired and unwelcome acts.

NOTES & REFERENCES

1 H.V. Hodgson, 'Sovereignty Demoted', *The Round Table*, No. 290, April 1984, pp. 130-138.

2 J. G. Starke, *Introduction to International Law*, Eighth Edition, 1977.

3 J. D. B. Miller, 'Sovereignty as a Source of Vitality for the State', *Review of International Studies*, Vol. 12, 1986, p. 80.

4 *Ibid.*, p. 82.

5 Communiqué of the Commonwealth Heads of Government Conference, *The New Delhi Communiqué 1983*, Commonwealth Secretariat, London, p. 9.

6 Hedley Bull (ed), *Intervention in World Politics*, Clarendon Press, Oxford, 1986, p. 191.

7 See Rosalyn Higgins, 'Intervention and International Law', in *ibid.*, pp. 29-44.

8 See operative paragraph 1 of UNGA Resolution 2131 (XX), 21 December 1965.

9 *Ibid.*, operative paragraph 2.

10 See Edward N. Luttwak, 'Intervention and Access to Natural Resources', in Bull (ed), *Intervention in World Politics*, pp. 79-94.

11 See George H. Quester, 'Trouble in the Islands: Defending the Micro-State', *International Security*, Vol. 8, No. 2, Fall 1983, p. 167.

12 International Court of Justice Report, cited by James Crawford, 'Islands as Sovereign Nations', *International and Comparative Law Quarterly*, Vol. 38, 1989, p. 290.

13 See Jenny Pearce, *Under the Eagle: US Intervention in Central America and the Caribbean*, Latin America Bureau, London, 1982; also H. Michael Erisman (ed), *The Caribbean Challenge: US Policy in a Volatile Region*, Westview Press, Colorado, 1984; and also Richard Newfarmer (ed), *From Gunboats to Diplomacy: New US Policies for Latin America*, Johns Hopkins University Press, Baltimore, 1984.

14 Anthony Payne *et al*, *Grenada: Revolution and Invasion*, Croom Helm, London, pp. 65-66.

15 Joan Edelman Spero, *The Politics of International Economic Relations*, George Allen & Unwin, London, 1985, p. 299.

16 Michael Manley, *Jamaica: Struggle in the Periphery*, Third World Media, London, undated, p. 68.

17 *Ibid.*, p. 237.

18 Anthony J. Payne, *Politics in Jamaica*, C. Hurst & Co, London, 1988, p. 87.

19 Cited in *Caribbean Insight*, Vol. 12, No. 3, March 1988.

20 Colin Clarke, 'Sovereignty, Dependency and Social Change in the Caribbean', *South America, Central America and the Caribbean, 1986*, Europa Publications, London, 1985, p. 24.

21 Evan Brown, *Caribbean Voices-Caribbean Images*, Report on the Caribbean Broadcasting Environment, UNESCO, July 1987.

22 Hopeton Dunn, 'Broadcasting Flow in the Caribbean', *Inter Media*, Vol. 16, No. 3, May 1989, p. 39.

23 CARICOM Secretariat Press Release 63/1989, Communiqué of the Caribbean Heads of Government Conference, Grenada, 7 July 1989, mimeo, p. 3.

24 Bruce Michael Bagley, 'The New Hundred Years War? US National Security and the War on Drugs in Latin America', *Journal of InterAmerican Studies and World Affairs*, Vol. 30, No. 1, 1988, p. 165.

25 James van Wert, 'The US State Department's Narcotics Control Policy in the Americas', *Journal of InterAmerican Studies and World Affairs*, Vol. 30, No. 1, 1988, p. 4.

26 Antigua and Barbuda (Recurrent) Estimates 1989, Ministry of Finance, Antigua, mimeo.

27 E. Charles Carter, Minister of Foreign Affairs, Statement to Bahamas Parliament, 12 April 1989.

28 From interview with Makeda Mikel, Personal Assistant to the Foreign Minister of Antigua and Barbuda, 29 June 1989.

29 Antigua Chamber of Commerce Publication, *Business Expressions*, Vol. 3, No. 9, May 1989.

30 In 1985, Norman Saunders, the Chief Minister of the Turks and Caicos Islands, was convicted in Miami on charges of assisting drug trafficking. See Tony Thorndike, 'When Small is not Beautiful: The Case of the Turks and Caicos Islands', *Corruption and Reform*, Vol. 2, No. 3, 1987, pp. 259-265.

31 See, for instance, Hugh O'Shaughnessy, 'Fidel's Faithless Heroes', *The Observer*, 2 July 1989, an account of how the third highest ranking military figure in Cuba was paid by the Medellin cartel of Colombia to smuggle drugs into the United States using Cuban facilities. He was subsequently executed.

32 See *Caribbean Insight*, Vol. 11, No. 8, August 1988, p. 2.

33 Report of a Commonwealth Consultative Group, *Vulnerability: Small States in the Global Society*, Commonwealth Secretariat, London, 1985, p. 21.

34 See Maumoon Abdul Gayoom, Address on the 24th Anniversary of the Independence of The Maldives, 26 July 1989, mimeo.

35 See *Caribbean Insight*, Vol. 2, No. 1, January 1979.

36 See *Caribbean Insight*, Vol. 4, No. 8, August 1981.

37 From an interview with Peter Penfold, West India and Atlantic Department of the Foreign and Commonwealth Office, 24 May 1989.

38 S.S. Ramphal, Commonwealth Secretary-General, speech at the opening of the Commonwealth Heads of Government Conference, New Delhi, 1983, mimeo.

CHAPTER FOUR

Options for Caribbean Small States

This chapter is concerned with exploring ways by which the Caribbean small states might, if at all, eliminate their vulnerability to intervention and constraints on their autonomy. It is clear that none of them individually has the capacity to deter intervention by larger states or coercion from TNCs and private groups such as drug traffickers. Thus, it appears that the only way they will be able to mount countering forces is by entering collaborative relationships with other states. The options for such collaborative relationships would seem to include the following possibilities:

A. THE ESTABLISHMENT OF A DEFENCE AGREEMENT AMONG CARIBBEAN SMALL STATES

The establishment of a defence agreement among Caribbean small states is a possibility for addressing the problem of mercenaries and drug traffickers, but it does not address the problem of armed intervention from a large power. In fact, paradoxically, the best defence which Caribbean small states have against military intervention by large powers, other than the United States, is the US's own determination to police the region in its own interest. It is most unlikely that any state, including the Soviet Union in its day, would attempt an armed intervention in a Caribbean territory for it would know full well that this would bring immediate reprisals from the United States.

It is significant that a scheme for mutual assistance was first discussed by the heads of government of Caribbean small states in 1973, but no attention was paid to it until 1981 when it appeared on the agenda of the Conference of Foreign Ministers. It was agreed to set up a working group which, however, did not convene until 1985.[1]

First written as part of MA thesis 'Caribbean Small States in the International System: Their Problems and Prospects', University of Sussex, August 1989.

According to one participant in the meeting, 'the difficulties of achieving agreement emerged not only as a consequence of differing perceptions of security needs but of the logistics which would be involved in a region-wide scheme'.[2] Consequently, 'the proposal no longer finds a place on the agenda of the Foreign Minister meetings'.[3]

However, the failure, thus far, to find agreement on security needs should not suggest that some arrangement is not possible. The intensity of the problem of drug-trafficking through the Caribbean should be sufficient to encourage governments to examine the issue again. The governments might find a scheme for mutual assistance more appealing if its activities were limited to dealing with drug traffickers, mercenaries and foreign fishing vessels which poach in Caribbean waters. In other words, the activities of any Caribbean defence mechanism, emerging from a mutual assistance scheme, might have to limit its concerns to matters which do not derive from local political concerns. Such a scheme, however, would only partially address the problems of the Caribbean small states. It would in no way meet the problems of intervention or coercion by the United States, nor would it address the constraints upon autonomy that flow from the asymmetry of relations between Caribbean small states and TNCs, and the structural constraints which derive from the dependence of these states because of the structure and size of their economies.

B. A MULTILATERAL MUTUAL DEFENCE AGREEMENT WITH LATIN AMERICAN COUNTRIES

A multilateral defence agreement between some Latin American countries and Caribbean small states would be beneficial to both groups of countries, but only in the context of security. It would not address the problems associated with economic coercion by larger states and private groups. But such an agreement would be able to call upon considerable military resources, particularly if Venezuela and Mexico were involved. In theory, it would be a deterrent to intervention even by the United States, since it would bring some degree of balance to the conventional military forces in the hemisphere. It would also address the problem of drug trafficking and the threat of mercenary invasion. However, such a multilateral defence agreement is most unlikely.

As explained in Chapter Two, the cultural and other differences between Caribbean small states and Latin American countries are considerable. And, even if these could be surmounted, there would be problems of which countries to include and which to leave out. It was inconceivable, for example, that, in the 1970s, the left-wing opposition political parties in the Caribbean would agree to any defence agreement, however limited, with what they saw as a right-wing fascist regime in Chile. By the same token, right-wing governments in the six smaller Caribbean islands – all of whom were associated with the Christian Democratic Union and the Republican Party in the United States – would have had profound difficulties associating themselves with the left-wing government in Nicaragua. Further, the territorial disputes between Belize and Guatemala, on the one hand, and Guyana and Venezuela, on the other, would immediately eliminate those four countries from a defence pact between Latin America and the Caribbean. In turn, the larger Latin American territories would have grave difficulties entering a defence agreement with Caribbean small states if such an agreement excluded other Latin American countries with which they share a history, culture and language.

Apart from these difficulties, in all likelihood the United States would oppose the arrangement and would actively work against it. The United States was the architect of the 1947 Rio Treaty, an Inter-American mutual defence agreement whose signatories are the US and the Latin American countries. But Caribbean small states have always perceived the treaty 'more as the occasion for intervention than as a source of security', and it therefore attracts little interest and few adherents.[4] Nonetheless, it is reasonable to assume that the US would view as hostile any mutual defence agreement in the hemisphere which excluded its participation. In that connection alone, it is unlikely that such an agreement would see the light of day.

C. A PROTECTIVE AGREEMENT WITH CANADA

A protective agreement between Caribbean small states and Canada might appear on the face of it to have great merit. Canada and the Caribbean small states are all Commonwealth countries, they share a long historical relationship of trade, Canadians holiday in the Caribbean, many Caribbean students attend university in Canada, there is considerable Canadian investment in the Caribbean, Canada is the second biggest aid donor to the area, and a large number of people from the Caribbean small states have migrated to Canada. However, there appear to be two obstacles to Canada entering an agreement to protect Caribbean small states. The first is that, in effect, protection against armed intervention from other states is already being given by the United States. Therefore, Canada would be giving Caribbean small states protection only from the United States. And it is very unlikely that Canadians would pit themselves against the United States for the benefit of the Caribbean. In any event, as one Canadian member of Parliament pointed out in 1984, Canada has 'only 20,000 fighting men and some of its Capital ships (are) in questionable combat shape.'[5] Moreover, as Lloyd Searwar again noted:

> On the specific issue of military security, Canada has yet to develop an effective bilateral and multilateral strategy for co-operation with those Caribbean governments whose policies have brought them into conflict with the United States.[6]

Secondly, the United States would undoubtedly be displeased about Canada usurping its policeman's role in the Caribbean. It is significant, for instance, that when in February 1974 US Secretary of State, Henry Kissinger proposed to a conference of the US, Latin American countries and Caribbean small states the creation of 'A Community of the Western Hemisphere', he excluded not only Cuba, but Canada as well.[7] And when it was suggested that such a community should include Canada to address 'the reality of inequality between the United States and the states of Latin America and the Caribbean',[8] Kissinger withdrew his proposal. Anyhow, a defence agreement with Canada would also not address the difficulties faced by Caribbean small states in terms of economic coercion. Further, a number of the TNCs operating in Caribbean small states, including those whose operations have restricted effective decision-making by states, are Canadian owned. When the operations of these TNCs are viewed in combination with reliance upon Canada for defence, it becomes clear that the Caribbean small states would be placing themselves in a situation akin to voluntary colonialism in which Canada would become the centre of effective decision-making power and the location of coercive power.

What is more, reliance upon a single country for defence has the tendency to restrict the capacity of a small state to exercise the rights

94

which flow from sovereignty, even if that restriction is self-imposed. An example of this is Belize which was for so long solely dependent on Britain for its defence against irredentist Guatemala. It is unlikely that Belize would have acted in some manner on the international stage that would upset the British government. Such an action would have been untenable to the British government and could have been used as a justification for removing the 1,800 troops and sophisticated military hardware stationed in Belize at a cost of some £31 million per annum to the British tax payer. Similarly, it would be fair to expect that if Caribbean small states relied solely upon Canada for their defence, their governments would be expected not to behave in a manner unacceptable to the Canadian government.

D. COLLECTIVE SECURITY UNDER THE UN

In theory, Article 47 of the UN Charter makes provision for collective security. In practice, the Charter provision is unworkable unless the permanent members of the Security Council are in agreement, for each has the power of veto. Thus, if the security of Caribbean small states is threatened by a permanent member of the Security Council, it would be impossible to invoke Article 47. And, as we have already established, since the United States already polices the Caribbean, it is only if the United States itself threatens the security of a Caribbean small state that a request for assistance would be made to the UN. Obviously, at that stage, the United States would vote against the invocation of Article 47.

E. DEFENCE BY EUROPEAN COUNTRIES

There would be little point in Caribbean small states looking to European countries for defence. The high costs of maintaining troops and equipment at such a great distance from home would be prohibitive, even if there were any interest by a European country in providing defence for Caribbean small states. But, given the past colonial link, and shared institutions and practices, it would be Britain to which Caribbean small states would turn in Europe. However, Britain would hardly be willing to pay such costs. Indeed, the British government's attitude suggests that it wishes to limit its military involvement in Caribbean small states to participation in joint efforts with other large countries. As early as 1983 its government was on record as saying that it stands 'ready to respond constructively and sympathetically to requests' for further training and 'assistance to the police, coastguard and security in the region', and it 'will continue to exploit any opportunities for international co-operation in securing countries of the area from external threat'.[9]

F. AN ACCOMMODATION WITH THE UNITED STATES

A final option for Caribbean small states if they wish to retain their formal status as independent, sovereign states is to reach an accommodation with the United States to provide defence. Such an accommodation would continue severely to restrict their capacity for independent decision making and is likely to increase their problems of coercion from the United States government and from US-based TNCs. In other words, as a consequence of such an arrangement, they would be sovereign and independent in name only; effectively they would become client states of the United States. The only merits in such an arrangement for Caribbean small states are: (i) they would be relieved of the necessity for defence against drug traffickers, mercenaries and other states; (ii) they would continue to enjoy a degree of autonomy over their local affairs providing that they adopt no ideological position or economic strategy regarded as hostile by the United States; and (iii) to the extent that it is important to the political elite in Caribbean small states to maintain the illusion of sovereign equality in the international system, they would continue to participate in international organisations, although they would be constrained from making decisions, or taking actions, unacceptable to the United States. However, while this option removes the vulnerability of Caribbean small states to all other interventionist forces, it intensifies their vulnerability to the United States and to US-based TNCs.

INDIVIDUAL SOVEREIGNTY NO LONGER AN OPTION FOR CARIBBEAN SMALL STATES

It should be obvious from the pitfalls posed by each of the above options that the maintenance of individual sovereign status does not provide Caribbean small states with enough room to manoeuvre against the structural constraints which they face. It seems that the only way they can maintain a high degree of autonomy is by re-entering some form of political union amongst themselves. As Dudley Seers argues:

> A more plausible way of escaping the constraints of size (and other constraints as well), at least in the short run, lies in political and economic integration which can take various forms from free trade associations through common markets and federations to monetary and political unions.[10]

A POLITICAL UNION FOR CARIBBEAN SMALL STATES

The arguments for a political union – particularly a federation – are compelling. In the words of Robert J. Leiber, 'a federal arrangement is said to exist when a set of political communities are united in a common order, but retain their autonomy'.[11] In a federal structure, Caribbean small states would be able to maintain some degree of local autonomy while pooling their economic and human resources into a relatively strong medium-sized state with a central government responsible for matters beyond the capability of the individual states. These matters could include defence, external affairs (especially representation and bargaining), economic planning and fiscal policy. The enlarged state would be quite considerable. Its combined resource base would include 'agricultural land, good climate for tourism, fisheries, forestry, other building materials, oil and natural gas, bauxite, hydroelectric and geothermal energy potential, and as yet undiscovered or unutilised natural resources'.[12]

If the powers given to the central government of an enlarged Caribbean state are adequate the participating units would benefit in several ways.

First, at the external level, while they would reduce their number of votes from twelve to one, they would be able to field a stronger diplomatic team by drawing upon the best people available to all of them. A better quality of representation would improve their bargaining capacity with other states. Further, the high cost of participation in international affairs would be shared, and they would, therefore, be able to involve themselves more fully in international conferences on issues of importance to themselves.

Secondly, they would be better able to bargain with TNCs which now take advantage of their smallness and lack of bargaining power to restrict their autonomy and flout their sovereign authority. In addition, the combined resources of the Caribbean small states would allow them more freedom of choice in terms of the conditions which they set for foreign investment.

Third, the automatic diversification of the economy as a whole, resulting from the creation of an enlarged state, would reduce their dependency on one or two commodities and allow for greater bargaining power in trade. They would also be able to qualify for, and service, larger loans from international financial institutions. In turn, this would make them less aid dependent.

Fourth, the different perceptions of security needs which now bedevil Caribbean small states and prohibit the formation of a regional defence mechanism would be removed. Federal institutions could include military and police forces which would deter all but the most determined drug traffickers and mercenaries. And, while the forces of an enlarged state would be unable to repulse an armed assault from a powerful state, they would be sufficient to inflict some damage, which should be enough to deter any state from contemplating armed intervention without sufficient cause to justify such intervention to its domestic community. It is worth noting here that, in Grenada, the United States committed 6,000 troops and took three days to hold the capital.[13] In the process they bombed the tiny island for a day and a night and killed 45 Grenadians. Eighteen Americans died and 116 were wounded.[14] Any state attempting armed intervention in an enlarged Caribbean state, stretching over a million square miles of sea and including two mainland territories, would have to contemplate a longer operation and a heavier casualty rate.

Fifth, while the considerable US media penetration which Caribbean small states now experience will not disappear with a political union, the greater resources available to these states should allow them to mount countering forces. The quality of their own radio and television programmes could be improved and daily newspapers could be made available in those territories which now have only weekly editions. In other words, resources would become available to compete with US media for knowledge creation and opinion formation.

THE THEORY OF INTEGRATION

In theory, political integration appears to offer Caribbean small states the best prospects for maintaining their autonomy and improving their status in the international system. Three of the basic assumptions which integration theory makes are:

- the nation state is incapable of carrying out certain tasks which are crucial to the well-being of mankind.[15] This has been established in the case of the Caribbean small states;
- man will be able to perceive the need for a revolutionary change in his governance and he will be willing to make that change. This has not been established with regard to Caribbean small states;[16]
- nations will forego the desire and ability to conduct foreign affairs and key domestic policies independently of each other, seeking instead to make joint decisions or to delegate. This too has not been established in connection with Caribbean small states.[17]

However, nine of the twelve Caribbean small states have experienced a political union before, and an analysis of that experience provides an indication of whether or not the latter two assumptions of integration theory hold good for the Caribbean.

INTEGRATION IN PRACTICE

At the end of the Second World War amid great agitation throughout the British colonies in the Caribbean for independence, and in the face of its own ailing economy, Britain 'was anxious to relieve herself of her burdensome overseas responsibilities'.[18] But, as a former Governor put it:

How could viable independence be possible for 15 colonies, each with its own legislature and government, spread over 1.75 million square miles of sea, when ten had populations of under 100,000 people and seven required annual grants from Britain to enable them to meet their day-to-day expenditures?[19]

99

The solution was to create a West Indian Federation in which all would be included.[20] As it turned out, the governments of the two mainland territories, Belize in Central America and Guyana in South America, as well as the governments of the Bahamas and the British Virgin Islands,[21] declined to join the Federation. Thereafter, it was a federation of ten, made up of the larger territories of Jamaica and Trinidad and Tobago, and eight smaller territories.[22]

The West Indian federal experiment differed from integration theory in two important ways. First, almost every integration theorist, including Ernst Haas and Amitai Etzioni, has stressed that while 'leadership of a union is not limited to member-countries', it is important that the leadership be internalised.[23] This was not the case with the West Indies Federation, which was a British idea, promoted by Britain.

Second, once federations have been created, the central government or 'the union-system' has what Amitai Etzioni calls 'utilitarian power' by which the elites guiding unification deliver benefits to the federating units, and thus attract greater utilitarian power.[24] Again, this did not occur in the West Indies Federation. A Conference in London of West Indian leaders and the British government in 1961 produced what 'could be more appropriately called a confederation rather than a weak federation'.[25] And when the already weak government attempted to introduce taxation measures, it incurred the ire of the two larger units in the Federation, Jamaica and Trinidad and Tobago. Lacking any coercive power, the central government had to stand idly by while Jamaica held a referendum to decide whether it would remain in the Federation where, as the largest country, it would be taxed the most. The Jamaicans voted to quit the Federation, whereupon the Chief Minister of Trinidad and Tobago, Dr Eric Williams, in a curious mathematical calculation proclaimed that 'ten minus one leaves zero'[26] and withdrew his country from the federal effort. His real fear was that his country would have to carry the burden of the poorer states. The West Indies Federation died less than four years after it was born.

The British government had tried to tie together ten units whose people had had relatively little experience of each other and whose remoteness and isolation had given them a strong sense of identification with the island of their birth. There was an elite – particularly those who had studied abroad in Britain – who had developed a sense of common West Indian identity, for there they were cast under that umbrella. But, apart from this elite, the only facet of West Indian life with which the people of the Caribbean small states had a common identification was the West Indian cricket team. As Amitai Etzioni observes:

> The federation was initiated with rather limited identitive powers in its support; the experience of federation, far from building up this power, actually further undermined it. The scope of the federation was so limited, the authority of the federal government so low, its budget so minuscule, its functions so restrictive that for most people most of the time there was no experience of federation at all.[27]

The collapse of the Federation started the process of independence for Caribbean small states – the very thing it was meant to avoid. The federal experience, however, was to have a lasting effect upon the Caribbean small states, for subsequent attempts to create a political union in the area, even though these were initiated by Caribbean leaders, foundered on the memory of the West Indies Federation.[28] This is illustrated by the attempt to create a political union initiated in May 1987 by the heads of government of the six smallest independent states and the British dependency of Montserrat.[29] These territories are all member countries of the Organisation of Eastern Caribbean States (OECS)[30] and, in an official publication explaining why a political union was being contemplated, the OECS Secretariat said:

> In recent years, the demands for economic and social development have outstripped the capacity of the individual OECS countries to deliver – their populations are too small, their natural resources too limited and their development costs too high. Moreover, independence proved that small states lack influence in the international community and are unable, in the main, to secure enough action to meet their development needs.[31]

Nonetheless, the attempt to form the political union ended in November 1988 and the reasons why the effort failed are explored in greater detail in the next chapter. Suffice it to say here that amongst the reasons for its failure was the memory of the collapse of the West Indies Federation, and the absence of education and information to allay the fears created by that memory. There was also no clear indication from the leaders of the benefits which would flow from such a union to each participating unit. But there was also an elite – particularly some political figures who regarded political union as a threat to their positions within their small units – who worked against a union. They promoted the idea at every level of their societies that the political union was 'part of a scheme hatched in North America'[32] to control the Caribbean states involved, and they pointed to the experience of the externally motivated West Indies Federation to underscore their contention that the proposed new union would fail.

NO SPILL-OVER FROM ECONOMIC INTEGRATION

It is also of some significance that, although the twelve Caribbean small states have operated an economic integration process since 1968, there has been no spill-over into political union. In fact, the largest country – Jamaica – remains resolutely opposed to any form of political union, and when, in July 1988, the then Prime Minister of Barbados, Erskine Sandiford, proposed the establishment of a purely deliberative Caribbean parliamentary assembly, the then Jamaican Prime Minister, Edward Seaga, accused him of attempting to re-establish the West Indies Federation 'through the backdoor'.[33] Seaga even opposed the integration of health, customs, police and judicial services as 'impractical'.[34]

On the evidence of the West Indies Federation, the failure of subsequent attempts to establish a political union, and the fact that, as yet, economic integration has shown no real signs of spill-over into a political integration, it is possible to conclude the following:

- the political elite in the Caribbean small states is not willing to make a change in their governance from single state to political union; and

- the political elite is not prepared to forego the certain prestige of national independence for the possible benefits of political union.

In this context, and unless they are finally deprived of the choice by economic collapse, it seems that Caribbean small states are very unlikely ever to opt willingly for a political union.

NOTES & REFERENCES

1 Lloyd Searwar, 'Foreign Policy Decision-Making in the Commonwealth Caribbean', *Caribbean Affairs*, Vol. 1, No. 1, 1988, p. 78.

2 *Ibid.*

3 *Ibid.*

4 Lloyd Searwar, *Peace, Development and Security in the Caribbean Basin: Perspectives to the Year 2000*, Report of a Conference held in Jamaica, 22-25 March, 1987, Canadian Institute for International Peace and Security, Ottawa, p. 7.

5 See *The Security of Small States*, Report of the Study Group of the Commonwealth Parliamentary Association, London, December 1984, p. 15.

6 Searwar, *Peace, Development and Security*, p. 8.

7 The Conference was held in Tlatelolco, Mexico in February 1974 on the theme 'The Role of the Hemisphere in the International Community'. See Ron Sanders (ed), *Inseparable Humanity: An Anthology of Reflections of Shridath Ramphal*, Hansib Publishing, London, 1988, p. 144.

8 Shridath Ramphal, 'The Realities of Inequality', in *ibid.*, p. 147.

9 Observations by the Secretary of State for Foreign and Commonwealth Affairs, presented to Parliament March 1983, Cmnd. 8819, HMSO, London, pp. 18-19.

10 Dudley Seers (ed), *Dependency Theory: A Critical Assessment*, Frances Pinter, London, 1981, p. 142.

11 Robert J. Leiber, *Theory and World Politics*, George Allen & Unwin, London, 1973, p. 39.

12 William G. Demas, 'Foreword', in Richard Millett and W. Marvin Will (eds), *The Restless Caribbean: Changing Patterns of International Relations*, Praeger Publishers, New York, 1979, p. xii.

13 *Grenada: Whose Freedom?*, Special Brief, Latin America Bureau, London, 1984, p. 90.

14 *Ibid.*, p. 92.

15 George A. Codding Jr, 'Federalism: The Conceptual Setting', in Paul Taylor and A. J. R. Groom (eds), *International Organisation*, Frances Pinter, London, 1978, p. 327.

16 *Ibid.*

17 Leon Lindberg's definition of integration. See James E. Dougherty and Robert L. Pfaltzgraff Jr, *Contending Theories of International Relations: A Comprehensive Survey*, Second Edition, Harper & Row, New York, 1981, p. 421.

18 Sir Kenneth Blackburne, 'Changing Patterns of Caribbean International Relations: Britain and the British Caribbean', in Millett and Will (eds), *The Restless Caribbean*, p. 204.

19 *Ibid.*

20 Anguilla was then attached to St Kitts-Nevis, and the Cayman Islands were attached to Jamaica.

21 Amitai Etzioni, *Political Unification: A Comparative Study of Leaders and Forces*, Holt, Rinehart and Winston Inc., New York, 1965.

22 The eight territories were Antigua (and its dependency, Barbuda), Barbados, Dominica, Grenada, St Kitts-Nevis (and Anguilla, then a dependency), St Lucia, St Vincent (and its dependencies, the tiny islands of the Grenadines), and Montserrat.

23 Etzioni, *Political Unification*, pp. 70-71; see also E. B. Haas, *The Uniting of Europe*, Stanford University Press, Stanford, 1968.

24 Etzioni, *Political Unification*, pp. 153-166.

25 Gisbert H. Flanz, 'The West Indies', in Thomas M Franck (ed), *Why Federations Fail*, New York University Press, New York, 1968, p. 93.

26 Cited by John Mordecai, *The West Indies: The Federal Negotiations*, George Allen & Unwin, London, 1968, pp. 426-7.

27 Etzioni, *Political Unification*, p. 169.
28 Between the end of Federation and the late 1980s there were eight separate plans by various groups for a political union in the Caribbean small states. These plans ranged from a political union of all 12 countries to proposals for a union of the six smallest states. For a good overview of these, see Patrick A.M. Emmanuel, *Approaches to Caribbean Political Integration*, Occasional Paper No. 21, Institute of Social and Economic Research (Eastern Caribbean), University of the West Indies, Barbados, 1987.
29 Montserrat had a population of 12,000 people.
30 The OECS is a treaty organisation brought into force in 1981. It provides for a free trade area amongst the participating states and for limited co-operation in external diplomatic representation. Its members are the six independent states of Antigua and Barbuda, Dominica, Grenada, St Kitts-Nevis, St Lucia, St Vincent and the Grenadines, and the British dependency of Montserrat.
31 *Why a Political Union of OECS Countries? The Background and the Issues*, OECS Secretariat, St Lucia, July 1988, p. 1.
32 Julian Hunte, Leader of the Opposition St Lucia Labour Party, speaking to news reporters in St Lucia. See Caribbean News Agency (CANA) report US2738, 3 July 1987.
33 See *Caribbean Insight*, Vol. 11, No. 8, August 1988, p. 2.
34 *Ibid.*

CHAPTER FIVE

Political Union in the OECS

A political union in the Commonwealth Caribbean – that is, the transformation of two or more territorial units into a single political entity, or a single state – is not a new concept. The issue of whether or not there should be a political union of countries in the Commonwealth Caribbean has been a part of the West Indian scenario since the 1670s when the first loose Leeward Islands Federation was established. For the convenience of one political elite or another the question was debated throughout the 19th and 20th Centuries. Over this period at least three political unions, involving groups of Caribbean countries, actually functioned, although with great dissension. The best known of these, of course, was the short-lived West Indies Federation which lasted from 1958 to 1962.

A significant feature of each of the attempts at political union is that they were motivated by concerns by a ruling group for the economic viability of the individual territories. It is that same concern which prompted a move between 1986 and 1988 for the creation of a political union: a union of the seven countries which are members of the Organisation of Eastern Caribbean States (OECS). These are the six independent territories of Antigua and Barbuda, Dominica, Grenada, St Kitts-Nevis, St Lucia, St Vincent and the Grenadines and the British colony of Montserrat. This attempt was spearheaded by the Prime Minister of St Vincent and the Grenadines, James Mitchell, in November 1986 and, to all intents and purposes, it was shelved exactly two years later in November 1988.

This is not surprising as this initiative to seek a political union in the OECS came against the background of past failures and the increasingly trying international environment in which these countries

First published in *Caribbean Affairs*, Vol. 2, No. 2, 1989, pp. 114-124.

exist. But the truth is that the initiative seems to have been squandered by a lack of cohesion on the part of the governments, and any further attempts at such a union by any group of Caribbean countries, based on the methods employed in this attempt, are doomed to end in the same way.

THE BACKGROUND

It is important to understand the economic background against which this attempt at political union was made in order to fully appreciate how the notion was given consideration at all. The independent members of the OECS came to sovereignty with the idea that independence would open up great opportunities for aid and finance. Freed from Britain, the governments envisaged using their new found sovereignty to access finance from Japan and countries in Europe, with which they had no previous relationship, and from international financial institutions such as the World Bank and the Inter-American Development Bank. It did not quite work out that way. The significant aid donors to the OECS sub-region remained the traditional ones of Canada, Britain, the United States and the European Community under the terms of the Lomé agreement between the Community and the African, Caribbean and Pacific (ACP) Group.

Further, the member states of the OECS have a relatively high per capita income and, because of this, the international institutions have categorised them as 'middle income countries'. They, therefore, do not automatically qualify for aid to least developed countries, although they are small island-states with minuscule populations and a very narrow resource base. By 1990, they were 'graduated' out of the soft loan window of the World Bank and it was, in fact, only intense lobbying that prevented this from being implemented a few years before.

Markets for their exports did not suddenly open up either. In fact, the two schemes, which became available to the OECS countries in the post-independence period – the US Caribbean Basin Initiative and the Canadian CARIBCAN – both offered little benefits since, from the outset, they excluded products, such as garments, which the Caribbean could best produce. The main exports of the OECS countries remained bananas, citrus and sugar, and their main guaranteed market remained the United Kingdom under the protocols of the Lomé Agreement. However, it was becoming increasingly clear that even this guaranteed market was under threat as the European Community advanced plans for the creation of a Single European Market in 1992. There was no certainty that the United Kingdom would be allowed to continue providing a guaranteed market for bananas and sugar from the Caribbean. Indeed, everything pointed to the unlikelihood of such a guaranteed market.

Beyond this, the prospects for employment in the Caribbean appeared bleak. Conservative estimates suggest that the growth of the labour force by the year 2000 will be as high as 54 percent in many countries and certainly no lower than 23 percent.[1] In the meantime, the average income in seven of the 13 Caribbean countries was lower in 1990 than it was in 1980.[2]

It was against this background that Prime Minister Mitchell proposed to a meeting of the Heads of Government of the OECS in November 1986 that they merge their states into a political union, or, as he put it, 'a single legal unit'.[3] He supported his proposal with a stark description of the severe limitations on their policy actions as follows:

> Economic realities now are clearly telling us that we will not mobilise the resources to fulfil our people's demands on a continuing basis as we are now structured.... Each of (our economies) is still largely mono-culturally oriented – sugar, bananas, cocoa, tourism. Within this framework we will simply be unable to make the structural adjustment to our economies required to enable us to recover from natural or economic shocks over an extended period. Our economies, no matter what we do, in the face of unfavourable external realities will continue to stagnate relative to our population growth at home, and the state of progress in the rest of the world.[4]

Mitchell's observations sufficiently impressed his colleagues for them to ponder his call for 'a single legal unit'. But there are two factors of great importance which need to be taken into account in analysing the events which followed. Firstly, the Prime Minister of Antigua and Barbuda, Vere Bird Snr., was not at the meeting, and secondly, the Leeward Islands group of Antigua and Barbuda, St Kitts-Nevis and Montserrat, is less dependent on exports than the Windward Islands group of Dominica, Grenada, St Lucia and St Vincent and the Grenadines. The main economic activity in Antigua and Barbuda and Montserrat is tourism which, at that time, was performing well enough to maintain employment at an acceptable level. Only St Kitts-Nevis of the Leeward Islands still depends on exports, but it did well in attracting enclave industries under the American CBI, and tourism to Nevis is satisfactory. Mitchell's suggestion, therefore, had a lukewarm response from the Leeward Islands whose leaders could see no reason, in their relatively better economic condition, to give up sovereign control of their affairs to a political union. I wish to stress the word 'relatively' in ascribing better economic conditions to the Leewards than to the Windwards. For the reality is that both of the groups of islands are heavily dependent on aid and borrowing to finance their capital development, and both groups have severe balance-of-payments deficits. However, the Leewards group has smaller populations, and at least one of the islands has financed development projects and employment through significant borrowing at high commercial rates of interest. The underlying structures of underdevelopment are, therefore, still as much a part of the economy of the Leeward Islands as they are of the Windwards.

In any event, when the OECS Heads of Government met in May 1987, again with Vere Bird Snr. absent, there had been considerable consultation among the Prime Ministers in the Windward Islands, particularly Dominica, St Lucia and St Vincent and the Grenadines, on the idea of 'a single legal unit'. Thus, the meeting was able to issue a communiqué in which it was stated that, following a discussion on closer political union among their countries, it had been decided 'that member governments would engage in a process of comprehensive consultations within their countries including a referendum on this matter before deciding on further appropriate steps.'[5]

It is important here to note that, while the Prime Minister of Antigua and Barbuda was not present at the two meetings, the Deputy Prime Minister, Lester Bird, attended. This is an important consideration, because in the Leeward Islands group of Antigua and Barbuda, St

Kitts-Nevis and Montserrat, Antigua has always been regarded as the leader, particularly by the Montserratians. In fact, when in 1965, attempts to form a federation in the Eastern Caribbean failed as Vere Bird pulled Antigua out, the Chief Minister of Montserrat followed suit with the rather picturesque declaration that: 'Where the Bird flies, there fly I.'[6] The presence of Lester Bird at the two meetings, and the fact that he had raised no objections to the proposal to seek a political union, would have caused the leaders of Montserrat and St Kitts-Nevis to go along with the idea, despite whatever reservations they may have harboured.

But it was obvious that the St Kitts-Nevis Prime Minister, Dr Kennedy Simmonds, was not keen to push the idea of a political union. Upon his return home after the May 1987 meeting, he talked of informing the Caribbean people of 'the pitfalls' as well as the benefits of regional co-operation, and he said that 'undue haste is to be avoided'.[7] Partly responsible for his attitude was the advice of his close friend and political colleague, Billie Herbert, who had stoutly opposed the participation of St Kitts-Nevis-Anguilla in a political union with Guyana and four other Eastern Caribbean countries proposed under the Grenada Declaration of 1971.[8] Later, in 1988, the government of St Kitts-Nevis established a committee to hold consultations on the proposed political union and Herbert was appointed Chairman. When in November 1988, therefore, Dr Simmonds announced to his fellow heads of government that Herbert's committee had found that there was an overwhelming feeling in St Kitts-Nevis that political union should not be pursued, few were surprised.

But, before this, in July 1987, Antigua and Barbuda's Prime Minister made his own position quite clear. He attended a meeting of the Heads of Government of the wider Caribbean grouping CARICOM – the Caribbean Community and Common Market – and there, during a discussion on political union of the OECS, he told his colleagues what he would later repeat in public: Antigua and Barbuda was not interested in a political union. Such a union represented, in Bird's view, a kind of colonialism.[9] At any rate, his statement appeared to signal the beginning of the end of the initiative. Once Bird's position was known, the Chief Minister of Montserrat, John Osborne, announced that his country could not be part of a union without Antigua and Barbuda.[10] In St Kitts-Nevis the government did not link itself to Bird's statement, but it moved very slowly in fulfilling its obligation, made at the May 1987 meeting, to 'engage in a process of comprehensive consultations.'

Meanwhile, in July 1987, the opposition party leaders had formed themselves into a single grouping – the Standing Conference of Popular Democratic Parties of the Eastern Caribbean (SCOPE). From the outset, the main opposition parties, particularly in the Windward Islands, were against the proposed union. Most of them, but particularly the St Lucia Labour Party led by Julian Hunte, felt that they were one general election away from winning office. They were, therefore, unhappy about the move toward a political union which could deprive them of power in their home states. But they had involved the far-left opposition parties in their consultations and these groups favoured a political union. For them, a political union of the Eastern Caribbean offered the chance for participation in parliament, if not involvement in government. This possibility became real when, in putting forward his idea of a single legal entity in the Eastern Caribbean, Prime Minister Mitchell had talked of elections 'on the basis of proportional representation.'[11] Therefore, despite their divided attitude, SCOPE issued a statement of support for the idea of political union, but through their Chairman, Julian Hunte, they wrote a letter to St Lucia's Prime Minister, John Compton, then Chairman of the OECS, asking for a meeting with the heads of government to discuss political union, and insisting on a number of facilities. These facilities included adequate and fair access to the radio and television stations owned or controlled by the governments, and the right to travel and address public meetings in OECS countries. Compton's decision not to reply, whether he took it alone or in consultation with other heads of government, gave the opposition parties a basis on which to question the governments' intentions. The matter then became a partisan political issue.

By mid-1987, it was clear that Antigua and Barbuda was out of the proposed political union and that the attitude of Montserrat was highly questionable. The Prime Ministers in the Windward Islands still held out some hope for St Kitts-Nevis, for, while they were aware that Dr Simmonds was not very enthusiastic, they also knew that the partner political party in his coalition government – the Nevis Reformation Party led by his Minister of Finance – favoured the proposed union. The Nevisians had traditionally been unhappy with their relationship as a 'ward' of St Kitts and would not have been averse to entering a political union in the Eastern Caribbean in their own right. It was also clear that the opposition parties were divided on the issue and therefore could not lead an all-out assault on the idea.

What followed over the next year and a half, until the idea was finally shelved in November 1988, was nothing short of a squandering of opportunities to make a reality of political union in the OECS sub-region.

THE BASIS FOR POLITICAL UNION

There is little doubt that there was, and remains, a basis for a political union in the OECS. In the years since the collapse of the West Indies Federation in 1962, the OECS countries have established and enjoyed a relatively high-level of co-operation in governmental and other areas. In the pre-independence period, the creation of the West Indies (Associated States) Council of Ministers in 1966 and the Eastern Caribbean Common Market in 1968 provided the fora for successfully establishing frameworks for co-operation in a range of fields, including free trade in a wide range of commodities, a common currency administered by a single Currency Authority, a common judiciary, and a common Directorate of Civil Aviation. This high level of integration, particularly in monetary union, went deeper than many of the then existing arrangements in the European Community. With the creation of the OECS in 1981, the collaborative relationship grew even stronger, and new dimensions were added including:

a. The upgrading of the Currency Authority to a common Central Bank serving all territories;
b. The establishment of a Regional Security System in 1982 relating to mutual assistance in matters such as threats to national security, national emergencies, prevention of smuggling, search and rescue, fisheries protection, and customs and excise control;
c. The establishment of a sports desk in the OECS Secretariat to organise sports events in the sub-region and provide technical assistance and equipment to national associations;

d. The establishment of the Eastern Caribbean Drug Service to reduce the cost of essential pharmaceuticals through bulk purchasing;

e. The initiation of the Eastern Caribbean Investment Promotion Service (ECIPS) designed to seek and promote investment to the countries of the OECS as a whole; and

f. The operation of joint diplomatic missions overseas by some of the territories. Four of them shared a common High Commissioner in London and six shared a single representative in Ottawa.

The point being made here is that over the years a pattern of co-operation had built up in the OECS. This pattern had spread beyond government into the private sector. Thus, an active Council of Eastern Caribbean Manufacturers operated 'to promote and encourage increased trade between OECS countries and promote investment in the islands through the indigenous private sector, regional and overseas investors, and joint venture or contract projects'.[12] This established pattern of co-operation at the domestic level was strengthened by much external goodwill and support for the proposed political union. For example, when the idea of creating the union became known, it was endorsed by the heads of government of the other Caribbean countries, by the heads of government of the Commonwealth, by the Caribbean Congress of Labour and, importantly for the Caribbean, by the bishops of the Roman Catholic Church.

OPPORTUNITY FOR UNION SQUANDERED

But this sound basis on which to build a climate of acceptability for political union was squandered. To begin with, insufficient attention was paid to the importance of the Prime Minister of Antigua and Barbuda, Vere Bird Snr. He was the longest serving leader in the region; he had been part of the early trade union movement in the Caribbean in the late 1930s; his government had been part of the West Indies Federation; and it was well-known that he had played a pivotal role in the decision to abandon efforts to form the federation of the 'Little Eight' in 1965.

Skilful diplomatic approaches to Bird, including a visit to him by Mitchell and Compton, who were the moving lights behind the initiative for a political union, may well have been helpful. They might have been able to convince him to accept a federation, even if he would reject, as he did, Mitchell's suggestion of a 'unitary state'. At least a federation would have left the local government in Antigua and Barbuda with considerable powers. That opportunity to talk with Vere Bird Snr. still existed between May 1987, when the heads of government made public their desire for a political union, and July 1987 when Bird declared his opposition to the idea. For, in the intervening period, his attitude became known in political circles. Yet no attempt was made to talk with him. But, had Bird been kept on board, the rest of the Leeward Islands group would have stayed. For the Nevisians would have pressed for participation in the union, and in those circumstances the St Kitts government would have had little choice but to go along with it. And, once Antigua was part of the union, Montserrat would have been happy to participate.

Even if diplomatic approaches to Bird had failed, the six remaining territories still had a chance to make the initiative work. But the key to this was the way in which the governments handled the opposition parties. The refusal of Compton, as Chairman of the OECS, to respond to the July 1987 letter from the leaders of the opposition parties, asking for a meeting with the heads of government to discuss the issue of political union, was ill advised. There had been several suggestions that a Constituent Assembly ought to be set up comprising representatives of the political parties in the parliaments of all the territories. This Constituent Assembly would have overseen administrative arrangements leading to a referendum on the question of political union, including the establishment of a Constitutional Commission to take evidence on the type of constitution which would best serve the union. The idea of a Constituent Assembly was rejected by the heads of government, and this led to alienation of the opposition parties who saw themselves being shunted aside. As Julian Hunte graphically put it: 'the governments were only interested in unity so far as it entrenched them in power and marginalised the opposition. We would not want and would not support OECS unity on those terms.'[13]

Some of the opposition parties were delighted, indeed, with the dismissive attitude of the governments, for political union was the last thing many of them wanted. One of them, Ralph Gonsalves, leader of a small political party in St Vincent, best describes how the opposition parties regarded political union:

> Three relatively small opposition parties are unequivocally for political union: Ralph Gonsalves' Movement for National Unity (St Vincent), George Odlum's Progressive Labour Party (St Lucia), and Tim Hector's Antigua-Caribbean Liberation Movement (Antigua). However, Julian Hunte's St Lucia Labour Party, Lee Moore's St Kitts-Nevis Labour Party, and Vincent Beache's St Vincent Labour Party are more concerned with their national politics than with any political union. George Brizan's National Democratic Congress (Grenada) and Mike Douglas' Dominica Labour Party stand somewhere between the pro-unionists and those who do not mind if the unity move falters. In short, the balance of political forces as represented in the political parties, in and out of government, favours the slowing down or even the halting of the unity train.[14]

It can be seen, therefore, that by not actively seeking to involve the opposition parties fully in the process toward a political union, the governments had wrong-footed themselves. For the parties, which never wanted union, could oppose the process on the basis that the governments were acting undemocratically. As Pat Emmanuel, a Grenadian academic, put it, the governments were operating a 'double standard' and approaching the issue in 'a secretive and high-handed manner'.[15]

But this alienation of the opposition parties could not practically serve the purposes of any government which was serious about political union. For the constitutions of all the OECS territories demand an affirmative vote of two-thirds of the members of some parliaments and three-quarters in others before a referendum can be held on any alteration to an entrenched clause of the constitution. Therefore, before the people of each state could be asked to vote in a referendum to alter the constitution allowing for political union, members of the opposition parties would have had to support such a motion in Parliament.

This active involvement of the opposition parties in the whole process leading to a referendum was important for another very crucial reason: the constitutions of each of the independent states concerned also require that any referendum to alter one of its clauses must have the support of two-thirds of the votes cast by the electorate. It is highly unlikely that any government would have been able to secure two-thirds of the vote without the support of the opposition parties. For, however much inter-state co-operation has expanded over the years in the OECS sub-region, a feeling of nationalism has also been fostered.

In the era approaching independence, political parties had instilled in their people the need for full control of their affairs and, in the period after independence, they had preached the value of national symbols and national heroes. Thus, while a sense of the value of regional co-operation had developed, nationalistic impulses remained a dominant characteristic of each of the societies. If the people of these territories were to be persuaded to subsume their nationalist feelings for greater benefit under a political union, it would require all their political leaders to convince them; no one faction could do it alone.

VAGUENESS EXPLAINED BY HINDSIGHT

There was a sense of vagueness in the way in which the governments approached the whole process of 'comprehensive consultations' to which they committed themselves in May 1987. That vagueness is fully explained with hindsight, and particularly with the knowledge that the Prime Minister of St Kitts-Nevis, Dr Simmonds, announced at a meeting of the OECS heads of government in November 1988 that his government would no longer participate in the efforts toward a political union.

It is now obvious that, throughout 1987 and 1988, decisions of the heads of government on the question of political union were being made to satisfy the least enthusiastic among them, and there was never any discussion, let alone agreement, on the substantive issues surrounding political union. Thus, the heads of government never laid out a clear course which they wanted to take except to say that there should be a preliminary referendum in each state in which, by a simple majority vote, the electorate would indicate whether or not they favoured the idea of a political union. And they could provide no answer when the electorate asked basic questions such as: what form of union? what type of government?

Indeed, at a meeting in June 1988 the heads of government 'took note of the view, widely expressed, that (they) should give more detailed information... on an appropriate form of union',[16] but they themselves produced nothing. Earlier in November 1987, they had announced that in January 1988 task forces composed of technical experts would be established to examine areas such as 'the constitution, public administration, external affairs and security, and finance'.[17] The task forces were never set up.

Thus the efforts toward creating a political union limped along throughout 1987 and 1988, often with conflicting statements being made by the various heads of government. Eventually it was brought to an end in November 1988 when they declared that 'it was agreed by the four governments of the territories normally referred to as the Windward Islands that they would continue to pursue the goal of political union.'[18] But, while it may have been clear that only the four Windward Island governments were interested in pursuing the 'goal of political union', it was equally clear that the goal would not be achieved if the methods employed so far continued. For even if the four governments were resolute, they would not achieve their purpose without the fullest participation of the opposition parties in Parliament. And that meant the establishment of a Constituent Assembly backed by funds and supported by good technical staff.

It also meant that political parties in those states would have to overcome their intense aversion to talking with each other. They would have had to learn that integral to operating the Westminster system of government is that, on important issues of national concern, political leaders from all sides of the house must hold dialogue as representatives of the people to whom they are accountable. If they failed to do so, as they did, the national consensus, which is an absolute prerequisite for altering their constitutions and proceeding to a political union, would never be achieved. Consequently, the people of the OECS sub-region may continue to face considerable and unnecessary economic hardship and retrogression in their separate states.

NOTES & REFERENCES

1   *Caribbean Development to the Year 2000: Challenges, Prospects and Policies,* Commonwealth Secretariat/Caribbean Community Secretariat, June 1988, London, p. 1.
2   *Ibid.*
3   James Mitchell, *Reuniting the Caribbean: Towards OECS Political Union,* November 1986, mimeo.
4   *Ibid.*
5   Conclusions of the Eleventh Meeting of the Authority of the OECS, Tortola, British Virgin Islands, 28-29 May 1987, p. 4, mimeo.
6   Cited by Howard Fergus in *Caribbean Contact,* Barbados, May 1988.
7   Caribbean News Agency report.
8   The Grenada Declaration proposed a political union of Guyana with the countries of Dominica, St Kitts-Nevis-Anguilla, St Lucia, St Vincent and the Grenadines, and Grenada.
9   Caribbean News Agency report US4068, 13 July 1987.
10 Reported in *The Voice* (St Lucia), 13 April 1988.
11 Mitchell, *Reuniting the Caribbean.*
12 Brochure of the Council of Eastern Caribbean Manufacturers.
13 Caribbean News Agency report US0181, 31 August 1987.
14 Ralph Gonsalves, 'Unity moves in limbo', *EC News,* 19 August 1988, Barbados, p. 5.
15 Caribbean News Agency report US 7562, 10 August 1987.
16 Conclusions of the Thirteenth Meeting of the Authority of the OECS, 2-3 June 1988, p. 3, mimeo.
17 Communiqué issued by the Twelfth Meeting of The Authority of the OECS, 26-27 November 1987, p. 3, mimeo.
18 Conclusions of the Fourteenth Meeting of the Authority of the OECS, 24 November 1988, St Lucia, p. 1, mimeo.

CHAPTER SIX

At the Crossroads of West Indian History

Jamaica's Norman Washington Manley asked a question over fifty years ago that ever since has been re-echoing throughout the West Indies. He asked: 'are we satisfied to be obscure and small nonentities in a world in which only larger groupings have the chance of survival and success?' That question has haunted the minds of West Indians ever since; not only Manley's generation, but also the generation that followed. For, in responding to Manley's question, the West Indies chose not the path to a 'West Indian nation standing shoulder to shoulder with all other nations of the world', which he advocated, but the road to small, weak countries in a world where to be small is to be unimportant and to be weak is to be ignored. Yet there have long been many West Indians who are convinced that the future progress and prosperity of the West Indies, and probably the region's cultural and political identity, depend upon the English-speaking Caribbean being integrated into a single political entity. For the problems, which urged political union on the agenda of the OECS between 1986-8, are shared by all the other West Indian territories, and their solution cannot be achieved by an economic grouping alone; they require joint and binding political action which can only come within a framework of political union.

It is right, of course, that the first step should be taken by the Leeward and Windward islands, for they have remained closely interlinked despite their separate independence – they have a common judiciary, a common Directorate of Civil Aviation, a common currency and a common Central Bank. The OECS, therefore, has the foundation upon which to quickly erect the pillars of political union.

In ignoring Norman Manley's call for one nation, separate independence was the path the West Indies chose; it seemed important

First published in *West Indian Digest*, No. 160, December 1988/January 1989, pp. i-iv.

for each state to achieve 'sovereignty' over its own affairs. But the sovereignty of St Lucia or St Vincent or Grenada has not made those islands richer or better off than the state of Texas which is not sovereign, or the province of Quebec which is not sovereign, or Scotland which is not sovereign. 'Sovereignty' did not give them equality even with small European states such as Yugoslavia or Denmark. 'Sovereignty' did not bestow upon them the capacity to defend themselves from revolution and invasion. Three mercenary attempts on Dominica in 1979, a plot in 1978 for Barbados, and a *coup d'etat* in Grenada in 1979 and again in 1983 followed by a military intervention, are ample evidence that Caribbean countries have no special immunity from invasion and their 'sovereignty' has not rendered them impenetrable. And this point is reinforced by the fact that most, if not all, of the Caribbean countries are now used as conduits for drug trafficking with governments and security services largely unable to combat it.

What the achievement of 'sovereignty' did for the OECS countries was to make them eligible to participate in international affairs. But being 'eligible' to participate and being able to 'effectively' participate are, as we have already seen, horses of a different colour; and, for the most part, OECS countries have not been able to participate in international affairs to any great effect. To participate effectively in international affairs, Caribbean countries require not only trained, human resources in diplomatic missions, they also need stronger economies, a basic defence capability and political clout; in other words, they need a degree of economic independence and bargaining power without which larger and more powerful countries will ignore them.

But are the Caribbean nations simply to give up – relegating themselves to the level of fourth-rate states in international society; beggars at the table of the rich, supplicants at the altar of the mighty? No self-respecting West Indian could choose to give up; no well-thinking Caribbean man could deny himself a place in the sun. But, if Caribbean people decide to fight for a share in the top prizes, they must also come to terms with the fact that separate states provide little, if any, chance; only a political union proffers such an opportunity, as did the West Indies Federation in 1958.

If the West Indies Federation had survived – forty or more years old by now – as a strong, vibrant nation with economic leverage and political clout, would it not, by now, have had at least an acceptable military capability to defend itself from mercenary attack? Would it not have been better able to fight for the presidency of the UN General Assembly? And, by the same token, would it not have been able to make stronger representations for its nationals in Britain who have been and still are subject to institutional as well as individual racism, by immigration, by the police, by the press and even by jailkeepers? Would not the government of Britain have to pay greater attention to a strong, vibrant country of more than six million people than it has to several small territories, some of which have populations of less than 200,000? Indeed, with the opportunities for employment that such a West Indian nation would have provided, would West Indians have come to Britain at all – would they have abandoned the warmth and comfort of the Caribbean for the cold and coldness of Britain? These are the questions that must be answered, for they are relevant to the merits of a political union both in the OECS and the region as a whole.

So we come to the question: why did a political union in the OECS come back on the agenda in the late 1980s? There is a fairly widely held belief that many countries in the OECS are much better-off than they were twenty or thirty years ago. It is undoubtedly true that physical conditions in many OECS countries have improved – there are more impressive buildings, roads where none existed before, modern airports and seaports, improved telecommunication and a wide spread of water and electricity supply. For these achievements every credit is due to the governments which skilfully negotiated and cajoled the financing of this infrastructure development from international financial institutions and friendly governments. But, in acknowledging the physical infrastructural improvements in the Eastern Caribbean, we cannot, at the same time, deny the reality of continuing poverty, slum dwellings, inadequate sewage and poor medical facilities. The sad reality is that the storm clouds of economic hardship that gathered over the West Indies as the region approached the end of the 1980s were even worse than those which loomed large at the beginning of the decade.

The average income of the people in seven of the thirteen Caribbean Community countries was lower than it was in 1980, and in two others the rate of increase was lower than three percent. This meant that, across the West Indies, the mass of people were poorer than they were eight years earlier. And, what is more, the prospects for improvement in the situation were growing bleaker every day: the rate of unemployment in every country was already high, but the indications were that the number of jobless would increase as the labour force expanded and the opportunity for emigration diminished.

Conservative estimates indicated that 'labour force growth is unlikely to be less than 23 percent in any country and may be as high as 54 percent'. The individual economies of the Caribbean – small as they are, dependent on one or two economic activities, and vulnerable to external forces – were hard-pressed; this led to 'contraction of expenditure on health, education and other social services'. There was, in short, a mask of affluence which hid an ugly face of underdevelopment. The mask was seen in the improved physical infrastructure, but below it remained dependent and fragile economies, organised on the basis of one activity – either agriculture or tourism – and surviving on the basis of external assistance, either aid or loans.

Official figures show that OECS countries have generally spent considerably more than they receive from taxes and other revenues. In this situation these countries have had to finance capital development programmes – roads, schools, ports, electricity expansion and so on – almost entirely from foreign resources, either through grants or borrowing.

There is a question here which begs itself: can any country or group of countries predicate development on the charity of others? Obviously, the answer is no, for while over the last few years, particularly in the wake of events in Grenada in 1979 and then again in 1983, the Caribbean attracted a greater deal of assistance than usual, the region cannot depend on the fears of others as a basis for its development. For, if tomorrow conditions in Latin America or South East Asia were to explode, the attention – and the assistance – would quickly turn away from the Caribbean as, indeed, it began to do in the early 1990s.

The problem of insufficient revenue was made worse by the fact that expenditure by OECS countries on imports is more than the earnings they get from exports. In 1986, they imported US$1.8 billion worth of goods and exported a meagre seven hundred and twenty-one million dollars in products. That meant that the deficit in visible trade in 1986 was just over US$1 billion.

What made matters worse was that the international trading environment was not helpful to the OECS countries. The much-vaunted Caribbean Basin Initiative, launched by United States President Ronald Reagan in 1982, did not produce the benefits it promised. Many goods of vital importance to the Caribbean were either denied duty-free access or were placed under quota restriction by the US Congress. The trade agreement between Canada and the Caribbean – CARIBCAN – had also not provided the expected market for exports from OECS countries, since from the outset it denied duty-free access to those goods, such as garments, which could most easily have been exported. Nor do Caribbean countries find any more cause for rejoicing in respect of trading prospects in Europe. At threat from the single European market which loomed on the horizon at the end of the 1980s was the preferential market, particularly for bananas and citrus, which they have enjoyed in Britain under the terms of the Lomé agreement between European Community countries and African, Caribbean and Pacific states. To save their markets, OECS countries with insufficient individual economic and political leverage needed to negotiate with the combined forces of the European Community countries. It was already obvious even then that no single OECS country had the capacity to conduct such negotiations successfully on its own.

OECS countries also needed, and still need, urgently to develop a joint capability for identifying their development needs on a rational basis, and for negotiating assistance to meet those needs. To do this, they have to agree on a programme of industry allocation; they have to set priorities in economic planning that take greater account of their potential in service industries; there has to be a realistic appraisal of their competitiveness, or lack of it, in the banana industry; and they have to diversify their agricultural production. And, very importantly, they have to jointly negotiate access to markets of other countries and financial assistance. But, to achieve all these things, the OECS has to take cohesive political action, and such action is only possible in the framework of a political union where binding decisions can be taken and fully implemented.

By comparison with the many processes of regional integration taking place in different parts of the world, the West Indies remains several small states – with an economic arrangement, it is true, but one requiring an overhaul that can most effectively be achieved in a more integrated political framework. In addition, they have tiny populations, little financial resources and are technologically backward. Given the large groupings that have developed and are continuing to develop in the world, how will the small countries of the West Indies cope? In particular, how will the disadvantaged islands of the OECS manage? How can they survive as dwarves in a world of giants?

It should be obvious that, as separate entities, the OECS countries will only survive on the aid of donors, but it is now accepted wisdom in international circles that aid is distributed not on the needs of the recipient but in the interests of the donor. Thus, the standard of living of the people of the individual states might deteriorate, and the standing in the world of the states themselves might recede into dependency until the very 'sovereignty', which they now hold so precious, may have to be pledged to the pawnshop of some larger power in return for sustenance. They might get a new master, but it is, nonetheless, to the old colonialism from which they scurried in the past that they will crawl in the future, shedding their dignity and self-respect in the process.

The countries of the Eastern Caribbean thus stood in the late 1980s at the crossroads of history: before them lay the path of political union and a future together or the path of separation and a fate alone. For a consequence of not deepening their present economic integration arrangements into a binding political framework could well turn out to be the unravelling of the tapestry of integration so painstakingly woven over the last twenty or so years. When the economic arrangements, which have now become inadequate, fail to continue to produce benefits, it is obvious that governments will be inclined to abandon them and, in the process, not only will integration end but each country will have to seek alliances and protection elsewhere. In these circumstances, it is to the colonialism of the past that they will be forced to return.

CHAPTER SEVEN

The Relevance and Function of Diplomacy

Several definitions of diplomacy exist in the literature on international relations, but many of them have been overtaken by changes in the nature of, and participants in, international relations. The classic definition is Sir Ernest Satow's, given in 1917, that 'diplomacy is the application of intelligence and tact to the conduct of official relations between the governments of independent states, extending sometimes also to their relations with vassal states'.[1] But Satow could not have foreseen circumstances in which states would recognise the Palestine Liberation Organisation (PLO) as being the official representative of the Palestinian people, even though there is still no Palestinian state. The same is true of the 1982 definition by Adam Watson that diplomacy means 'the dialogue between independent states'.[2] Both definitions fail to take cognisance of the international organisations, such as the United Nations and the Commonwealth, which play important roles in international politics. In my view, Hedley Bull captured the substance of today's diplomacy by defining it as 'the conduct of relations between states and other entities with standing in world politics by official agents and by peaceful means'.[3] Bull's definition introduced two elements which, it is now generally agreed, are essential to the process and purpose of diplomacy: (i) the concept that there are entities in world politics other than states; and (ii) the idea that diplomacy is a 'peaceful' activity.

From the outset it should be established that diplomacy is only one of the instruments available to a state in the execution of its foreign policy. For the sake of convenience, and because it covers the ground, this chapter adopts Adam Watson's definition that foreign policy is 'the substance of a state's relations with other powers and agencies and the purposes it hopes to achieve by these relations'.[4] In executing its foreign policy, there is general agreement that a state has three

First published in *The Round Table*, No. 312, October 1989, pp. 413-24.

instruments available to it: (i) military capability – the pursuit of its purposes through force of arms; (ii) economic capability – the pursuit of its purposes through the use of economic measures; and (iii) diplomacy – the pursuit of its purposes through negotiation.

But, in the execution of their foreign policies, small Caribbean states cannot call on the instruments of military or economic force; diplomacy is really the *only* tool available to them. For, as the Commonwealth Consultative group put it:

> Since these states have no military or economic power to wield they are forced to rely on diplomatic means in order to convey to other countries the nature of their national interests in the different areas of international relations that are vital not just to their security but to their very survival.[5]

As we have amply seen in earlier chapters, the geopolitical setting in which these states have to operate is one that makes them very sensitive to US disapproval of the actions which they may take. In a sense, this sensitivity to US disapproval places an even greater relevance on diplomacy for small Caribbean states. For it is only by concerted diplomatic efforts that they can hope to allay US fears that, in seeking to pursue their own purposes, they are not placing US interests at risk.

Clearly, then, an important function of the diplomacy of small Caribbean states would be constantly to persuade the US administration that nothing would be done to pose a threat to the security interests of the USA. This is simply good sense, for experience has shown that any action by Caribbean states, which encourages US distaste, could result in punitive measures being taken against them. Such measures could be to destabilise the government, and, as we know, there are several such recorded incidents in Latin America and the Caribbean as a whole.[6] Other measures could be economic as occurred in Grenada when the Marxist government of Maurice Bishop came to power by a bloodless *coup d'etat* in 1979. The US cut off aid to, and trade with, Grenada, and encouraged its close allies to do likewise. And, in the absence of protective security arrangements under the auspices of the United Nations, a pretext could be found by a determined US government to intervene militarily. A precedent was thus set in Grenada in 1983 when US President Reagan claimed to have taken decisive action in order to 'protect innocent lives including up to 1000 Americans (students and tourists) whose personal safety is, of course, my paramount concern'.[7]

By the same token, a similar argument could be used for relations with Cuba, at least during the years of Cold War. In that period the potential threat which it posed to the stability of small states in the Caribbean could not be ignored. For instance, the Cuban Communist party maintained strong links with left-wing parties in all of the Caribbean small states and provided their members with training, including the use of weapons. Therefore, as in the case of the US, one of the functions of diplomacy for these small states should have been to have official dialogue with Cuba through the normalisation of relations. It would also have been prudent for those states which had not done so to establish diplomatic relations with the Soviet Union. For in a world dominated to a large extent by the United States and the Soviet Union as super powers, it made little sense not to have normal relations with both. In neither of these cases would the establishment of diplomatic relations have necessarily led to resident embassies. As happens in other cases, representatives to the United Nations could have been charged with responsibility for carrying out the dialogue between the states concerned.

Two factors emerge from consideration of the functions of diplomacy for small Caribbean states. The first is that of the three instruments generally accepted as available in diplomatic negotiations – persuasion, the offer of rewards, and making threats[8] – only persuasion is available to poor, small states. Therefore, it places vital importance on the development of well-trained and competent diplomatic personnel. And, since in small countries the exercise of diplomatic functions is not limited to professional diplomats, but also extends to officials from other government departments, they too should be properly trained.

The second factor which emerges is that the foreign policy of a small Caribbean state is based primarily on its domestic need for security, and economic and social development. Thus, at this point, we can conclude that diplomacy is extremely relevant to the small Caribbean state, and its purpose is to negotiate by persuasion with states and agencies to safeguard the country's security and promote its economic and social development.

THE FUNCTION OF DIPLOMACY

In this section, I will set out how diplomacy might function for small Caribbean states in ideal circumstances, and I will describe how diplomacy actually operates given the severe limitations faced by these resource-poor states.

Apart from the function of reassuring their neighbours that they would pose no threat to their security the primary function of bilateral diplomacy for small Caribbean states should be to negotiate substantial levels of aid and favourable terms of trade. Similarly, the function of multilateral diplomacy should be to contribute to global negotiations for an improved economic deal for developing countries through agencies such as the United Nations, the Generalised Agreement on Tariffs and Trade (GATT), the United Nations Conference on Trade and Development (UNCTAD), and the African, Caribbean and Pacific (ACP) and the European Economic Community (EEC) Council of Ministers.

Some Caribbean small states already try to utilise diplomacy in this way. They have done so by targeting their efforts in areas of special interest. Therefore, the establishment of bilateral overseas missions has been linked to considerations of aid, trade and, as Lloyd Searwar aptly puts it, 'whether or not the host country's friendship and goodwill are important for their security'.[9] With regard to multilateral relations, some Caribbean states have sent resident missions to the United Nations in New York and to the UN agencies in Geneva, for it is in these organisations that crucial negotiations mostly take place on trade, aid and development issues.

However, it would be incorrect to assume that all small Caribbean states effectively utilise diplomacy, or even recognise its primacy in their survival. Because, in many cases, the importance of diplomacy is not fully appreciated, some diplomatic appointments overseas, on a resident basis, are made as a reward to faithful political cronies, or as a banishment for troublesome political rivals. Consequently, the diplomat often does not have Satow's required 'intelligence and tact' and, in any event, is ill-suited to carry out the diplomatic functions which are vital to his country's security and economic and social development. Further, when small states are fortunate enough to appoint good diplomatic representatives abroad, some of these states constrain their diplomats from functioning effectively by placing greater emphasis on petty protocol matters, such as meeting ministers at the airport, than on the substance of the diplomat's job. The fact is that foreign ministries in many small Caribbean states are little short of being nominal institutions. They are hopelessly understaffed, deficient in trained and able personnel, and incapable of dealing with the range of issues with which a foreign ministry is beleaguered. This observation is not a condemnation of foreign ministries in small states; it is merely a description of the reality of underdevelopment. They, themselves, would like to be better, but lacking the financial and trained resources they do the best they can.

ASSOCIATIVE DIPLOMACY

One way in which Caribbean small states have attempted to overcome the problems of fear of disapproval from powerful neighbours, and lack of trained and qualified diplomats, is by employing what R.P. Barston describes as 'associative diplomacy'. His full description is as follows:

> Associative diplomacy serves one or more of a number of purposes including the creation of a larger grouping, the co-ordination of policies and mutual assistance within the grouping. Other purposes are maintenance of the political, economic or security influence of the 'primary' grouping, limiting the actual or potential coercive power of other groupings (damage limitation) and enhancement of the individual identity of members of the grouping.[10]

The small states in the Caribbean, aware of their own limitations, have entered into a number of forms of 'associative diplomacy'. For example, as we have already noted, when in 1972, four of them – Jamaica, Guyana, Trinidad and Tobago and Barbados – decided to establish diplomatic relations with Cuba, they did so together. The government of each country knew that, had it established relations with Cuba on its own, it would have suffered the wrath of the USA. Their collective action was an attempt at damage limitation. It should be noted here that in 1981 a new government in Jamaica, determined to enjoy the closest possible links with the US, broke diplomatic relations with Cuba.

With regard to policy co-ordination and mutual assistance, all of the Caribbean small states are members of CARICOM – a treaty organisation under which they are pledged to 'co-ordinate' their foreign policies. Representatives of the states meet at the level of heads of government and at ministerial levels. Prior to multilateral negotiations, representatives of the states meet to co-ordinate their positions and strengthen their negotiation team by pooling their human resources and appointing a single spokesman. In the past they have done so with remarkable success. For instance, in the ACP-EEC negotiations in 1973-74 leading to the signing of the first Lomé Convention in 1975, it was the representative of a Caribbean small state, Guyana, who convinced the African, Caribbean and Pacific countries that they should create a single grouping to negotiate with the European Community.[11] The initial agreement, which institutionalised the economic relationship between the EEC and ACP, opened the way for subsequent agreements which are still in force today. These agreements have allowed the Caribbean to be able to plan development projects with some level of certainty of economic assistance. This co-ordination has been repeated in other international fora, particularly with regard to the election of Caribbean officials to seats in international bodies. In these situations, the 'smaller' of the small Caribbean states benefit from the expertise of the more developed foreign ministries and longer experienced diplomats in the 'bigger' Caribbean small states.

Even at a bilateral level, some Caribbean small states have experimented with 'associative diplomacy' through joint representation. Thus, in London, St Kitts-Nevis, St Lucia and St Vincent and the Grenadines shared a common High Commissioner at one time, and these three countries and Dominica have a single representative in Ottawa.

However, there are limits to associative diplomacy. In the area of 'low' politics, such as support for a Caribbean candidate and global negotiations on the new international economic order, small Caribbean states have shown no reluctance to pool their sovereignty in order to strengthen their bargaining power. But in the area of 'high' politics, such as their relations with the superpowers or how they vote in the

United Nations on international political issues, there has been a marked unwillingness to harmonise their positions. In 'high' politics, individual 'sovereignty' comes to the fore, and each state feels it has greater benefits to gain from dealing directly with those countries which seek its support. This is underscored, for instance, by the fact that though some countries have a common representative in some capitals, they each insist upon their own ambassador in Washington.

CONCLUSION

Small Caribbean states, then, will continue to be a feature of the international system, and without military or economic muscle, diplomacy remains the only instrument available to them in international politics. Yet, in the aftermath of the US invasion of Grenada a trend emerged, and it still persists, that small states should basically mind their own business and stay out of international politics. As the Commonwealth Consultative Group which studied small states after events in Grenada put it:

> An activist role may have its perils as, unless there is a careful choice of issues for support, it might attract the hostility of larger powers. It is important therefore that in playing such a role small states should plan their international activities on a highly selective basis and focus on issues that have a *direct bearing* (my emphasis) on their national interest.[12]

This argument would suit those who have a vested interest in maintaining the current international system and those who, like Hans Morgenthau, see the membership of the UN by new states and particularly small ones as 'the vice of the majority'.[13] But prospects for the survival of small states in economic and security terms depend very much upon their active participation in the United Nations, particularly in support of the principle of the non-use of force, and in advancing new concepts and systems of collective security under the UN as proposed, for instance, by the Palme Commission.[14]

It is true that small Caribbean states will always be under the threat of hegemony from many quarters. But they will not reduce that threat by not taking principled positions on issues such as apartheid in South Africa in the past or conflicts in the Middle East today which, arguably, do not have a direct bearing on their interests. Yet, if they stand aside from these issues, they run the risk of being ignored by other regions of the world when the Caribbean may need international support to withstand hegemonic forces or aggression.

The threat of hegemony could be kept at bay if Caribbean small states demonstrate that they are sincerely unaligned between the major powers; if they collectively espouse principled positions in international affairs; and if they make greater use of the opportunities presented by associative diplomacy. These opportunities exist in extending their joint efforts for better terms of trade and aid beyond the ACP-EEC, into negotiations with the United States, Canada and Japan. But, apart from economic issues, the Caribbean could use associative diplomacy to try to achieve a better balance of power in the hemisphere and thus attain more room for diplomatic action free of security concerns. One way of doing this could be to collectively deepen and strengthen their relationship with the larger countries in Latin America, such as Mexico, Venezuela, Colombia and Brazil, on the basis of mutual assistance.

An important dimension in achieving these purposes through diplomacy will be the quality of the representatives of Caribbean small states on the international scene. For, as R.P. Barston points out, representatives of small countries

Perform major roles at international conferences, sometimes far in excess of the apparent capabilities or importance of the country. Diplomatic power and influence, defined through organisation and negotiating reputation, are quite separate from other elements of power.[15]

Similar roles could be played by able diplomats at the bilateral level. The Caribbean has clearly demonstrated that it has such people. For instance, at the beginning of the 1980s, Caribbean men and women from small states occupied the positions of Commonwealth Secretary-General, Under-Secretary-General UN (Women's Affairs), Assistant Secretary-General of UNCTAD, Deputy Administrator of UNDP, Deputy Secretary-General of the ACP, and Assistant Secretary-General of the OAS, with numerous other senior positions being held in international organisations.

In the end, diplomacy is not the instrument of last resort for small Caribbean states, but the primary instrument. Neither its relevance nor its function in international politics can be overstated. Commonwealth governments may have recognised this in providing funds for the Commonwealth Secretariat to facilitate the presence in New York of Permanent Missions to the UN from small countries which would otherwise have been under-represented, or not represented at all. Nine Commonwealth small states are at the moment facilitated in this way; four of them small Caribbean states.

NOTES & REFERENCES

1   Lord Gore-Booth (ed), *Satow's Guide to Diplomatic Practice*, Longman, London, 1979, p. 3.
2   Adam Watson, *Diplomacy: The Dialogue Between States*, Eyre Methuen, London, 1982, p. 11.
3   Hedley Bull, *The Anarchical Society*, Macmillan, London, 1977, p. 163.
4   Watson, *Diplomacy*, p. 14.
5   Commonwealth Secretariat, *Vulnerability: Small States in the Global Society*, Report of a Commonwealth Consultative Group, Commonwealth Secretariat, London, 1985, p. 68.
6   Cf. Jenny Pearce, *Under the Eagle: US Intervention in Central America and the Caribbean*, Latin America Bureau, London, 1982.
7   Cited by Anthony Payne, *The International Crisis in the Caribbean*, Croom Helm, Beckenham, 1985, p. 164.
8   K. J. Holsti, *International Politics: A Framework for Analysis*, 2nd edition, Prentice Hall, New York, 1974, pp. 198-9.
9   Lloyd Searwar, *Administration of Foreign Relations*, Occasional Paper No. 1, Institute of Social and Economic Research (Eastern Caribbean), University of the West Indies, November 1974, p. 5.
10 R. P. Barston, *Modern Diplomacy*, Longman, Essex, 1988, p. 108.
11 Paul Sutton, 'From Neo-colonialism to Neo-colonialism: Britain and the EEC in the Commonwealth Caribbean', in Anthony Payne and Paul Sutton (eds), *Dependency Under Challenge: The Political Economy of the Commonwealth Caribbean*, Manchester University Press, Manchester, 1984.
12 Commonwealth Secretariat, *Vulnerability*, p. 74.
13 Hans J. Morgenthau, *Politics Among Nations*, 5th edition, Scientific Book Agency, Calcutta, 1973, p. 537.
14 *Common Security: A Programme for Disarmament*, report of the Independent Commission on Disarmament and Security Issues under the Chairmanship of Olaf Palme, Pan Books, 1982.
15 Barston, *Modern Diplomacy*, p. 5.

CHAPTER EIGHT

The Drugs Problem in the Caribbean

The illicit trade in narcotics is now the biggest contributor to crime in the Commonwealth Caribbean. Since the early 1980s, the Caribbean has been a transhipment point for drugs from South America to North America and Europe. In the early stages, Caribbean governments stood aloof from the problem. They regarded it as an issue for the governments of the demand countries, such as the United States. However, over time, drug trafficking has spawned increased crime, violent crime, the spread of illegal weapons and drug addiction throughout the Region. The problem is now as real for Caribbean governments as it is for the governments of the United States. It threatens to destabilise the area, and it could get worse unless it is tackled comprehensively by the Region as a whole with international help.

Many of the problems of the smaller islands of the Caribbean in relation to the illicit trade in, and abuse of, narcotics are not different in type from the difficulties experienced in the rest of the world. The essential difference is that, in smaller countries, the problems have a greater impact because populations are smaller and far fewer resources are available to meet the awesome challenge posed by the narcotics trade. In support of this assertion, it might be useful if we establish a typology of the problems posed by drug trafficking and drug abuse and compare the consequences faced by smaller countries with those encountered by larger states.

Generally speaking, the problems are of the following five broad types: the lack of financial resources to mount an adequate general response to the problem of drug trafficking; the insufficiency of resources to police territorial waters or borders, ports and airports effectively; the corruption of officials; threats to the security of states from external forces; and internal instability caused by drug-related crimes.

LACK OF FINANCIAL RESOURCES

Dealing first with the proposition that small islands lack the financial resources to respond adequately to the problems of drug trafficking, it should be noted that experts have suggested for some time now that the trade in illicit drugs is bigger than world trade in arms or oil. Some have put a figure on it of US$500 billion a year. Since the early 1980s, a substantial portion of that trade has originated in three South American countries: Peru, Bolivia and Columbia which produce virtually all of the trafficked cocaine. In addition, Latin American and Caribbean countries supply one-third of the heroin and 80 percent of the marijuana used in the United States. Three-quarters of the United States drug market, worth in excess of US$100 billion annually, is fed by the production of Latin American and Caribbean countries. The lucrative US market, and the increasing demand in Europe, for cocaine and cannabis from South America has placed the Caribbean in the centre of transhipment activities. While some cannabis is grown in a few of the smaller islands, these islands are not regarded themselves as major producers.

Against a figure of US$500 billion in world trade in narcotics of which the United States contributes at least US$100 billion, the total expenditure of the government of Antigua and Barbuda – which will be used in this chapter as indicative of the Caribbean's smaller islands – was US$99 million for the financial year 1988-89, with its expenditure on the police and military reckoned to be no more than US$6.2 million. Of this US$6.2 million, less than a third, or US$2 million, would have been allocated specifically for combating the illegal traffic in drugs. Antigua and Barbuda's performance is thus a measure of the sheer inability of smaller Caribbean countries to respond adequately to the drug threat. But inadequate responses are not limited to the smaller islands. Of the larger territories, the Bahamas spends more money than any other on combating drug trafficking; yet, with 13 percent of its national budget allocated to the problem, and with the collaboration of US agencies, the Bahamas has only succeeded in closing down 'certain drug corridors'. It is worth noting as well that in the same period the United States allocated a total budget of about US$4 billion annually for dealing with all aspects of drug related activity. This sum represented less than four percent of the money spent by Americans to purchase illicit drugs every year.

In summary, then, the lack of sufficient resources to address the problems of narcotics is not unique to small Caribbean countries. What is different about the problem is that, whereas larger and more developed countries, such as the United States, have the capacity to secure the necessary resources by either re-allocating sums in the national budget, or by new financial measures, small Caribbean islands – already underdeveloped, operating in budget deficits, and subject to the vicissitudes of the external economic environment – do not have the means to raise more money. And, even if they did, their severely limited resources would ensure that the maximum funds they could muster would still be inadequate to compete with the vast sums available to drug traffickers. This observation is equally true of the larger Caribbean countries which are themselves beleaguered by mounting debt and worsening terms of trade.

Let us now turn to the problem of the insufficiency of the necessary resources to police their waters, ports and airports. Here again, in terms of the type of problem, the smaller Caribbean islands share the same difficulties experienced by larger territories not only in the region, but everywhere, including North America and Europe. Given the large quantities of illicit drugs that continue to enter the United States, and are now increasingly entering European countries, these larger and richer states are more successful than smaller territories at effectively policing their borders, ports and airports only by degree. But the degree of difference is great. For instance, basic policing materials that are taken for granted in larger countries simply do not exist in small islands. An example of this is a lack of forensic material for identifying narcotics disguised as something else. Similarly, inexperienced dog handlers can nullify the capacity of sniffer dogs where such dogs exist. The point being made here is that the mere possession of dogs is not sufficient for the detection of drugs – the handler has to be as well-trained as the dog, and in many cases he is not. These, however, are surmountable difficulties if governments are prepared to divert resources into purchasing supplies and training.

What is not easily overcome is the problem of policing the waters of small islands. The many coves that characterise the topography of

Caribbean islands lend themselves to drug traffickers whose light aircraft drop shipments into the sea where they are uplifted by fast boats which return to the island undetected. Such coastguard services as exist in the smaller islands are hopelessly under-equipped and under-funded.

CORRUPTION OF THE SYSTEMS

A deep conviction that governmental systems have been corrupted is shared throughout the Eastern Caribbean. But the point should be made that suspicion also abounds in the larger Caribbean territories and within the United States. Evidence of this is revealed in a joint US/British report compiled in 1987 which stated that concern over corruption of local government officials had prevented Federal agents from co-ordinating their work with them. Further, a Commission of Inquiry in Trinidad and Tobago in 1987 claimed that police officers were deeply involved in drugs.

Writing in Britain in *The Observer*, in the wake of the revelation that a top figure in the Cuban military establishment had helped the Medellin cartel in Colombia to smuggle six tonnes of cocaine into the United States, Hugh O'Shaughnessy posed a question which, he said, 'must terrify the governments of the whole Western World'. The question was: 'how have the cocaine merchants of Colombia become so immensely powerful that they can corrupt and subvert the leadership of the army of a Marxist-Leninist state which has beaten a US-sponsored invasion at home and outshone the Soviet forces routing a South African army on battlefields thousands of miles from Cuba?' The answer to that question is less relevant to me as a basis for analysis than is the claim which it makes: that the cocaine merchants are powerful enough to subvert and corrupt even those who appear above such subversion and corruptibility. It is obvious that the cocaine merchants are powerful. Their power is measurable in their capacity for coercion through terrorism and murder, their military strength and the vast sums of money at their disposal for corrupting officials in many countries.

Let us consider their power to corrupt. It is easy to understand how traffickers corrupt policemen and customs officers in small islands. Pilots flying light aircraft on behalf of the Colombian drug traffickers were reported to be earning US$5,000 a kilo and their planes carried an average of 300 kilos. That translates to US$1,500,000 per shipment. If we take the pilots on the one hand, and the police and customs officials on the other, as the representatives of the front line in the battle of drug trafficking, it becomes clear that small countries cannot win. In the first place, the police and customs officials lack the attractive financial motivation to do their duty, and in second place they are very susceptible to bribery. Indeed, even large countries would have profound difficulties, for, as one US academic has pointed out, 'an offer of US$100,000 or US$150,000 to a commanding officer (of the US military) to look the other way while a load of cocaine is brought into the United States could prove irresistible to some officer(s)'. But the difference between small countries and large ones is that, in the small ones, fewer people need to be corrupted to facilitate trafficking, for the simple reason that fewer people are engaged on the front line of law enforcement and fewer still in the back-up and cross-checking roles. Correspondingly, the corruption of a few can cover a wide field in island terms.

SECURITY AND INTERVENTION

Let us now move to the security problem which drug trafficking poses to smaller islands. Again, though the smaller islands are not unique, they are particularly vulnerable. As already indicated, it has been estimated that 50 determined and well armed men could take over any of the smaller Caribbean islands. But it is unlikely that narcotic barons would want to go to the long-term trouble and expense of taking over an island and defending it from attack by forces – either rival traffickers or large neighbouring countries unhappy with their presence – which would like to dislodge them. For, paradoxically, the sovereignty of the states in which they operate provides traffickers with protection from those countries whose military forces are capable of eliminating them. For example, the United States could not intervene militarily in Colombia to stamp out the Medellin cartel while a legitimate government holds office. Such an intervention would be regarded as an outrage and would subject the United States to widespread international criticism. It should be remembered that, when the United States sent military units into Bolivia at the invitation of the government to destroy cocaine laboratories there in 1986, the

American administration was severely criticised by Latin American governments and the Paz Estenssoro administration in Bolivia was almost toppled. However, looking at the matter theoretically, if the cartel were to overthrow a government by force of arms and establish a narcotic state, the scenario would be very different. For, at that point, the distinction between that country's internal affairs and the threat posed by such a state to the well-being of other states would be blurred. In such circumstances, it is possible to envisage sufficient international support for intervention. Therefore, not taking over a state, but hiding behind its sovereignty, would appear to be in the interest of the drug barons.

A much more likely scenario is one in which the narcotic barons demonstrate their capacity for terror to a government of a small island in order to prevent it from becoming too aggressive in its interdiction activities. For instance, a handful of well-armed narcotic soldiers, or mercenaries, could make a lightning trip to a country, wreak destruction, and fly out before a defence could be mounted by states friendly to the small island. When, in January 1989, a group of Colombians were held in the British Virgin Islands, several policy makers both inside and outside the Caribbean entertained the thought that narcotic barons might mount a rescue operation of the sort I just described. Such an operation is, of course, highly possible in the smaller islands where there are no prisons for such dangerous criminals. Indeed, if we are to believe one travel writer while he was in Anguilla on a recent visit, 'a prisoner broke out (of prison) to buy coconuts at the market and then broke back in again'. And, while in the 'larger' of the smaller islands prisons are somewhat more secure than in Anguilla, they are certainly not high security institutions. It is not surprising, therefore, that immediately after being convicted, the Colombians who had been held in the British Virgin Islands were transferred to a high security prison in Britain. Further, the police and military forces in the smaller islands – in the case of those who have such military forces – are small and poorly armed. They would be unable to match the superior weapons and battle experience of narcotic soldiers or mercenaries.

But the security of the smaller islands is not limited to military considerations; economic, social and political factors are perhaps even more important. Drug trafficking is capable of undermining each of these. In the first place, trafficking has resulted in the abuse of drugs by a growing number of young people. This debilitation of the youth of a small country – already short of skilled and qualified labour – must, over time, have an adverse effect on the country's productive capacity. Moreover, as the number of addicts increase, small countries will have to devote a greater portion of their scarce resources to rehabilitation. Alongside the increased cost of rehabilitation will be the attendant increase in the costs of law enforcement, for drug addiction has brought with it an increase in crime. The tourist industry – the mainstay of the economy – has also been hit. There have been reports of tourists being harassed on beaches by drug vendors, but even worse, there has also been an increase in the number or tourists being robbed by addicts seeking the means to buy their 'fix'. Already a fragile flower, it would not take many more of these incidents for tourism to begin to wilt. Apart from the loss of income from economic activity, such as tourism, the diversion of scarce resources from the productive sector into law enforcement and rehabilitation can have both short- and long-term effects on the economic development, social equilibrium and political stability of a small country. In this sense, the security of the state could be jeopardised by a process akin to 'destabilisation'.

DRUG TRAFFICKING HAS INCREASED DOMESTIC CRIME

Drug trafficking has also dramatically increased crime, particularly violent crime, in the Commonwealth Caribbean. Traffickers have armed their 'soldiers' with weapons which, in some cases, are more sophisticated than the armoury of the Police. Turf wars and executions are now more prevalent in countries such as Jamaica and Trinidad and Tobago, and they are beginning to occur in the smaller Eastern Caribbean islands. But, crimes are not restricted to rivalry between drug gangs; they have spread into the wider community with significant increases in hold-ups of business places and break and entry into homes. There are now 'no-go' areas in some countries where Police dare not enter, and where the only order that prevails is that which is set by gang leaders.

While the situation I have just described is not unique to small states; they also exist in large and powerful countries, such as the United States and Britain, the difference is that small states lack the resources and the capacity to cope with the problem. Large states can allocate increased resources to law enforcement agencies; small states have limited resources to allocate, and if they do re-allocate such scarce resources, some other vital element of their social or economic development programme suffers.

The United States convinced many Commonwealth Caribbean countries to sign up to what came to be called 'The Shiprider's Agreement', under which US coast guard vessels could pursue the ships of suspected drug traffickers in the territorial waters of Caribbean countries, and make arrests. This was a controversial agreement at the time. There was genuine concern among Caribbean countries – not only the smaller ones – that the United States was attempting to use the battle against drug trafficking and money laundering as a means of political manipulation, including infringements of the sovereign authority of governments in their own territory.

Nonetheless, Caribbean governments had to recognise that, even though some attempt was being made to use the battle against drugs to manipulate Caribbean countries, there is a genuine problem of drug addiction in the United States – one which the US administration is determined to stamp out. Thus, while acknowledging that they lack the resources to effectively interdict drug trafficking through their territories, or to hold certain types of traffickers in their prisons, Caribbean governments signed up to the 'Shipriders' Agreement'. Given their own lack of capacity to cope with drug traffickers in their own waters, they accepted that they needed the US to provide assistance.

WHAT INTERNATIONAL SOLUTION?

Caribbean governments did try to find a way to respond to the problems caused by drug trafficking that did not rely solely on the United States. In 1989 led Prime Ministers Michael Manley of Jamaica and A.N.R Robinson of Trinidad and Tobago proposed respectively the establishment of a 'multilateral force, under the aegis of the United Nations, which would provide assistance in particular situations regarding intelligence and interdiction capabilities beyond the resources of individual states', and Commissions of Inquiry and an International Criminal Court 'which would be capable of investigating and adjudicating on the criminal responsibility of persons engaged in offences such as drug trafficking'[1]. Basically, the problem that both Manley and Robinson were trying to grapple with in their proposals was how to reconcile their fear of being swamped by the United States with their need for help in dealing with the drug problem – in other words, how to protect the sovereignty of Caribbean states from erosion while meeting US pressure for interdiction. It remains a real dilemma, but it is arguable that the United Nations may not be the most effective mechanism for a multilateral solution to a problem of such urgency. Its record to date on providing collective security, given the reluctance of superpowers to act, certainly does not commend it.

One other approach to the problem may be a regional one, involving the governments of the Caribbean, the United States, Canada and Latin American countries, along with the residual metropolitan powers in the area – Britain, France and the Netherlands – in a multilateral commission to police the area, allowing for joint interdiction and imprisonment upon conviction in one of the developed territories. Among the participating Latin American countries in such a commission one would expect to see Cuba whose government, by the conviction and execution of its third highest ranking military officer for involvement in drug trafficking, has demonstrated that it can be relied on to fight the illicit trade in drugs. At the executive level, the commission could be made up of plenipotentiaries of the participating governments, and, while its force should be drawn from all the countries involved, the command structure of its operations should be smaller to render it effective. No one would pretend that getting agreement on such a commission would not be fraught with problems, but the joint exercises which have been taking place since the early 1980s among forces from Britain, the United States and Caribbean countries provide a basis on which such a regional commission could be built. Short of the adoption of one of the multilateral approaches identified here, it is difficult to see how the Caribbean region will avoid the United States 'Americanising' the battle against drugs, with all the infringements of the sovereignty of the Caribbean states which that might entail.

DIVERSION OF SCARCE FOREIGN EXCHANGE RESOURCES
In an article entitled, 'The Colombian Nightmare: Drugs and Structural Adjustment in the Caribbean', Dennis Pantin powerfully reiterated the point that combating drug trafficking severely taxes the foreign exchange resources of Caribbean countries.[2] All of these countries

face significant balance of trade deficits, and the three largest in population terms – Guyana, Jamaica and Trinidad and Tobago – have also long had overwhelming debt problems. Moreover, foreign exchange is vital in all of the Caribbean countries for the maintenance of their productive sectors, which still fail to offer jobs to half the young people seeking employment. Combating drug trafficking is therefore a further demand on already scarce foreign exchange. And, while precious foreign exchange in ailing economies is being diverted to coping with drug trafficking, it has been observed that the presence of drug-related resources 'enables some of our countries to better resist the economic crisis as they generate employment, inject foreign exchange into dollar-starved economies and enable investment to be made in other productive areas; in short, temporarily to cushion the crisis.'

MEASURES TAKEN

In the late 1990s, Commonwealth Caribbean governments established strong regimes designed to curb drug trafficking. The legislative frameworks are in place, and the penalties for drug offences are severe. Many countries have also established special units of the Police force or stand-alone bodies to combat drug trafficking. They have also established Mutual Legal Assistance Treaties with the United States and other countries to allow for co-operation in the exchange of information and for joint action to arrest suspected drug traffickers. In addition, the governments of the United States, the United Kingdom and Canada have provided technical assistance, including training and equipment to several Caribbean countries. The British government has been particularly active in providing training and assistance to the coast guards of the Eastern Caribbean countries. The Caribbean Region also established the Caribbean Financial Action Task Force (CFATF) in 1996. This body was charged with monitoring the machinery of member countries in the fight against money laundering and drug trafficking. It does so through a peer review or mutual evaluation. Each country is assessed by representatives of a group of others using objective criteria for evaluation. The CFATF evaluation, along with monitoring by the US government which publishes an annual report, has pushed Caribbean governments to make the machinery for fighting drug trafficking more effective.

However, two aspects of the anti-narcotics regime remain weak.

The first is the lack of adequate resources for law enforcement both by coast guards and police and the second is co-operation between authorities within countries. Often there is insufficient co-operation between police and customs or the coast guard and the police.

But, as one Jamaican minister has pointed out, the measures taken by all the Caribbean countries individually 'fall short of a regional response which will be necessary in the development of a sustained Caribbean initiative. The Caribbean countries do not possess either the facilities or the resources to achieve this most important objective.'[3]

A SUSTAINED INITIATIVE

A sustained Caribbean initiative to deal with the drug problem would seem to require several important components, including:

1. the ability to police Caribbean waters effectively and particularly to pursue and arrest vessels carrying illicit drugs;
2. the capacity to police ports and airports to guard against the transit of illicit drugs;
3. well-manned, well-financed, and well-equipped narcotics units;
4. the capacity for sharing intelligence within the Caribbean and with extraregional territories;
5. the maintenance of the sovereign authority of Caribbean states;
6. bilateral extradition treaties with non-Caribbean states for the extradition of citizens and non-citizens from and to each other's jurisdiction;
7. the continuous education of the entire population – through the mass media, the education system and interpersonal communications – about the dangers of drug use; and
8. a vigorous diplomatic process designed to mobilise the United States, Canada, European countries and international agencies into providing additional resources to Caribbean countries dedicated to helping them more forcefully to interdict drug traffickers, to provide acceptable alternatives to the financial benefits of the drug trade, and to mount effective anti-drug education programmes throughout their communities.

It is obvious that, apart from adopting stringent and common legislation for dealing with drug traffickers, Caribbean countries individually do not have the capacity to implement successfully the measures mentioned above. As we have pointed out, they simply lack the financial resources. Even at the diplomatic level, while the government of Jamaica enjoyed some success in getting the United Nations General Assembly to accept a Resolution on a Global Programme of Action against Illicit Narcotic Drugs in January 1990, it fell short of Michael Manley's original intentions. The Jamaican Prime Minister had proposed the establishment of a 'multilateral force, under the aegis of the United Nations, which would provide assistance in particular situations requiring intelligence and interdiction capabilities beyond the resources of the individual states.' The General Assembly agreed to consider 'the feasibility' of such a United Nations facility.[4]

THE NEED FOR A REGIONAL AUTHORITY

The countries of the Caribbean could more effectively formulate and implement a narcotics policy containing the elements outlined above if they did so collectively and in a cohesive fashion. But this would require a regional authority with supra-national powers capable of establishing the bodies required; managing the policy, including supervising the drug enforcement units; drafting the necessary anti-narcotics legislation; negotiating equal bilateral extradition treaties with other states; executing an education programme against drugs; and mounting a diplomatic *démarche* on behalf of all the Caribbean states.

The acceptance and implementation of this concept, or something similar to it, should not be impossible. There is an undisputed acknowledgement throughout the region that individual states cannot cope with the drug problem. Similarly, there is an increasing recognition that acquiescence to US demands is not an acceptable remedy for the lack of capacity to deal with the problem. For, while close co-operation with the United States is evidently required, simply caving in to US demands seriously threatens the autonomy of Caribbean governments.

Caribbean countries have periodically displayed the readiness to deepen their integration arrangements under the umbrella of CARICOM. Governments might thus consider the establishment by treaty of a commission made up of a governing body of ministers and a small, high-quality secretariat to formulate and implement a narcotics policy for the region as a whole. Decisions of the governing body would have to be legally binding on every government and would best be made by a majority vote of two-thirds of the membership.

While this concept would surely place the Caribbean countries in a more advantageous position to deal with the drug problem, it would require considerable support from the international community. For, even though the implementation of such a concept would undoubtedly improve the region's capacity for decision making and action, as well as for bargaining, the area would still lack the financial resources to man, equip and maintain the necessary programme of interdiction, education and rehabilitation. However, the commission conceived above, closely focused as it would have to be, would be more able to attract both programme and project financing for its work from major donor states and international agencies. Certainly, it would be able to forge co-operation agreements not only with the United States but also with Canada and the residual metropolitan powers in the Caribbean. These co-operation agreements could include exchange of intelligence among drug enforcement units, supply of equipment and funds to the Caribbean and joint policing of the Caribbean waters.

THE URGENT NEED FOR INTERNATIONAL SUPPORT

Given the lack of financial resources and the dire conditions of most of their economies, it is difficult to see what else Caribbean governments could do at the individual level to combat the drug problem. Even the urgent task of anti-narcotics education and rehabilitation of drug addicts is beyond the financial capability of many of these states. There is, therefore, a pressing need for international support. In this context, the UN Resolution on a Global Programme of Action Against Illicit Narcotic Drugs, which began with Michael Manley's proposal for a multilateral force, among other things, is very useful. But, as indicated, the United Nations committed itself only to considering the feasibility of such a force, and it has stressed that account has to be taken 'of its ability to perform its increasing tasks in the light of existing mandates.'[5]

Against this background, the United States, as the major purchaser of the illicit narcotics that transit the Caribbean, should take a lead role in mobilising international support to help ease the economic burdens of Caribbean countries. Such support would place individual Caribbean states in a better position to deal with drug trafficking. Among the measures that major donor countries and international agencies could implement are debt forgiveness and special and differential treatment for in organisations such as the World Trade Organisation and the World Bank. These small and vulnerable countries should be given genuine assistance in trade and economic matters that would allow them to allocate adequate resources for building capacity to fight the daunting problem of drug trafficking.

Unless such assistance is forthcoming, Caribbean governments will be able to do little more than scratch the surface of the drug problem in the region. Their inability to act will pose great dangers to their fragile democracies, dangers that may ultimately render the region unstable. At the same time, the United States, Canada and the countries of the European Union will continue to confront the reality of a Caribbean gateway to their countries for hundreds of tons of narcotics, with all the adverse effects for their populations that flow from such a situation.

NOTES & REFERENCES

1   Television statement by the Prime Minister of Trinidad and Tobago, Rt. Hon. Mr A.N.R. Robinson, on 25 June 1988, to launch the First International Day Against Drug Abuse and Illicit Trafficking, observed on 26 June 1988, mimeo.

2   See 'Drug Addicts on the Rise', *Barbados Advocate*, 20 September 1989, p. 32.

3   Kenneth McNeil, 'Development of Cocaine Trafficking in Jamaica,' keynote address at World Ministerial Summit to Reduce the Demand for Drugs and to Combat the Cocaine Threat, London, 9-11 April 1990, p. 8, mimeo.

4   For Manley's original proposal, see communiqué of Tenth CARICOM Heads of Government Conference, Grenada, 7 July 1989, mimeo. For the General Assembly's response, see UN General Assembly, Resolution A/RES/44/141, 12 January 1990.

5   See UN General Assembly, Resolution A/RES/44/141.

CHAPTER NINE

Britain and the Caribbean

The modern-day relationship between Britain and the English-speaking countries of the Caribbean falls into two distinct periods. The first period straddled two decades between 1962-82 beginning with the granting of independence to Jamaica and Trinidad and Tobago and ending with a constitutional conference in 1982 to give independence the following year to St Kitts-Nevis, the last of the Associated States. The second period, which is still continuing, began with the 1982 'Falklands War' between Britain and Argentina.

The outstanding feature of the first period was Britain's obvious determination to withdraw from the Caribbean, giving up influence over the area, and responsibility for policing it, to its NATO ally, the United States. The second period has so far revealed a desire by Britain to once again exert some influence in the region. The reasons for Britain's new interest were clearly expressed in 1987 by Timothy Eggar, the Under-Secretary of State in the Foreign and Commonwealth Office, who eschewed any 'romantic idea of what the relationship used to be' in identifying 'hard-headed mutual interest' for taking the region seriously. Specifically, Eggar identified four areas of British interest as:

- the Caribbean's influence in the UN;
- the importance of the area as a transit point for trade and re-supply from the United States to Europe in the event of hostilities;
- the value of the Caribbean as a market for British goods, particularly as the British share of exports to the Caribbean had gone down from over 50 percent to between 9 to 15 percent; and

---

First published in Paul Sutton (ed), *Europe and the Caribbean*, Macmillan, London, 1991, pp. 173-186.

- the rapid development of the region, including the British dependencies, as a centre for drug trafficking and money laundering.[1]

I shall later deal in detail with these four areas of British interest, suffice to observe for now that an important reason for the British government's renewed interest in the region was its recognition that, with twelve votes in the United Nations and ten in the Organisation of American States (OAS)[2], the Caribbean could be generally helpful to Britain on a wide range of issues and particularly useful in the continuing diplomatic struggle with Argentina in the wake of the 1982 Falklands war.

For the Caribbean's part, the governments of the twelve English-speaking countries of the region no longer place Britain at the centre of their foreign policy concerns. This development did not occur overnight, nor was it engendered in the Caribbean; its source and impetus stemmed from the British government's policy of indifference to the region which in 1987 the Barbados Prime Minister, Erskine Sandiford, described as 'some neglect, not only in trade, but also in the broad cultural contacts that go back for hundreds of years'.[3] However, by virtue of their countries' smallness and lack of resources, Caribbean governments need development assistance. Therefore, they rely upon Britain as an aid donor, although they have for some while been dissatisfied with the quality and quantum of British aid. But the basis for the current Caribbean relationship with Britain does not go much beyond aid, and there is a big question mark over the extent to which Britain could be helpful to the advancement of the region's economic aspirations in the future. I shall return to this point in greater detail.

As has been mentioned, Britain began to withdraw from the Caribbean in the 1960s with the granting of independence to its larger territories in the area. This process of withdrawal might have ended there had Britain shown an interest in the development of its remaining colonies; instead, not only was Britain stingy with aid, but successive governments made it clear that they wished to be free of the remaining non-independent states. An example of this was a journey to the region in 1976 by the then Under-Secretary of State for Foreign and Commonwealth Affairs in the Labour government, Ted Rowlands, to persuade the governments of the Associated States to proceed with independence.[4] Faced with what they saw as Britain's neglect, while at the same time restricted by their non-independent status from seeking assistance in the wider international community, the Associated States accepted the British offer and elected to fend for themselves. Thus, when the Deputy Premier of Antigua, Lester Bird, justified his government's decision to seek independence, he did so on the basis that:

> Avenues will be opened for membership of institutions like the Inter American Development Bank (IADB), providing us with the opportunity for direct financing of development projects; we will be able to reap benefits from the World Bank and the specialised agencies of the United Nations such as UNESCO, UNDP and FAO.[5]

Britain demonstrated its determination to extract itself from the region in other ways. The British Council offices in the area were closed between 1967 and 1974, daily broadcasts to the Caribbean from the BBC's World Service were terminated and, as part of a policy applied to all Commonwealth students, fees for Caribbean students attending university in Britain were raised to prohibitive levels forcing them to seek higher education in the United States and Canada. Further, new British legislation stopped immigration from the Caribbean, including from Britain's remaining colonies whose people were deprived of the right as British citizens to live in the United Kingdom. Given this scenario in which British doors were being constantly closed in Caribbean faces, governments in the region had little option but to turn away from Britain.

Despite these developments Caribbean countries might still have pursued a close relationship with Britain, particularly since, traditionally, some of their major exports such as sugar, bananas and rum were sent to the United Kingdom on preferential terms. However, the necessity for such efforts was significantly reduced by the British government's decision to join the EC and by the institutionalisation of aid and trade relations between the Caribbean and the EC under the Lomé Conventions. Caribbean governments had harboured misgivings about Britain's entry to the European Community in May 1972, but their fears were allayed with the conclusion in 1975 of the first Lomé Conventions, between the EC and ACP countries, which continued to guarantee preferential access to the British market for bananas, rum and sugar. In a real sense, however, the 1975 Lomé Convention and its successor agreements shifted the focus of Caribbean economic attention in Europe away from London to Brussels. This was tangibly demonstrated in 1985 by Dominica's establishment of a permanent resident mission to the EC in Brussels, and the downgrading of the High Commission in London to an Honorary-Consulate. Other developments confirmed the shift in Caribbean priorities: for instance, the missions in Brussels of the larger English-speaking Caribbean countries have more staff than the missions in London, and where, for reasons of economy, some of the smaller territories have accredited one person as High Commissioner to London and Ambassador to Brussels, the greater portion of his time is spent on EC matters.

The consequences for the Caribbean of the single European internal market, which came into effect in 1992, now underscore the Caribbean view that Brussels, not London, should be the focus of their economic attention in Europe. Caribbean governments cannot any longer negotiate bilaterally with the British government for preferential access to the British market; such negotiations have to be done with the Commission in Brussels. The future of banana exports to Britain is a case in point. A great deal of uncertainty has long surrounded the 'Banana Protocol' to the Lomé treaty under which bananas from Jamaica, Belize and the Windward Islands enjoy preferential access to the UK market. The one certain thing in all of this was that the Protocol would not be allowed to continue; for, as one Commission official put it:

> The present regime, applied within the Community as regards imports of bananas, is certainly not compatible with the objectives of the internal market; it is based on divergent national legislation and largely excludes free circulation of bananas within the community.[6]

While Caribbean governments initially took some encouragement from a statement by the British Prime Minister, Margaret Thatcher, that Britain 'will continue to fight hard in the European Community to make sure that Jamaica and other Caribbean countries go on enjoying preferential arrangements for sugar and bananas',[7] they recognised that Britain alone could not deliver the guaranteed access they desired. They were also conscious of the qualification to Mrs Thatcher's statement made by her Minister for Overseas Development Administration (ODA), Chris Patten, who said that Britain

> Has made it clear to the Commission... that it is essential any regime for bananas after 1992 safeguards the interest of the ACP suppliers *and contributes to the objectives of the single market* (my emphasis).[8]

Patten's qualification raised the question of whether safeguards for the interest of ACP suppliers were compatible with the objectives of a single market, particularly as many European countries, who are keen to promote a market for Central American states, agreed in the GATT in April 1989 to remove barriers to imports of tropical products from all sources. It was difficult to see how such a commitment would allow the EC to continue to privilege Caribbean bananas especially as, with the possible exception of Belize, bananas from Caribbean countries cannot be produced as cheaply as bananas from Central America. Nonetheless, prime ministers from the Windward Islands have subsequently mounted extensive personal lobbying campaigns to Brussels seeking to persuade European officials to allow their countries to continue to enjoy preferential arrangements for bananas. It is worth noting that representatives of the British government have actively urged Caribbean leaders to mount these campaigns: an indication that the British government recognises that its voice alone in Brussels is not sufficient.

What all this points to is a considerable diminution of the importance of Britain in the Caribbean's foreign relations. This is encouraged by Britain's parsimonious aid policy to the region. In arguing that Britain continues to be concerned about the development of the region, British ministers have been fond of stating that British aid to the English-speaking Caribbean is the highest they give on a per capita basis anywhere in the world.[9] This is an argument rejected by Caribbean governments who retort that British aid is small and has remained static in real terms for more than a decade. British aid to the region certainly lagged behind assistance from Canada and the

United States during the 1980s, British aid to the entire English-speaking Caribbean, including four of its five remaining dependencies, amounting to only £29 million in 1987.

But, apart from its size, other aspects of British aid contributed to the irritation of Caribbean countries. For example, it was a sore point with the six former Associated States that the so-called independence gift of £10 million each from Britain was not negotiated with them, but unilaterally imposed by London. Of even greater contention was the fact that only £5 million of the so-called 'independence gift' was a grant; the other £5 million was a loan. Further, none of the 'gift' was additional aid; it was the *only* aid Britain was prepared to give, and it had to be delivered on a pro-rated basis from an annual global sum for the entire area pre-determined in London.[10] Some regional governments complained that the prior determination of the amount of money to be spent in each country restricted the projects which could be undertaken and favoured the selection of small and relatively insignificant projects, thereby reducing the potential economic impact of the aid received'.[11] Caribbean governments were further peeved by the fact that their role in the use of British aid was limited simply to the submission of project proposals, and their priority projects 'often do not meet the approval of the British ODA.'[12] Consequently, it has been the British Overseas Development Administration, and not Caribbean governments, which determined sectoral priorities. In the light of this aid relationship, it should be obvious that, while Caribbean countries want British aid, it has not been substantial enough, nor the procedures for its delivery unrestricted enough, to command great influence for the British government in Caribbean capitals. The only exception to this has tended to be Belize which remained heavily dependent for a long period on Britain's maintenance of a military presence there as a deterrent to the claims of Guatemala to the entire country.

In analysing the relationship between Britain and the Caribbean, there is also a danger of according too much significance to the large Caribbean population in Britain. On the face of it, the presence of such a large Caribbean population should form a basis for a special relationship between Britain and the English-speaking Caribbean. But the fact is that neither the British government nor governments in the Caribbean place much emphasis on it. There are several reasons for this, the most significant being that the Caribbean population has had to assume British nationality or lose the right to citizenship of the United Kingdom. Having assumed British nationality, they have placed themselves fully under the jurisdiction of the British government while they are in Britain, and accordingly deprived Caribbean governments of the right to intervene with the British government on their behalf, even though they may also hold the nationality of their birthplace. In a sense this constraint on intervention by Caribbean governments has been a boon to relations between British and Caribbean governments. For if Caribbean High Commissions in London could act on the many complaints of racial harassment or discrimination they receive from Caribbean-born persons, a great deal of their time would be spent in acrimonious debate with the Home Office, and this in turn could sour relations between Britain and the Caribbean.

Of further significance is that, to the extent that the Caribbean population in Britain is a political community, it is concerned with black-white relations in the context of the United Kingdom; it has not taken on the issue of relations between Britain and Caribbean countries. Even the election in 1987 of two Caribbean-born members to the British Parliament did not result in significantly greater advancement of matters of concern to Caribbean governments; the members of Parliament in question have tended to preoccupy themselves with issues related to the black community in Britain.

Another consideration, which is often overlooked, is that the Caribbean populations in Canada and the United States are now at least as large as the group in Britain. Therefore, if the mere presence of a Caribbean population is the criterion for a special relationship, equal grounds exist for such a relationship with the United States and Canada. But, in fact, since both the United States and Canada continue to accept Caribbean immigration, however limited, these countries assume greater importance than Britain in the minds both of Caribbean people and their governments who still regard emigration as a safety valve for growing populations whose economic and social demands cannot be satisfied by the limited resources at home.

Other traditional links between Britain and the Caribbean have inevitably been slackened with the independence of its former colonies. In the past, the educational curricula of Caribbean secondary schools replicated the British system with pupils sitting the British General Certificate of Education (GCE) to qualify for employment and further education. The obvious result of this was that Caribbean children imbibed British poetry and literature; they learned British history and geography. In their eyes, Britain appeared to be the centre of the world. With independence, and the need to make education relevant to the development aspirations of new nations, the GCE was replaced with the tests of the Caribbean Examinations Council (CXC) and the curricula ceased to be dominated by Britain. To the new generation in the Caribbean, England became simply a distant place lacking the sentimental attachment which had influenced previous generations. In the course of time, other institutional links began to weaken. Thus Caribbean governments, with the support of the Caribbean lawyers, have for some time been considering the establishment of a Caribbean Court of Appeal to replace appeals to the British Privy Council. It is also not without significance that three of the twelve independent Commonwealth Caribbean countries opted to become republics, ending the relationship with the British Monarch as their Head of State. And it cannot also be without some import that, when proposals were put forward between 1986 and 1988 for a political union of the seven Leeward and Windward Islands, all of them, including the official proposition from the Prime Minister of St Vincent,[13] suggested the creation of a republic. This seems to suggest that, while enough of a mystique still surrounds the Queen to attract curious crowds on her infrequent visits to the Caribbean, this final link with Britain has largely become an anachronism in Caribbean thinking.

At a non-governmental level, the relationship between Britain and the Caribbean is no better. British private sector investment in the region is very small, and in relation to similar investment from the United States and Canada it is becoming even smaller. Efforts by the Foreign and Commonwealth Office to urge new investment by British businessmen in the region have produced no great result, except an expansion of the telecommunication operations of Cable and Wireless in several islands. In recent years the businessmen who have demonstrated an interest in the Caribbean have been more keen to sell British goods and services in the region than to invest in it. However, Caribbean countries share some of the blame for this state of affairs. The nationalisation of the British-owned sugar estates in Guyana, and the movement towards socialism which characterised Jamaica in the 1970s, created a perception for a time that the larger Caribbean countries did not want foreign private investment. It is only in recent years that Caribbean governments have sought to turn around this image. But not enough has been done, for only a few Caribbean governments have signed investment protection agreements with Britain, and even fewer mount regular high-powered promotion campaigns in British cities to attract investment. Their focus has turned to the United States.

This focus on the United States is understandable and, in a sense, was engineered by Britain. Undoubtedly, as Britain withdrew from the English-speaking Caribbean, its policy makers fully expected the United States to fill the vacuum they were leaving. After all, extending American influence to Britain's former colonies was consistent with the 'Monroe Doctrine' under which the United States defined Latin America and the Caribbean. Anxious to be rid of its Caribbean colonies, Britain encouraged Caribbean governments to look toward Washington. Most of them did, although Jamaica and Guyana, in trying to pursue a socialist path domestically and a non-aligned course internationally, incurred the displeasure of Washington which regarded both socialism and non-alignment as links to communism. Already deeply disturbed by a communist Cuban state in their Caribbean 'backyard' which they saw as a threat to their security, successive United States administrations worked to so destabilise Guyana and Jamaica that they would return to the American fold. The Americans achieved their objectives in Guyana and Jamaica by economic pressure: less spectacular but just as effective was the 1983 invasion of Grenada which brought that country to heel after a four-year Marxist government. How this was done is sufficiently recorded elsewhere.[14] It is sufficient for me to note here that, by the end of the Reagan Presidency in January 1989, all of the English-speaking Caribbean countries were firmly in the grip of the United States.

In any event, the United States has fully replaced Britain in Caribbean thinking at all levels. Diplomatically, every independent English-speaking Caribbean country is individually represented in Washington; whereas in the United Kingdom, three countries shared a High Commissioner until 1998, and, as already pointed out,

Dominica did not have a resident High Commissioner until 1989. In economic terms, sixty per cent of Caribbean tourism comes from the United States with only twelve per cent originating in Europe including Britain.[15] American private investment in the Caribbean is larger than that from any other country and Caribbean concentration is on securing even more. While aid from the United States to the Caribbean has been falling in recent years, it remains larger than aid from the United Kingdom. With regard to security, the United States has been actively involved in training military and paramilitary forces throughout the English-speaking Caribbean, and has provided soft loans for the purchase of American weapons. And, especially significant, is that in eight of the twelve independent Caribbean territories, American television is transmitted into virtually every home twenty-four hours a day. The remaining four countries also transmit American television programmes though on a more restricted basis. As we have had cause to note before, in the absence of national media with the resources to compete for audiences, the understanding of international events in the Caribbean is being shaped largely by American broadcasters whose values and beliefs are fashioned by cultural, economic and political interests completely different from those which have traditionally obtained in the Caribbean.

In the early 1980s, when Britain looked again at the Caribbean, it saw a region in which its influence had given way to that of the United States; although it is worth noting that Canada is well regarded by governments in the region because of its high level of aid and the few demands it makes on them. However, events had taken place which encouraged renewed British interest in the region. The first was its war with Argentina over the Falklands. The British government clearly hoped that it would be able to influence the English-speaking Caribbean countries, with the sovereign competence to do so, to support Britain against Argentina in the UN, the OAS and even in the Non-Aligned Movement which Argentina quickly joined in the wake of the Falklands war.

The second event was the invasion of Grenada by the United States with the backing of some Caribbean territories. I do not subscribe to the view that British interest in the region was revived because the government was deeply upset by America's invasion of a Commonwealth country where the Queen was still Head of State. I certainly got no inkling of this during my first term as a Caribbean diplomat in London which covered the period of the Grenada invasion and its aftermath. It was well known that the Thatcher government was as offended as the Reagan administration by the Marxist government in Grenada, and had reduced aid to that country to a nominal sum. Mrs Thatcher herself did not make a statement of criticism of the American or Caribbean governments during the debate on Grenada at the Commonwealth Heads of Government Conference one month after the invasion.[16] My own belief is that the United States, no longer excited by the communist spectre which Grenada once presented, became reluctant to carry sole responsibility for the security of the region and encouraged Britain to help share the burden in the English-speaking Caribbean. This is why, for instance, in 1987 Timothy Eggar identified as a British interest in the Caribbean 'the importance to the United States and NATO of the Caribbean being a stable area'.[17] And, of course, immediately after the Grenada invasion, Britain did become active in Caribbean security in a limited way by providing training, building coastguard facilities in the Eastern Caribbean and participating in joint training exercises with American and Caribbean forces.

The third event was a clear statement in the early 1980s from four of the five remaining British dependencies in the Caribbean that they had no wish to seek independence. The British government had to reconcile itself to the fact that Britain would have to maintain a presence in the region for some time to come.

The fourth event was the rapid and widespread development of the Caribbean, including British dependent territories, as a transit point for drug trafficking and for laundering drug money through casinos and shell banks. Until the end of the 1970s, the Caribbean was not a major route for drug trafficking, but the revolution in Iran (1979), the invasion of Afghanistan (1979) and the *coup d'état* in Turkey (1980) caused the production of hard drugs to shift from heroin, traditionally produced and refined in those countries, to cocaine. The farming of coca, which up to 1970 had been concentrated in Bolivia and Peru, increased in output and expanded to other Latin American states. By 1982, the production of coca in Bolivia alone rose to 80,000 tons; in 1972 it was reported to be as low as 200 tons. In the course of transporting the drugs from Latin America to destinations in the West, the Caribbean became a major transit point. Today the resources of traffickers are so immense that they can afford to transport drugs over long and complex journeys, often leaving shipments in-bond in some countries for some months at a time before moving them to their ultimate destination. By this process, Britain itself has become a major destination for illicit drugs from Latin America.[18] Evidence of the government's growing worry over the extent of illicit drugs entering Britain was the introduction in 1986 of the Drug Trafficking Offences Act under which 'anyone accused of drug trafficking can have his assets restrained *before he is convicted*'.[19] Therefore, the British government's desire to stop the transshipment of drugs in the Caribbean is very much in its own self-interest. And this was reflected in a visit to the area in 1987 by Timothy Eggar when he placed drug trafficking at the top of his agenda for discussion with governments.[20]

The British government was directly alerted to the extent of the problem of drug trafficking in the Caribbean when Norman Saunders, the Chief Minister of one of its dependencies, the Turks and Caicos Islands, was arrested by American authorities in Miami on charges of drug trafficking in 1985. A year later, it carried out a survey of its five dependencies and was sufficiently troubled by its findings to provide facilities 'to help the local governments combat drugs and narcotics trafficking'.[21] In 1987, the British and United States governments undertook a joint review of the independent Caribbean territories and found that not one of them was immune from drug trafficking. There is certainly evidence that the large sums of money involved have corrupted government officials and members of the police force and customs in several territories. For example, the Prime Minister of St Lucia in October 1988 publicly declared that in his country 'there is a type of mafia within the police force, a number of people who use their uniforms for criminal activity'.[22] In addition, drug abuse among young people has become commonplace and crime, including violent crime, has increased.

As previously noted, Caribbean governments lack the resources to mount an effective response to so major a problem. Only the government of the Bahamas is spending considerable sums from its national budget to fight drugs. According to the Bahamian Foreign Minister, 'in excess of 13 percent of the national budget is dedicated to law enforcement' and the Bahamas has a '270-man strong Police Drug Unit'.[23] But few other Caribbean countries have the resources to fight drug trafficking on the same scale as the Bahamas and the assistance being given to them, primarily from the United States and Britain, is inadequate to deal with the problem.

For its part, the United States has been active in fighting drug trafficking in the Caribbean since the early 1980s and has been more active than any other country; although it should be noted that some of its activities, including covert operations, have shown scant regard for the authority of Caribbean governments in their own territory. Britain became involved in 1986 and Canada began to show an interest in 1987. The United States administration has provided specialist training and equipment and the Drug Enforcement Agency maintains a special liaison with the units concerned with illicit drugs in Caribbean territories. Some countries have given the United States the right of 'hot pursuit' in their territorial waters and have signed agreements to give banking information to US authorities when the laundering of funds from drug-related activities is suspected. However, not all Caribbean countries have been as co-operative as the United States would like, and in 1986 a law was passed requiring the President to certify to Congress by March of each year whether major drug-producing countries and countries through which drugs transit have co-operated fully with the United States. Many Caribbean countries have since been placed on the list of transit countries.

Apart from the fact that their own countries are the ultimate destination for illicit drugs, both the British and United States governments are concerned about drug trafficking in the Caribbean because they recognise that it is the single most important problem that will confront the independent countries of the Caribbean for the foreseeable future. For not only are drugs now readily available to young people in the area, but traffickers are using their vast resources to corrupt the society including the system of justice. What is more, narcotic armies in Latin America are reported to be sizeable, and certainly larger than the forces of Caribbean countries; they also possess modern weapons, including surface-to-air missiles. Caribbean governments would be unable to withstand raids from such armies determined, for instance, to liberate any of their traffickers who might be caught and held in Caribbean prisons. Yet every Caribbean country is under pressure to introduce laws similar to the British Drugs Trafficking Act and to interdict offenders. Hanging over their heads, if they do not, is the possibility that they would be regarded as 'un-co-operative' and, therefore, ineligible for certification by the United States President. The consequences could be a loss of aid or worse. But it is difficult to see how improved interdiction can do anything but add to the region's problems of insufficient resources to combat drug trafficking, for they would have to build new jails for convicted drug offenders, and train and equip special forces to man them. One alternative would be to enter agreements with countries such as the United States and Britain to transfer convicted offenders to prisons in those countries. However, in such cases, the governments of the Caribbean would have to pay the costs involved and they simply do not have the means to do so.

In conclusion, then, Britain has renewed its interest in the independent states of the English-speaking Caribbean in the years since 1982. It has shown its rekindled interest in several ways: the number of ministerial visits to the region has increased in recent years; in 1987 the BBC World Service restarted a five-days-a-week broadcast directly to the Caribbean; and the British Council has re-opened an office in Jamaica to serve the Commonwealth Caribbean[24]. But the focus of Caribbean attention has been turned toward the United States and the European Community through the Commission in Brussels. Therefore, while the majority of Caribbean countries continue to need development assistance, and they certainly need help in combating drug trafficking, the level of British assistance is not sufficient to give the British government great influence over Caribbean governments. That being said, it is important to note that, to the extent that the British government is able and willing to help Caribbean countries to meet their concerns by championing their case in the EC for trade access to Europe, by providing investment, aid and technical assistance for economic development, and by providing meaningful resources for combating drug trafficking, Caribbean governments are still and will remain keen to maintain a close relationship with Britain. They will also give Britain diplomatic support on issues where such support would not compromise their own interest. But, at the end of the day, British influence over the English-speaking Caribbean has weakened considerably. And on present trends it looks set to weaken still further as Caribbean governments strengthen their links with the United States and Canada and seek to develop closer relations with other European capitals in order to safeguard their aid and trade relationship with the European Community as a whole. Britain might still reverse these trends; but it will require a major act of political will to do so backed up by substantial resource flows. Neither appears to be forthcoming from Britain.

NOTES & REFERENCES

1   Timothy Eggar, Speech to the Caribbean Parliamentary Group and the West India Committee in London, 15 July 1987, mimeo.
2   Guyana and Belize were initially debarred from membership of the OAS because of border disputes with existing members, Venezuela and Guatemala respectively. Hence, of the 12 independent Caribbean states, only ten became early members of the Organisation.
3   Caribbean News Agency (CANA) report US7024, 16 September, 1987, of Erskine Sandiford's remarks during talks with Timothy Eggar in Barbados.
4   See Ron Sanders, *Antigua and Barbuda: Transition, Trial, Triumph*, Archives committee, Antigua, 1984
5   Lester Bird, *A Declaration for Development*, Statement to the Antigua Labour Party Convention, 7 September, 1978, mimeo.
6   Tony Fairclough, EC Deputy Director-General for Development, *The Courier*, No. 113, January-February 1989.
7   Margaret Thatcher, Speech at Dinner in Jamaica, 18 July 1987, mimeo.
8   Chris Patten, The Lomé Renegotiation – Trade and Transformation, Speech on 9 February 1989, mimeo.
9   Eggar, Speech; and Chris Patten, Speech to the British Caribbean Parliamentary group and the West India Committee, 22 July 1987.
10 Memorandum from Ronald Sanders, High Commissioner for Antigua and Barbuda, in *Bilateral Aid: Country Programmes*, Second Report, Session 1986-7, House of Commons Foreign Affairs Committee, 22 April 1987, HMSO, London.
11 Memorandum from the Economic Affairs Secretariat of the Organisation of Eastern Caribbean States (OECS) in *Bilateral Aid: Country Programmes*.
12 *Ibid.*
13 See James Mitchell, Prime Minister of St Vincent and The Grenadines, *Two Decades of Caribbean Unity*, Government Printing Office, St Vincent, 1987.
14 See Michael Manley, *Struggle in the Periphery*, Third World Media, London, undated,; and Anthony Payne, *The International Crisis in the Caribbean*, Croom Helm, Beckenham, 1984.
15 *Caribbean Insight*, Vol. 12, No. 4, April 1989, p. 6.
16 The writer attended the Executive Sessions of the Commonwealth Heads of Government Conference in New Delhi in 1983 as part of the Antigua and Barbuda delegation.
17 See Eggar, Speech.
18 From conversation with officials of the Foreign and Commonwealth Office.
19 Foreign and Commonwealth Office, background brief, *International Drug Trafficking: Attacking the Profits*, December 1987, mimeo.
20 CANA report of Eggar's statement at the conclusion of his 1987 visit to the Caribbean.
21 See *Hansard*, written answer by Timothy Eggar to Mr Page on 27 January 1989.
22 *Caribbean Insight*, Vol. 11, No. 11, November 1988, p. 2.
23 E. Charles Carter, Minister of Foreign Affairs, Statement to the Bahamas Parliament, 12 April 1989, mimeo.
24 In 1998, the UK and CARICOM countries created the 'UK-Caribbean Forum' under which Foreign Ministers would meet every two years to discuss and act on matters of mutual interest. Heads of Government agreed to meet in the years in-between the Foreign Ministers Meeting, and Caribbean High Commissions in London and the Caribbean Unit of the UK Foreign and Commonwealth Office met twice a year to oversee the implementation of decisions.

CHAPTER TEN

The Growing Vulnerability of the Caribbean in the 1990s

More than a decade ago when the Commonwealth Secretariat produced the study *Vulnerability: Small States in Global Society*, it did so against a background in which the Commonwealth Heads of Government, in the words of the then Secretary-General, 'were deeply concerned about the precarious state of the international situation'.[1] The Secretary-General observed at the time that 'small states continue to be buffeted politically, economically and socially from both internal and external forces with the world taking little heed of their special needs'.[2]

However, looking back on it, Commonwealth Caribbean small states might seem to have been in a relatively privileged position at the time. On the economic front, they enjoyed special trading relationships with the countries of North America and the European Community. These relationships were embodied in the Lomé Conventions and in special arrangements with Canada and the United States. Under these arrangements, Caribbean small states were able to sell certain of their products at a preferential price on a quota basis and they enjoyed a guaranteed market in the European Community, particularly for bananas, sugar and rum. In the case of the US and Canada, they exported certain products on a duty free basis with no requirement to reciprocate similar treatment.

In the heady days of the Cold War, the Caribbean enjoyed a pivotal geo-strategic significance for the United States and what was then Western Europe because much of the oil requirements of the US had to transit Caribbean waters and the Caribbean was an important passageway for US military supplies to Western Europe. In the context of the US only, the Caribbean was its so-called 'backyard', and US preoccupation with countering the 'communist menace' in that backyard rendered the Caribbean very important to Washington

First published in *The Round Table*, No. 343, July 1997, pp. 361-74.

decision makers. It should be recalled that it was after the US invasion of Grenada in 1983 that Commonwealth Heads of Government, at their meeting in New Delhi, mandated the Secretariat to undertake a study of the vulnerability of small states.

Apart from trade advantages, Caribbean small states also benefited from a relatively high level of aid flows from the European Community and North America whose governments were intent on countering communist influence in the area. These same governments actively encouraged investment of private capital into the Caribbean.

Comparing today's reality with 12 or 14 years ago, the 1980s, for all the 'buffeting', represented a decade of opportunity for the Caribbean. The really tough times were yet to come. Today, with the Cold War at an end and Europe configured very differently, with administrations in the United States and Russia both resisting communism, the geo-strategic importance of the Caribbean has diminished. Aid and investment flows into the region have declined rapidly and the Caribbean's preferential market access in both the European Community and North America has eroded. In the case of US aid to the Caribbean, this dropped nearly 90 percent from US$225 million to US$26 million over the decade 1986-96.[3]

On the economic side, as the Prime Minister of Barbados, Owen Arthur, recently put it:

The precepts which now inform the reform of the world's trading system – the new emphasis on reciprocity, non-discriminatory practices, liberalisation and the like, strike at the very basis of the preferential arrangements which have hitherto been the pivot around which the Caribbean Basin economies relationship with its traditional and main trading partners has turned.[4]

When the present Lomé Convention expires in February 2000, it is most unlikely that the Caribbean will continue to enjoy the preferential prices and market share in the European Community that it did in the past, particularly for bananas which is an important export for the Windward Islands of the Caribbean and to a lesser extent Jamaica and Belize.[5] World Trade Organisation (WTO) rules, geared as they are to the trade liberalisation policies of its more powerful member states, will see to that. A WTO interim report in March 1997 upheld several elements in a complaint from the United States and four Latin American countries challenging the European Union's marketing regime for bananas. The role of the US in this matter particularly worried Caribbean small states which pointed to the fact that the US is not a banana exporter but that a US multinational corporation owns banana plantations in Latin America and is a big contributor to US Presidential and Congressional elections. One Caribbean ambassador to the European Union summed up Caribbean feelings as follows:

> Small countries like mine have no power… All that is on offer to us is rough justice. The interest of ACP banana farmers were not being allowed to prevail against the ambitions of a multinational corporation which happens to be politically influential.[6]

In the event, the 'colonial conscience' which fuelled aid and market access from the European Community for Caribbean countries is fast disappearing with both the expansion of the membership of the European Community and the increasing view that the colonial obligations, if not met, are not longer relevant. The European Commissioner with responsibility for relations with ACP countries, João de Deus Pinheiro, has made it clear that the ACP countries are not now a priority for the European Union. According to him:

> Recent years have seen greater priority being given within the European Union, and a short time ago at the Essen Summit, to relations with countries in Central and Eastern Europe, paving the way for further expansion, and to relations with Mediterranean countries, in other words our closest neighbours.[7]

The creation of NAFTA between the US, Canada and Mexico has already had a detrimental effect on the competitiveness of Caribbean products into the US market. Certain Caribbean-produced goods are being driven out of the US market by similar Mexican products by virtue of that country's unrestricted access under NAFTA. The Caribbean Textile and Apparel Institute says that, over the two-year period, 1995-96, more than 150 apparel plants closed in the Caribbean and 123,000 jobs were lost as a direct result of trade and investment diversion to Mexico.[8] Promises of membership in NAFTA for

Commonwealth Caribbean small states, posited by US President Bill Clinton at a Summit of the Americas in December 1994, have remained unfulfilled, primarily because the US Congress has opposed fast-track authority for NAFTA expansion. In any event, the unrestricted free trade and market liberalisation envisaged by NAFTA would close fledgling Caribbean businesses making many small states mere markets for goods from the United States, Canada and Mexico. Two or three Caribbean small states may be able to survive, but the region as a whole would undoubtedly suffer.[9]

Responding to concerns by small states in Central America and the Caribbean, the Clinton Administration sought to have Congress accord them 'parity' status with Mexico in order to address the problem of diversion of trade and investment. This notion was rejected by Congress.

Although Canada continues to allow duty-free access for almost 90 percent of Commonwealth Caribbean products, these products represent less than ten percent of the region's major exports. The area's beneficial exports are still restricted from duty-free entry to Canada. Further, Canada no longer appears to have a well-defined constructive policy toward the Commonwealth Caribbean, and its own global trade liberalisation posture is inimical to the economic development prospects of many of the countries of the region. For the countries of the Commonwealth Caribbean, this is a regrettable development since, in the past, Canada was always regarded as a dependable ally and champion.

While Caribbean small states have experienced severe erosion of the markets for their goods and the prices they have enjoyed, they have equally faced increased costs for the goods and services which they import. This has led to a widening balance of payments deficit and to burdensome debt as they seek to finance much needed social and economic development through borrowing.

The international financial institutions, such as the IMF and the World Bank, have been unhelpful to the worsening economic conditions in Caribbean countries. Except for Guyana and Jamaica, Commonwealth Caribbean countries have been graduated from eligibility for borrowing on soft terms on the basis of their per capita income. The Caribbean countries have long argued that the use of per capita income as the formula for determining such eligibility is flawed since it fails to take account of the fact that a small number of persons earn the bulk of the income while the greater number exist at a subsistence level. They have also contended that the international financial institutions should create a mechanism for debt forgiveness, especially for those debts which, onerous interest excluded, have been repaid several times over. These countries have also pleaded for debt repayment to be linked to an acceptable percentage of export earnings to give them a chance to finance development without further borrowing. None of these arguments or pleas have elicited a sufficiently favourable response.

On the security side, apart from Cuba, the primary interest that the US administration retains in the Caribbean is in making sure that conditions in the region do not produce an adverse effect on the United States. The US is concerned about the flow of increasing numbers of unskilled Caribbean people to its inner cities, the consequent increased demand on its welfare system, the intensifying of racial tension and mounting crime. Hence, US activity in the region in recent time was focused on Haiti more because of the constant flow of Haitian refugees to US shores than because of strong desire to address the inherent economic and political problems in Haiti which sparked the flow of refugees in the first place. It is well known, for instance, that, before the Cold War ended, successive US administrations tolerated repressive regimes in Haiti, including the notorious ones led by Francois 'Papa Doc' and Jean-Claude 'Baby Doc' Duvalier, who declared themselves allies of the US in the anti-communist battle. As one commentator put it, 'one United States Administration after another held its nose against the stench but tolerated the Duvaliers as the alternative to possible communist penetration'.[10] Further evidence of US determination to stem the flow of Caribbean immigrants is the new Illegal Immigration Reform and Immigrant Responsibility Act of 1996. Under this act immigration officials are empowered to remove an arriving alien without any further review and aggressively pursue and deport criminal aliens, even if they are landed immigrants. The act also requires sponsors of alien relatives for immigration to have higher incomes than was previously necessary.[11]

US deportation of Caribbean-born criminals to their native countries has bothered Caribbean governments considerably. They have argued that these criminals were created in the peculiar conditions of the United States and it is unfair to ship them back to the Caribbean which is ill-equipped to deal with sophisticated and violent criminals and was not responsible for their development as criminals in the first place.

All this profound global change that has affected the Caribbean is worsened by the fact that there is a weakening of key international institutions and the role they play in global affairs, particularly as guardians of the interests of small states. The UN General Assembly, for instance, was once an effective forum for developing countries, including small states. Today, it has slipped to a low place in global diplomacy. The doctrine of sovereignty and the inviolability of the nation state have also been eroded, with the case for intervention over a wide range of issues being arbitrarily interpreted by the world's only remaining military superpower – the United States.

Apart from the United Nations itself, other international organisations – long the champions of causes dear to the developing world, and, therefore, to small states – have fallen by the wayside. The Non-Aligned Movement no longer enjoys the authority it did in the decades of the 1960s and 1970s. Other UN bodies, such as UNESCO and UNCTAD, which sought to challenge the pervasive influence of individual states such as the USA, have been whipped into submission either by the withdrawal of the more powerful countries or by the creation of other organisations, such as the WTO, whose organisational ideology and rules suit the larger states better. The result of this is that small states are marginalised in international fora along with the issues which most concern them.

Even in organisations where small states are in the majority, such as the Commonwealth, they no longer enjoy the heightened concern for their viability and survival that prompted Commonwealth Heads of Government to commission the 1985 study. Not until March 1997 did the Commonwealth Secretariat announce – after considerable urging – that it was appointing an expert group to update the 1985 report in time for the Edinburgh Commonwealth summit in October 1997. However, there was little or no consultation with small states on the membership of the expert group or its terms of reference. Indeed, representatives of small states had to press hard at a senior officials meeting in October 1996 to focus the attention of the Secretariat and some Commonwealth governments on the clear and present problems of small states.

Since the 1985 Commonwealth study on the vulnerability of small states, several other developments have taken place, making the Caribbean even more vulnerable than before. These include:

- the use of the region as a transit point for illicit narcotics from Colombia, Peru and Bolivia destined for lucrative markets in North America and Europe;
- an increase in the number of countries offering offshore banking services and the potential for money laundering perceived by the United States in particular;
- the diversion of investment to Cuba by Canada and European nations, especially the United Kingdom;
- an increase in the frequency and intensity of natural disasters; and
- the weakening of states in terms of their capacity to serve the needs of their communities adequately.

Each of these developments is discussed below. Paradoxically, the first two developments have caused both Europe and North America to resume greater interest in the Caribbean, albeit for selfish reasons. Drug trafficking has become important and has already been extensively discussed in earlier chapters. Money laundering has also become a major consideration because, in an effort to diversify their economies away from a reliance on clearly threatened preferential trading relationships with Europe and North America, many small Caribbean countries have established financial service sectors including offshore banks and trust companies. Governments in North America and Europe have linked these financial services sectors to drug trafficking. While there is evidence to support the view that some banks have been used for laundering drug-related money – as have many banks worldwide – it has not been established that this is true for all banks and all countries. There are some officials who believe that the assault on the Caribbean financial services sector, particularly by the United States, is concerned more with the flow of funds out of the US than it is with money laundering.

Whatever the whole truth, both these developments create problems for the region domestically and internationally. Domestically, a drug problem has been created in the region and is having a debilitating effect on Caribbean youth. Drug trafficking is a prime contributor to increased crime in Caribbean societies and, as we have seen, has led to corruption at many levels of the societies, including police, customs officials and even political parties and governments. Internationally, money laundering and transshipment of drugs in the Caribbean encourages the intervention of large countries in the region, giving them the opportunity of being seen to be doing something about the drug problem when the real remedy lies in curbing demand at home. In the case of the United States, under the Foreign Assistance Act, the President 'certifies' to Congress that countries are co-operating fully with the US in combating drug trafficking and money laundering. If he determines that a country is not doing so, that country is 'decertified' – a process by which US assistance is officially denied to that country. Commonwealth Caribbean countries – Belize, Antigua and Barbuda and Jamaica – have all been threatened with such 'decertification'.[12]

Unofficially, US agencies also mount unsubstantiated media and other campaigns designed to coerce unwilling governments to co-operate in the manner required by the US. In November 1996, the Prime Minister of Antigua and Barbuda, Lester Bird, accused the US State Department of 'encouraging if not orchestrating' a negative press campaign against his country in an effort to pressure the government to sign a Mutual Legal Assistance Treaty giving US agencies jurisdiction in certain instances in Antigua and Barbuda.[13] Eventually, the government yielded and the agreement was signed on 31 October 1996. Another instance was a media campaign, attributed to an official of the US State Department, against the Jamaican government because it was unwilling to sign a 'Shipriders Agreement' according to the US coast guard the right to patrol and effect arrests in Jamaican territorial waters. Barbados, which had also declined to sign the Shipriders Agreement, had its international airport – undoubtedly the best in the Caribbean – downgraded by the US Federal Aviation Authority to a Category B airport. In each case, US representatives denied any intention to coerce Caribbean governments, and representatives of two governments – Trinidad and Tobago and Grenada – openly defended signing the Shipriders Agreement, saying that, rather than undermining the sovereignty of their countries, the agreement 'saves sovereignty'.[14] However, the majority of Caribbean governments remain convinced that the US authorities have little regard for their sovereignty. The Prime

Minister of St Vincent and the Grenadines is on public record declaring: 'we've surrendered our sovereignty. We've given the US all the co-operation in the world. What else do they want?'[15] In the case of Belize, which was accused by a US Assistant Secretary of State of 'falling short of the standards' for counter-narcotics performance, the government issued a public statement saying that 'the true reason for decertification is... Belize's refusal to sign a new Extradition and Mutual Legal Assistance Treaty *in the form dictated by the US*'.[16]

On the face of it, the treaties which the US government sought to conclude with Caribbean governments appear reasonable. For, if countries are committed to fighting drug trafficking and combating money laundering, they should all be ready to co-operate with each other to combat such activity, especially if they lack the financial and human resources to do it alone effectively. The problem for Caribbean countries is that the US did not seek to negotiate these treaties; they sought simply to impose them. In the case of the six smaller Commonwealth Caribbean states, their heads of government were urged to sign the treaties without review or change by their attorneys-general. Thus, the issue is not about co-operating to stop drug trafficking and money laundering; it is about the nature of the relationship between the US and Caribbean countries and the respect to which Caribbean countries feel entitled as sovereign states. Caribbean heads of government said as much at a special conference held in Barbados on 16 December 1996 specifically to discuss what appeared to be undue pressure upon Caribbean governments to sign treaties with the US. In their communiqué, they declared:

> Heads of Government recognised the fundamental coincidence of interest of CARICOM member states and the US in a peaceful, stable and prosperous Caribbean. To that end, they reaffirmed the importance of a healthy relationship with the US based on respect for sovereignty and territorial integrity, dialogue, consultation and mutually beneficial co-operation.[17]

They went on to state that:

> Heads of Government recognised the right of sovereign countries to enter into mutually acceptable agreements. They also rejected

any suggestion or threat of coercive measures as a means of extracting compliance with predetermined policies. They warned that unfounded allegations, innuendoes and the threat of punitive measures, aimed at the economic welfare of Caribbean States, would only weaken the collective effort against drug trafficking and undermine the foundations of the good relations which the Region has enjoyed and seeks to maintain with the US.[18]

On the matter of Cuba, Caribbean countries all acknowledge that it poses no threat to their security. US commentators also acknowledge that Cuba poses no real threat and that 'the continuation of the punishing American economic embargo, a form of intervention, reflects domestic politics in the United States rather than foreign policy'.[19]

However, Cuba does pose a threat of an economic kind to Commonwealth Caribbean small states. There has undoubtedly been a significant diversion of investment by Canada and certain European countries, most recently Britain, from the Commonwealth Caribbean to Cuba. The Cubans themselves report that joint ventures and other foreign investment projects rose from 212 to 260 in 1996. In February 1997, Foreign Investment Minister, Ibrahim Ferradaz, said that 150 additional projects were being negotiated.[20] In turning their attention to Cuba, investors from Canada and some European countries are taking advantage of the low wage levels and other costs that flow from the system in operation in Cuba. Unlike the Commonwealth Caribbean, Cuba has no trade unions and, therefore, no concerted demands for increases in wages and improvements in the conditions of work. What is more, unlike Caribbean governments, the Cuban government does not have to face general elections where the electorate chooses between contending political parties on the basis of promises for improved conditions. Cuba, therefore, can continue to keep its costs of labour and production at a much lower level than its competitors in the Caribbean. This includes tourism which passed the million mark for the first time in 1996, a 35 percent increase over 1995.[21] The result is that Commonwealth Caribbean countries and Cuba are not competing on a level economic playing field for investment or for tourists. Cuba's low costs make it more attractive to investors and for tourists seeking a relatively low-cost holiday.

Furthermore, the governments of countries investing there pay only lip service to the Castro regime's continuing disregard for democracy.

Caribbean small states have been very helpful to Cuba. As far back as 1972, as we have seen, Barbados, Guyana, Jamaica, and Trinidad and Tobago established diplomatic relations with Cuba despite clear messages from the US that it would look askance at such a move. This step by four Caribbean states in the height of the Cold War did much to improve Cuba's acceptability in the Caribbean and Latin America. The Caribbean also stood firm when the US signalled its unhappiness over Cuba's admission as a founder member of the Association of Caribbean States (ACS) in 1994. Previously in 1993, Caribbean small states voted in favour of a resolution asking the United States to modify its policies toward Cuba including repealing or invalidating laws or measures 'aimed at strengthening and extending the economic, commercial and financial embargo against Cuba'. Therefore, having helped to bring Cuba in from the cold, Commonwealth Caribbean countries now find themselves a casualty of investor attention which has been diverted to Havana and a victim of their own adherence to the Western democratic system.

Despite all this, Cuba also presents an opportunity for Commonwealth Caribbean countries if they encourage their business people to invest in the Cuban economy now. Commonwealth Caribbean countries have some expertise in gearing industries for markets in Europe and North America. This expertise could be utilised in combining Cuban raw material and labour with Caribbean capital and know-how in joint ventures which could benefit Cuba and the region as a whole. Investment by Commonwealth Caribbean hoteliers in the Cuban tourism industry would also be beneficial in eventually promoting Cuba and other Caribbean destinations as multi-stop destinations.[22] However, opportunities for the Caribbean are ebbing away. Despite a commission made up of representatives of Cuba and Commonwealth Caribbean countries and several private sector missions to Cuba, there has yet been no major Caribbean investment in Cuba. Apart from other constraints, the Helms-Burton legislation authorising US sanctions against any firm and individual doing business with Cuba – legislation universally condemned – will operate with impunity against Caribbean small states.

In 1992 and 1993 Caribbean small states voted overwhelmingly at the UN in favour of condemning human rights violations in Cuba. Thus, if they decide to encourage their business people to invest in Cuba, Caribbean small states will also have to push the Cuban government to address issues of human rights and the need for a democratic system of government. This is important not only for the Cuban people, but also for Caribbean economies which, otherwise, will continue to compete with Cuba on a playing field that benefits only the Cuban regime.

Natural disasters, particularly hurricanes, in the Caribbean region have increased in frequency and intensity in recent years. Each disaster causes hundreds of millions of dollars in damage and reverses development of these countries by several years. For instance, in 1995, Hurricane Luis packing winds of 210 miles per hour wrecked Antigua and Barbuda causing over US$500 million in damage and closing every hotel. The population of the country is 65,000 and more than 90 percent of its gross domestic product is derived from tourism. Apart from the civil service, much of the workforce on Antigua and Barbuda was unemployed for nearly six months. What is worse is that the effect of these disasters on the economies of small states causes skilled and qualified manpower to seek jobs abroad. Often, they do not return and the countries have to re-invest scarce capital in training a new cadre of skilled personnel. Moreover, governments, already strapped for cash, are forced to spend money on rehabilitating vital infrastructure, such as roads, power and water supplies and buildings, thus postponing expenditure on social essentials like health and education. Consequently, the capacity of the country to produce healthy, well-trained people to spur economic activity is eroded and development is retarded even more. It is a cruel irony that, according to the Intergovernmental Panel on Climate Change, these increased natural disaster hazards are attributable in no small measure to global warming – itself the consequence of CO_2 emissions by the industrial countries of North America and Europe.

Increasingly, the economic and security conditions described in this chapter are weakening the capacity of Caribbean small states to serve the needs of their people in the way that responsible sovereign states should. It is clearly true for all Caribbean small states that they lack the capacity to protect themselves from the incursions of drug traffickers and, then, from coercion by larger countries which impose their requirements on Caribbean governments. There is little point in looking to the international organisations, such as the United Nations, for such protection. As was said earlier in the chapter, these organisations have been severely weakened. A Regional Security System exists between Barbados and the six independent countries of the Leeward and Windward Islands, but it would be incapable of mounting any real defence of the countries concerned. As it is, they are not fully able to patrol their own waters against drug traffickers which, in part, is why the US sought to impose the Shipriders Agreements. In any event, coercion of governments of small states by larger and more powerful countries is now more economic than military.

The cost of full participation in the international community is greater than many Caribbean small states can afford. At the United Nations, for instance, five Commonwealth Caribbean small states and other Pacific island-nations share premises partly funded by Australia, Britain, Canada and New Zealand through the Commonwealth Secretariat. Without the financial assistance of these countries, it is unlikely that these small states could sustain a meaningful presence in New York. Beyond this, there are many international organisations in which Caribbean small states are not represented even though matters vital to their survival are discussed every day: the WTO is a case in point. For the most part, the active participation of Caribbean small states in the international community is limited to the UN, the Organisation of American States and the work of the ACP Group with the European Community in Brussels.

In the domestic context, governments are finding it very difficult to provide the basic services required by their people. Police forces lack the manpower and equipment to fight crime effectively. Judicial and prison services are also inadequately staffed and equipped. Hospitals also lack the equipment, drugs and trained medical personnel to cope properly with serious illnesses and grave accidents. Schools are also under-equipped and under-staffed with trained teachers. In many Caribbean small states, computers are still to be introduced as part of the normal equipment in schools. There are, of course, exceptions. Some small states do better than others in certain areas, but as a general observation the conditions described here hold good.

A further dimension of the domestic situation is the relationship between governments and opposition political parties. The

Westminster system of adversarial politics adopts an unwholesome confrontational character in small states and the Caribbean is no exception. The intense political rivalry between parties causes the opposition in many of these small states to oppose government policies often whether they have merit or not. Similarly, governments tend not to consult, or involve, opposition parties in decision making for fear of strengthening them. This reluctance to set aside political differences for the national good further weakens the state which, in turn, frightens potential foreign investors, injures the investment climate even for local entrepreneurs and dilutes the country's capacity to resist external forces. On the latter point, had governing and opposition parties been able to set aside domestic political differences to arrive at a consensus, each country might have been able to resist the types of treaties imposed on them as well as the conditions dictated by the IMF and World Bank for structural adjustment programmes.

As economic growth and prosperity continue to elude Caribbean countries, the capacity of the state to provide services is further eroded. Although there is no imminent danger of Caribbean small states becoming 'failed states', should their economic difficulties go unattended by the international community, that spectre might well arise early in the 21st Century at a greater financial burden to the world's richer nations than the cost of remedying the current problems.

What, then, are the prospects for Caribbean small states and in what international forum can their situation be addressed? The Commonwealth is an obvious place. The theme of the CHOGM in Edinburgh in October 1997 was 'Trade, Investment and Development'. Strikingly, it was originally mooted as 'Trade and Investment'. It was representatives of Caribbean small states at a meeting of senior officials in London in October 1996 who urged that 'development' be added. However, unlike New Delhi in 1983, the plight and prospects of small states was not part of the main agenda of the Heads; instead it was discussed by a Committee of Ministers whose report was then submitted to Heads for consideration. Leaders of small states were not, therefore, given the opportunity personally to sensitise their fellow heads of government from larger states to their situation. Regrettably, since the period for this Heads of Government Meeting was shortened, with an abbreviated 'retreat' by the Heads, the possibility of discussing such matters was significantly curtailed. Within the UN system, for its part, there are already numerous recommendations on small states, many of them implemented. Indeed, one of the recommendations from the 1985 Commonwealth study was the appointment of a UN Assistant Secretary-General for small states – a recommendation already ignored for 12 years. There is, in short, no ready international forum for addressing the particular problems and prospects of small states.

Where, then, does the solution to the problems of small states lie? Initially, it lies with them. As far as Caribbean small states are concerned, they already have an institutional arrangement in the form of CARICOM on which they could build. They are in the process of establishing a single market and they have taken some actions to bring a greater level of coherence to their decision making, particularly in external economic negotiations. At a meeting in Antigua in February 1997, the CARICOM Heads of Government decided to appoint the former Commonwealth Secretary-General, Sir Shridath Ramphal, as their chief negotiator on external negotiations such as those with the European Community on the successor arrangements to Lomé IV or with the United States and others on NAFTA and the proposed Free Trade Area of the Americas.

This decision to act together, rather than as individual units, points the way for a process by which Caribbean small states might jointly address all their external relations. For instance, had Commonwealth Caribbean countries adopted a uniform and institutional approach to the treaties which the USA sought to impose upon them, more acceptable terms might have been jointly negotiated. The CARICOM treaty itself already provides for the 'co-ordination and harmonisation' of foreign policies. It now only requires the will of heads of government to act in concert in all external matters which affect their sovereignty and territorial integrity.

A beneficial development would be a strategic coalition of small states throughout the international system. If these small states act in unison on the issues that most concern them, they could achieve much more for themselves. An early opportunity presents itself in the negotiations for the successor arrangements to Lomé IV. In the past, the African, Caribbean and Pacific countries have negotiated together. European countries have been suggesting to the Africans that they should separate from the traditional grouping and negotiate by themselves to get a better deal. Small states from the Caribbean and Pacific must resist this notion and do all in their power to persuade their African colleagues that there is danger in division – danger as much for Africa as for the Caribbean and Pacific – as their bargaining strength is diluted.

Essentially, small states throughout the world must meet and establish a common agenda supported by collaborative diplomacy in every international forum. Such an initiative has now become urgent. In the early 1990s an Association of Small Island States (AOSIS) was launched at the UN by delegations in New York. Essentially, AOSIS was a pressure group of small states which collaborated in advancing environmental issues at the UN. AOSIS is a useful example of how small states might work in every international organisation to secure better conditions. Of course, there will always be matters where agreement among small states might not be possible, but if they could agree a common agenda on a cluster of important issues their bargaining strength would be considerably enhanced, as would be their prospects for improving their situations.

Beyond what the Caribbean small states must do for themselves, there are measures which the international community could take now that would strengthen small states and spare richer nations the greater costs of redeeming these tiny economies in the future. Both the members of NAFTA and the European Union should recognise that trade liberalisation will not benefit all small states; some will suffer. Therefore, neither the European Union nor the NAFTA countries should expect all small states to allow reciprocity in trade. Further, both NAFTA and the European Union should continue trade preferences to those same small countries with limited resources and restricted export potential, recognising that without such preferences their economies will wither, with all the social and political consequences of such a development including an exodus of people by legal or illegal means. The USA and the European Union could continue to strengthen their already stringent immigration legislation, but it is impossible to legislate borders against refugees.

International financial institutions should establish natural disaster funds to help small states rebuild when they are struck by hurricanes, earthquakes and flooding. The countries that control the IMF and World Bank should also allow those international financial institutions to give debt relief to small states. The richer countries should themselves consider relieving small states of bilateral debt, particularly where onerous rates of interest have been applied. Furthermore, the international community should adopt a standard by which small states would repay debt at a reduced rate of interest and from a fixed percentage of their export earnings to allow them the opportunity to invest in their economic and social infrastructure. It should be recalled, as British economist Mike Faber points out, that 'in 1946 the terms of a large US loan to war-torn Britain stipulated that interest payments should be waived – not reduced, but forgiven entirely – should that interest exceed two percent of British export revenues in any given year.'[23]

Finally, where richer and more powerful nations require the collaboration and co-operation of small states to help combat problems which affect such rich and powerful nations, they should recognise that there is no need to threaten them or to deny them economic assistance. Many, if not all, small states will readily co-operate with larger countries in combating any pernicious activity; small states, therefore, do not need to be controlled. But they do need help. Treaties and other arrangements designed to combat problems such as drug trafficking and money laundering should be accompanied by the resources necessary to do the job effectively.

Without such co-operation and assistance from richer nations, small states will not be integrated into the world economy and the stormy seas on which they toss at present will soon capsize them. The operation to salvage them will be a considerable cost to those nations and institutions which neglect them now.

NOTES & REFERENCES

1   Foreword by the Commonwealth Secretary-General, Sir Shridath S. Ramphal, to Commonwealth Secretariat, *Vulnerability: Small States in the Global Society*, report of a Commonwealth Consultative Group, Commonwealth Secretariat, London, 1985, p. v.

2   *Ibid.*

3   Larry Rohter, 'Caribbean Nations Find Little Profit in Aiding US Drug War', *The New York Times*, 24 October 1996, p. A13.

4   Owen Arthur, Prime Minister of Barbados, 'The Economic Realities of the Caribbean Basin', address to the Wilton Park Conference on 'The Caribbean Basin: New Relationships Within and Beyond the Caribbean', 21 September 1996, mimeo.

5   1987 figures show that the percentage of the population working in the banana industry was 46 percent for St Lucia, 54 percent for St Vincent and 50 percent for Dominica. In 1988, the contribution of banana production to gross domestic product was 36.5 percent for St Lucia, 24.9 percent for St Vincent and 32.1 percent for Dominica.

6   St Lucia's Ambassador to the European Union, Edwin Laurent, cited in 'Banana Trade Under Fire from WTO Panel', *Caribbean Insight*, Vol. 20, No. 4, April 1997.

7   Cited by Michael B. Joseph, 'Post Lomé IV Arrangements must mirror the Principles and Instruments of Lomé: A Perspective from the Banana Sectors of the Windward Islands', European Centre for Development Policy Management Working Paper No. 18, The Netherlands, April 1997.

8   Larry Rohter, 'Caribbean Reels in NAFTA's Wake', *International Herald Tribune*, 31 January 1997.

9   Trinidad and Tobago and Jamaica with larger populations and better developed manufacturing and agriculture are probably the only exceptions.

10   Gaddis Smith, 'Haiti: From Intervention to Intervasion', *Current History: A Journal of Contemporary World Affairs*, Vol. 94, No. 589, February 1995.

11   See The Illegal Immigration Reform and Immigrant Responsibility Act of 1996, Pub L. 104-208 enacted on 30 September 1996.

12   See Statement on Belize made by US Assistant Secretary of State for International Narcotics and Law Enforcement Affairs, Richard S. Gelbard, on 28 February 1997.

13   See Don Bohning, 'Antigua Condemns US for Bad Press About Drug Efforts', *Miami Herald*, 21 November 1996.

14   See CANA report by Linda Hutchinson, 21 March 1997, from Port of Spain.

15   Cited by Rohter, 'Caribbean Nations Find Little Profit'.

16   Press release from the Belize Information Service, 4 March 1997.

17   Communiqué at the conclusion of the Fifth Special Meeting of the Conference of Heads of Government of the Caribbean Community held in Bridgetown, Barbados on 16 December 1996, issued by the CARICOM Secretariat, Georgetown, Guyana, 17 December 1996.

18   *Ibid.*

19   Smith, 'Haiti'.

20   See 'Cuba Aims at External Deficit Reduction', *Caribbean Insight*, Vol. 20, No. 2, February 1997.

21   *Ibid.*

22   For fuller discussion of this, see Ron Sanders, 'Cuba: Ripe for Caribbean Community Joint Ventures', *CANA Business: The Financial Magazine of the Caribbean Community*, September 1993.

23   Cited in Susan George, *A Fate Worse Than Debt*, Penguin Books, London, 1990, p. 245.

CHAPTER ELEVEN

The Commonwealth
and Small States

If there is one multi-national organisation in which the leaders of small states ought to invest their energies and resources, it is the Commonwealth.

Thirty-two of the 54 members of the grouping of Britain and its former colonies are small states, 12 of them from the Caribbean. There is no other multi-national organisation in which small states predominate in this way.

It is now a cliché to say so, but it is nonetheless true that the Commonwealth bridges the world with membership in Africa, Asia, the Pacific, the Caribbean, Europe, the Mediterranean and North America. The Organisation and its councils link people of developed and developing countries, of every religion under the sun, and provide an entrée into practically every multinational grouping in the world.

Sidelined as they are, in international organisations, because of their smallness and lack of any sort of clout, the Commonwealth presents the leadership of small states with unique opportunities to advance their concerns in the international community. They have equal status in the Commonwealth with the Prime Minister of Britain, a major power, and with the leaders of influential countries such as Canada, Australia, India, Nigeria and South Africa. They can advance their causes in formal sessions of meetings and in informal gatherings.

Through Britain, Commonwealth small states have the opportunity to have their concerns raised in the councils of the European Union (EU). Britain, Australia, Canada and New Zealand can advance the interests of small states in the Organisation for Economic Co-operation and Development (OECD) and the Financial Action Task Force (FATF). By apprising Commonwealth African and Asian countries

A version of this Chapter was first published in The Round Table, No. 345, January 1998, pp. 39-44 as 'Commonwealth Edinburgh Summit: A Beneficial Encounter for Small States'.

of their challenges, small states issues can be raised in the Organisation of African Unity, and in the ASEAN group. Similarly, Commonwealth countries which have representatives on the Boards of the IMF and World Bank could be asked to speak-up for small states.

What is more, because small states comprise the greatest number of Commonwealth members, the Commonwealth Secretariat is the closest thing they have to a Secretariat for small states. The work programme of the Commonwealth Secretariat pays special attention to giving technical and other assistance to small states, and there is no other organisation whose councils always include small states on its agenda as the Commonwealth does. This is not to suggest that small states predominate the attention of the Commonwealth. The organisation is concerned with many other issues including good governance and democracy, alleviation of poverty in poor countries, trade facilitation, education, the environment and youth.

Don McKinnon, the present Commonwealth Secretary-General places importance on the membership of small states in the Commonwealth. He contends that: "The Commonwealth itself is made stronger by its small states membership. Small states enrich the Commonwealth. They are an integral part of the Commonwealth's diversity. They extend its range of influence and allow the Commonwealth to play a crucial role as a consensus builder. That is why the partnership between small states and the Commonwealth is at the heart of the organisation and is so crucial to its future.[1]

However, Commonwealth experts such as Peter Lyon, a learned academic and commentator on Commonwealth matters, argues that "there is no intrinsic reason why the Commonwealth should be especially attentive to the interests of the small states beyond the fact that over half the entire membership today comprises small states".[2] He concedes that his argument "is an analytical fact rather than a political or humane point".[3] Nevertheless, there is great substance to Lyon's point that there is no intrinsic reason why the Commonwealth should pay special attention to small states. The resources of the Secretariat come mainly from Britain, Canada, Australia, New Zealand and the lager developing member countries. Obviously, they have interests in the work of the Commonwealth well beyond the concerns of small states.

This is why the leaders of small states and their diplomatic representatives have to make the decision to invest in the Commonwealth as an important tool in their international political and economic policies.

It makes sense to do so for all the reasons stated earlier in this Chapter.

The historical relationship between the Commonwealth and small states emphasises the great value of the organisation to these powerless nations. As small states became independent and joined the Commonwealth, the Organisation which established a formal secretariat in 1965 in London, began to pay attention to the peculiar problems of its new members. In 1979, the Secretariat published, *The Commonwealth: Its Special Responsibilities to Small States*. The publication reflected the concerns of the time. It dealt primarily with problems of development and international representation.

By 1983, triggered by the US intervention in Grenada after a military coup, these concerns, while remaining valid, had grown to include security issues including the vulnerability of small states to external attack and interference in their internal affairs. The 1983 Commonwealth Heads of Government mandated a study of the new difficulties facing small states and, in 1985, *Vulnerability: Small States in the Global Society* was produced by a Consultative Group. The study remains a seminal work on the challenges confronting small states, and the measures to tackle them. It recommended, for instance, that 'the World Bank should adopt more flexible criteria for graduating small states from its lending especially from the International Development Association (IDA)'.[4] This recommendation remains unfilled today, and is still a major concern of small states. The study also recommended that 'small states should be freed from all limitations that apply to their access under the Generalised System of Preferences, and exempted from all organised marketing arrangements and voluntary export restraints".[5] This issue, expressed today as 'special and differential' treatment, is still a burning and crucial issue for small states.

While many of the recommendations of the *Vulnerability* report were not implemented, others were. The Commonwealth Secretariat put in place special programmes for small states across the broad vista of its work programme, and in this way maintained attention on their development needs in particular. Through its various officials, the Commonwealth Secretariat became an advocate of the causes of small states and represented their views in high-level contacts with UN agencies, the European Union, the IMF and the World Bank. But, the developed countries and the international agencies largely ignored the recommendations which only they could execute.

Ten years later, the problems confronting small states had grown. The cold war had ended establishing the United States as the world's only super-power; global warming had become a reality threatening small island states in particular through both natural disasters such as hurricanes and flooding; drug trafficking and money laundering had escalated as cross-border crimes adversely affecting the legal and financial integrity of states; terms of trade had worsened, and small states in the Caribbean and Pacific found themselves losing preferential markets.

In 1997, the *Vulnerability* report was updated, but only after agitation by ministerial and diplomatic representatives of small states. *A Future for Small States: Overcoming Vulnerability* was produced by another consultative group. This report went to the 1997 CHOGM in Edinburgh. Again, the recommendations of the second report were far seeing. Among them were:

- Small states should investigate and encourage innovative approaches to insurance in disaster-prone areas. Urgent consideration should be given to the introduction of an international insurance scheme for small states;
- Small states, while being mindful of the position of global powers should seek security assistance from them in areas where there are overlapping interests, such as combating global crime, subject to safeguarding national sovereignty;
- In determining eligibility to concessional finance, bilateral and multilateral donors should recognise the special position of states by taking account of a broader set of criteria other than per capita income;
- Small states should seek the establishment of a compensatory financing scheme within the UN system to provide funds for rehabilitation and reconstruction following natural disasters which affect them.[6]

Again the recommendations went unimplemented by the developed countries and the international agencies. But, small states themselves also failed to pursue the recommendations with the vigour that implementation required.

Nonetheless, the Edinburgh CHOGM, which considered the report, was a beneficial encounter for small states. This was a view universally held by their representatives at every level. Edinburgh will be remembered as the summit that returned small states firmly to the Commonwealth agenda and renewed for them the worth of Commonwealth membership. Prior to the Edinburgh CHOGM, small states, already marginalised in international institutions, were beginning to feel that, even within the Commonwealth where they constituted the majority, they were being sidelined.

Among the many elements which constituted positive developments for small states was a clear acknowledgement by the Commonwealth and its member states in the Edinburgh Commonwealth Economic Declaration that:

- special measures are needed by small states to help integrate them into the global economy;
- they must be helped to participate effectively in economic decision making in key international fora, particularly the World Trade Organisation (WTO);
- official development assistance (ODA) is still an essential instrument for poverty reduction and for creating conditions for increased trade and investment, including skills and infrastructure development in small states;
- debt constitutes a burden for small states and they require relief if they are to secure a sustainable exit from it;
- natural disasters are increasing in frequency and magnitude in small states and the Commonwealth should initiate action in the international community to strengthen disaster relief mechanisms for the provision of urgent and adequate assistance.[7]

The items listed above did not relate to small states only; least developed countries (LDCs) were also rightly included, but, unlike previous CHOGMs whose economic utterances focused on the plight of the LDCs only, this summit took real account of the problems of small states.

Three other matters were also of special importance to small states. First, for some years before, representatives of small states had been arguing in the international financial institutions (IFIs) that per capita income should not be the sole criterion by which they are judged for graduation from eligibility for concessionary finance. In the Economic Declaration heads of government not only 'encouraged' the IFIs to 'review their graduation policies' and 'establish a task force to address the concerns of small states'; they also agreed to 'set up a small ministerial group to discuss small states' concerns with major multilateral agencies and to report to governments on the outcome as soon as possible'.[8] This represented a major breakthrough for small states for it represented a commitment from Britain and Canada – two influential members of the IFIs – to work for a change in policy that would bring tangible benefits to small states. Further, the small ministerial group was given an important action-oriented task to perform for small states, one which can be monitored for its effectiveness. This development is a far cry from the Ministerial Group on Small States (MGSS) which was established at the Cyprus CHOGM in 1993, and which did little but meet ritualistically in the wings of CHOGM and routinely present a report to the summit.

The second matter was a resolution to 'work for a successor arrangement to the Lomé Convention which... gives African, Caribbean and Pacific (ACP) countries, particularly small states, adequate transitional arrangements; and in particular encourage the European Union (EU) and WTO members to accommodate the legitimate interest of the ACP banana producers and facilitate the diversification of their economies'.[9] This represented a strong commitment particularly from Britain, which was shortly to assume the Presidency of the EU, to work in the interests of small states whose preferential prices and market in the EU were being threatened by both the desire of some EU members to change the existing arrangements, and rulings of the WTO that the arrangements are not compatible with its rules.

The third matter of benefit to small states was the decision to establish a Trade and Investment Access Facility to provide technical assistance to help countries manage trade liberalisation and fulfil WTO requirements.[10] This facility could be of immense help to all developing countries, but particularly to small states in coping with the demands of trade liberalisation and managing the process of integration into the global market.

These were the commitments, resolutions and agreements declared at the Edinburgh CHOGM that gave small states reason for satisfaction. But it should not be assumed that these benefits to small states flowed from a sudden desire by larger Commonwealth member states to focus meaningful attention on them. Small states – particularly Caribbean small states – worked well in advance of the meeting to ensure that they would not be ignored at the summit and that there would be some substance in it for them.

Since January 1996, Commonwealth Caribbean High Commissioners in London had met on at least a monthly basis to co-ordinate their positions in relation to bilateral issues with the United Kingdom and on multilateral issues in the Commonwealth and other agencies with which they interface in Britain. This process of 'associative diplomacy' helped to strengthen the positions of small Caribbean states. High Commissioners were able to draw on each other's strengths and benefit from debate on a range of issues which affect their countries individually and collectively. Where it was appropriate, they adopted a common stance, including on matters related to the Commonwealth.[11]

As far back as the Commonwealth Senior Officials Meeting in London in October 1996, the representatives of Caribbean small states decided that they would not accept marginalisation in the Commonwealth in the same way that they were being sidelined in other international bodies. Their efforts to ensure this, started with the theme proposed for the conference by the British government – 'Trade and Investment: The Road to Commonwealth Prosperity'. There was no mention of development or any of its ancillary subjects such as environment, official development assistance or debt. The representatives of the group of Caribbean small states at that meeting vigorously argued for the inclusion of 'development' in the theme. Support from African and Asian Commonwealth countries ensured that the theme was broadened to include 'development'.

At that same meeting, representatives of small states also argued for the 1985 *Vulnerability* report to be updated. Delegates contended that, a decade on, small states were still confronted by many of the challenges identified in the 1985 study and a range of new ones, among them: natural disasters which had increased in frequency and magnitude, the effects of drug trafficking and money laundering, the evolution of a multilateral trading system which fails to take account of their special circumstances, and international financial institutions that deny them access to concessionary financing.

In January 1997, at a meeting between the then Commonwealth Secretary-General, Emeka Anyaoku, Commonwealth High Commissioners in London and a representative of the United Kingdom, the representatives of Caribbean small states made it clear that the terms of reference for consultants to produce a paper on the theme of 'Trade, Investment and Development' for the Edinburgh CHOGM was not acceptable to them because it failed to take sufficient account of development issues. Again, with the support of African and Asian Commonwealth countries, it was agreed that any paper which was produced would be only a 'background paper', not a 'working document'. In this way, the Edinburgh CHOGM would not be bound to take the paper into account in its decision making.

Representatives of small states, suspicious of the theme paper which seemed to be moving in the direction of simply repeating the positions already elaborated in the international financial institutions and the World Trade Organisation (WTO), again called for the vulnerability study on small states to be updated. It was as a result of representations at this meeting that the Secretary-General decided to constitute an independent advisory group to do what he later described as 'a comprehensive analysis of the vulnerability of small states in all its dimensions, including political, economic, social and environmental aspects'.[12]

The representatives of Caribbean small states in London then set themselves two tasks. The first was to ensure that the background theme paper reflected as much of their concerns as possible, and the second was to make certain that the new study of small states would be taken seriously. High Commissioners, therefore, asked for a meeting with the consultants on the theme paper. It seemed evident from that meeting and the terms of reference given to the consultants that small states would be given little consideration and certainly no detailed analysis. This was confirmed when the draft of the theme paper was circulated to all Commonwealth High Commissioners who then met and sent a detailed response to the Secretariat itemising their concerns and setting out counter-arguments on many points.

By then, representatives of Caribbean small states feared that an attempt would be made to base any Declaration of Economic Principles that might emerge from CHOGM on the theme paper which was regarded as unhelpful. It was decided therefore to consult with other Commonwealth representatives in London, particularly the Commonwealth African countries, partners with the Caribbean in the ACP, and Canada, a traditional close Commonwealth ally. These consultations revealed as much unease with the theme paper as was felt by the Caribbean. The African and Caribbean groups feared that some attempt would be made to produce a Declaration of Economic Principles in advance of CHOGM, one which would be presented to an already abbreviated conference so curtailing discussion. The two groups, therefore, set up a joint working group to create the sort of economic declaration they would like to see.

Mention should also be made of the fact that the British Prime Minister, Tony Blair, wanted an economic declaration to emerge from CHOGM, particularly after his newly elected government had made much of it. He instructed the British Foreign and Commonwealth Office to get their High Commissions to ascertain from governments their view of the substance of the declaration. Certainly, in the Caribbean, they heard concerns about the WTO and the need for Commonwealth support for ACP countries in negotiating the new Lomé Convention on economic relations with the EU.

It subsequently came to light that the Secretariat was in possession of a draft Declaration of Economic Principles which, while helpful in parts, contained many elements that were unacceptable to Caribbean small states and to other developing countries in Africa. It is inconceivable that Britain, as the host country, did not have a hand in the Secretariat's draft, and it is most unlikely that Canada and Australia and a few other hand-picked countries were not asked for an opinion. The African and Caribbean groups therefore submitted their draft to the Secretariat with the request that its contents be taken into account in any draft declaration, 'so as to ensure consensus in Edinburgh'.

As it turned out, the draft declaration, subsequently refined at the conference, was largely acceptable to the African and Caribbean groups and it contained many of the elements covered in the draft they submitted to the Secretariat. The point is, however, that had this collaborative work not been done, there would have been either no economic declaration at all, or one which did not take sufficient account of the real challenges and problems being faced by small states and other developing countries.

On the matter of the new small states' study, *Overcoming Vulnerability*, Caribbean small states certainly welcomed it. The report was a synthesis of the body of literature that had been produced on the vulnerability of small states since the 1985 Commonwealth study had been conducted. It benefited from work published in the journal, *The Round Table*, which deserves much credit for keeping the issue of small states alive in the academic and governmental circles, and from the tireless inquiry into the subject by Dr Paul Sutton, one of its consultants.

As the President of the Maldives, Abdul Gayoom, put it, the 1985 study 'was born of concerns that small states faced in confronting threats posed by military adventurism and terrorism'.[13] The Caribbean island of Grenada had been invaded by the United States in 1983; and in countries in both the Caribbean and the Pacific, there had been attempts by mercenaries to seize power. Against this background, Commonwealth Heads of Government meeting in Delhi in 1983 were focused on the security of small states in military terms. While the 1985 study did take account of the structural constraints on small countries for economic growth and development, this was not its primary focus. In any event, the 1980s represented a period of relative economic prosperity for small states especially those in the Caribbean; the worst was yet to come. By comparison, the significance of the new small states' study lay, in the words of the Prime Minister of St Lucia, Dr Kenny Anthony, 'in its advocacy for a priority to be created on the international agenda in favour of states that are becoming increasingly vulnerable and finding it increasingly difficult to survive in an environment that is becoming insensitive'.[14]

Once the report was completed, the question then arose as to how to ensure it received full attention at the Edinburgh summit. It was scheduled to be discussed as item 4 on the agenda following the economic discussion and the debate on political values of the Commonwealth (including the report of the Commonwealth Ministerial Action Group on Nigeria, Sierra Leone and The Gambia) and the criteria on new membership along with applications from Rwanda, Yemen and the Palestine Liberation Organisation (PLO).

The representatives of the Caribbean small states feared that the already considerably shortened meeting would pay little attention to the report if it was taken so late in the conference. What is more, they considered that the recommendations of the report were absolutely vital for inclusion in the Economic Declaration which the Secretariat had suggested be issued on the afternoon of the conference's second day. This meant the Declaration would be released before the special problems of small states could be discussed. Therefore, in a meeting of senior officials on the eve of the opening of the conference, Caribbean small states argued for the small states' study to be moved up the agenda and for the economic debate not to be closed until the Chairman of the Ministerial Group on Small States (MGSS) had made a report. Arising out of their previous consultations with the African group with whom this strategy had been argued, African countries spoke in support of the Caribbean proposal and it was carried.

This was accepted by senior officials and, when the MGSS met on the morning of the conference's opening, the new arrangement was settled with Robin Cook, the British Secretary of State for Foreign and Commonwealth Affairs, who was elected chairman. Thus the small states' study formed part of the consideration of the economic debate and many of its key recommendations found a place in the economic declaration. These very points had also been included in the draft declaration which the African and Caribbean group had submitted to the Secretariat prior to the meeting.

At the Summit itself, the leaders of small states were strengthened by the thoroughness of the new study of small states. They argued a case for special attention that was difficult to resist. The Edinburgh CHOGM was, therefore, a beneficial encounter for small states, but it was not achieved without careful diplomatic work prior to the conference.

The experience reinforces the argument that diplomacy is the primary instrument of small states in pursuing their objectives in the international community. And, it also demonstrates that the Commonwealth is the best vehicle in the international community for the advancement of the interests of small states. Therefore, leaders of small states should use it more effectively by investing in it as a tool for advancing the interests of their countries.

NOTES & REFERENCES

1   Opening Remarks by the Commonwealth Secretary-General, Don Mckinnon,to the Commonwealth Ministerial Group on Small States, 29 November 2003, Abuja
2   Lyon, Peter; 'Foreword' in *Small Statehood and the Commonwealth Reconsidered*, published for The Round Table by Carfax Publishing Ltd, October 1997
3   *Ibid.*
4   *Vulnerability: Small States in the Global Society,* Commonwealth Secretariat, London, 1985; p. 112
5   *Ibid.*, p 113
6   *A Future for Small States: Overcoming Vulnerability,* Commonwealth Secretariat, London, 1997; *page xiii to xvii*
7   *Promoting Shared prosperity: Edinburgh Commonwealth Declaration,* Commonwealth Secretariat, London, 24-27 October 1997
8   *Ibid*, paragraph 8
9   *Ibid,* paragraph 4
10 *Ibid*
11 For a discussion of how Commonwealth Caribbean countries have used 'associative diplomacy' in the past, see Chapter on 'The relevance and function of diplomacy in international politics for small states'.
12 Press Conference Statement by Commonwealth Secretary-General, Chief Emeka Anyaoku, at the launch of the Report on 'A Future for Small States: Overcoming Vulnerability', Edinburgh, 24 October 1997
13 At the Press Conference referred to in reference above
14 *Ibid.*

CHAPTER TWELVE

The Fight Against Fiscal Colonialism: The OECD and Small Jurisdictions

This Chapter offers a Caribbean perspective on the so-called 'Harmful Tax Competition Initiative' (HTCI) of the Paris-based Organisation for Economic Co-operation and Development (OECD)[1] – an instance of fiscal colonialism that the Organisation intends should be fully implemented by 2005.

The OECD's HTCI is nothing less than a determined attempt by the world's wealthiest economies to bend powerless countries to their will. It is a form of neo-colonialism in which the OECD attempts to dictate the tax systems and structures of other nations for the benefit of its member states. Through this initiative, the OECD is seeking to curb the rights of sovereign small states and autonomous jurisdictions, defying the norms of international rules and practice.

The OECD is a multinational grouping of thirty of the world's richest countries. It is not an international organisation and it has no legal authority to speak for the world or to establish rules, norms or standards for any State except its own members. Nonetheless, its HTCI launched in 1998, dictated terms on what, in short, could be described as cross-border tax matters.

In 1999 the OECD identified 41 small jurisdictions, mostly in the Caribbean and the Pacific, as 'tax havens' and said quite categorically that, if they did not submit to its terms, sanctions would be imposed against them. In other words, wherever the OECD met resistance to its unilaterally ordained 'rules', it would invoke economic power to force surrender.

As one commentator put it, "when a powerful international political organisation officially brands a small nation as 'harmful', trouble is brewing. Defamation anticipates oppression, conditioning suggestible minds to accept it".[2] The evidence supports that observation. Throughout the principal OECD countries – the US, the UK, Canada, Germany, France

First published in *The Round Table*, July 2002.

and Japan – the media characterises these 41 jurisdictions as "harbouring tax cheats", and "providing secure bases for tax dodgers and other criminal activity". The media, playing handmaiden to their Governments, characterise these small jurisdictions as 'rogue states'.

As far back as 1834, a US Senator described this with prescient clarity. He said, "power marks its victim; denounces it; and then excites public hatred and odium to conceal its own abuses and encroachments". By seducing the media into characterising these 41 jurisdictions as rogues, the OECD clothed itself in the armour of a moral champion and covered up its real intention – to force small countries into surrendering their autonomy.

Alarmingly, neither the OECD as an Organisation, nor its members States, seemed to pay any attention whatsoever to the fact that these small jurisdictions developed financial services, at the urging of several OECD countries and international financial institutions, as a means of diversifying their mostly one-product economies, and maintaining democracy and civil order in their societies. They were already faced with significantly reduced aid programmes and had seen their share of the world's market for primary products disappear. There was not much else they could turn to and rapid deterioration in their standard of living stared them in the face. As Economist Bishnodat Persaud describes it: "Offshore financial services have become a significant part of the economy of many small states. These activities generate a substantial amount of licence fees which belie the notion of a no tax situation. They also generate employment involving secretarial, administrative, accounting, information technology and professional skills. They encourage business and leisure visits and the skills developed have wider favourable economic impact. Much rental income is also generated by the sector."[3]

Eighteen of the 41 jurisdictions are Commonwealth member-states, and another ten had a relationship with the Commonwealth by virtue of being overseas territories or colonies of the United Kingdom or New Zealand[4]. The Commonwealth, therefore, had to take an interest in the issue especially as almost half of its membership were in direct confrontation – its four largest members who are also OECD countries, Australia, Britain, Canada, and New Zealand, and the eighteen independent Commonwealth states. The Commonwealth's role will be examined later in this chapter.

THE BEGINNING OF THE OECD'S HTCI

In 1998, the OECD produced a Report entitled, *Harmful Tax Competition: An Emerging Global Issue.*[5] The report listed what it called "key factors" in identifying and assessing harmful preferential tax regimes and tax havens. These were:

"No or low effective tax rates
a low or zero effective tax rate on the relevant income is a necessary starting point for an examination of whether a preferential tax regime is harmful. A zero or low effective tax rate may arise because the schedule rate itself is very low or because of the way in which a country defines the tax base to which the rate is applied. A harmful tax regime will be characterised by a combination of a low or zero effective tax rate and one or more other factors such as set out below.

Ring fencing of regimes
Some preferential tax regimes are partly or fully insulated from the domestic markets of the country providing the regime. The fact that a country feels the need to protect its own economy from the regime by ring-fencing provides a strong indication that a regime has the potential to create harmful spill over effects. Ring fencing may take a number of forms including:

- a regime may explicitly or implicitly exclude resident taxpayers from taking advantage of its benefits
- enterprises which benefit from the regime may be explicitly or implicitly prohibited from operating in the domestic market.

Lack of transparency
The lack of transparency in the operation of a regime will make it harder for the home country to take defensive measures. Non-transparency may arise from the way in which a regime is designed and administered. Non-transparency is a broad concept that includes, among others, favourable application of laws and regulations, negotiable tax provisions, and a failure to make widely available administrative practices.

Lack of effective exchange of information

The lack of effective exchange of information in relation to taxpayers benefiting from the operation of a preferential tax regime is a strong indication that a country is engaging in harmful tax competition."[6]

Having produced its report, the OECD then set about, in a unilateral and arbitrary manner, identifying jurisdictions that it considered to be competing in tax matters in a way that was harmful to its member-states. In 1998 the Organisation actually indicated that there were 47 jurisdictions it deemed to be tax havens. Later that year six of these jurisdictions were dropped but the OECD never disclosed their identity. It can only be surmised that the OECD decided to exclude these six undisclosed jurisdictions for political reasons such as the reluctance of its member-states to engage in a confrontation with the Governments concerned. It is noteworthy, for instance, that Hong Kong was never named as a tax haven, yet, by every criteria that the OECD established, Hong Kong should have been a prime target. Was Hong Kong's omission an indication that the OECD did not want to offend the Peoples Republic of China?

In the event, the Co-Chairs of the OECD's Forum on harmful tax practices wrote to the remaining 41 jurisdictions in February 1999 stating that their harmful tax competition project had "been endorsed by OECD Ministers and G7 Heads of State".[7] It is significant that the OECD wrote to "jurisdictions" and not "countries" or "states". The reason for this is that the OECD member-states did not wish to be held responsible for the activities of their overseas territories or colonies. Indeed, in the case of the UK, the government appeared to welcome the cover of the OECD for insisting on change in the financial services offered by the jurisdictions in its charge. In the February 1999 letter, the OECD informed the targeted jurisdictions that "the tax haven list is expected to be agreed at the Forum's November meeting" and it produced a timetable of events, beginning on 1 March, in which a report on the jurisdictions would be unilaterally written by the OECD, comments would be invited from the jurisdictions, the reports revised and the list of tax havens issued.

Faced with the threat of appearing on an OECD blacklist and the consequent dangers to their reputation and standing in the capital and investment markets, the 41 targeted jurisdictions – many of them very small states or overseas territories of OECD states – decided to respond by agreeing to talk with the OECD's Forum on Harmful Tax Practices. The OECD organised the talks by inviting each jurisdiction to appear before its Forum on Harmful Tax Practices between July 1999 and April 2000. In an inquisition-type setting, representatives of these small jurisdictions were arrayed before senior Treasury officials of the OECD countries and presented with an OECD researched report describing their territory as 'tax havens'. Dwarves before giants – and unsympathetic giants at that – the arguments of these small jurisdictions fell on deaf ears. Six jurisdictions – Bermuda, Cayman Islands, Cyprus, Malta, Mauritius and San Marino – committed to "eliminating their harmful tax practices". In a vulgar display, the OECD published on its Internet website, letters of commitment that its officials had dictated and demanded from the Heads of Government of these jurisdictions. It is well known that Bermuda and the Cayman Islands – two British Overseas territories – experienced considerable pressure from London to sign the commitment letters. In addition, both Cyprus and Malta were urged to sign the commitments in the context of their interest in becoming members of the European Union (EU) which had adopted a Council Directive to tackle harmful tax competition.

The EU directive dealt, *inter alia,* with "the difficulty of ensuring a minimum of effective taxation of interest payments in the Community". It proposed a single system of withholding tax throughout the Community. Although pressed by France and Germany, it failed to win unanimous agreement. The UK government was particularly opposed to this idea because of the effect it would have on employment and on the operations of the City of London where no taxes are paid on dividends and interest earned from savings of non-residents. The UK Treasury Department, led by the Chancellor, Gordon Brown, fought hard to win acceptance of 'exchange of information' between the tax authorities of the European Union countries as the governing principle of the Savings Directive rather than a common system of withholding tax. Indeed, on 9 May 1998, he issued a statement endorsing the OECD's recommendations "and the complementary EU Code of Conduct on business taxation".[8] Other elements of the European Union package were: "the scope for non-taxation of cross-border interest payments in the Community" which was seen as causing economic distortions that were "incompatible with the proper functioning of the single market", and "the erosion of tax bases linked to the absence of guarantees concerning a minimum of effective taxation on the cross-border investment of savings".[9] The European Union project to level the playing field on taxation in the Community therefore lay at the heart of the OECD initiative, and intertwined the OECD HTCI and the EU Code of Conduct as a complete package. If the OECD HTCI were abandoned or significantly altered, commitment to the EU Code by countries such as The Netherlands, Belgium, Austria and Ireland would evaporate in the face of what they considered direct competition from the targeted jurisdictions particularly Jersey, Guernsey and The Isle of Man.

As it turned out, the targeted jurisdictions were right to be concerned about both the content of the OECD HTCI and the manner in which the Organisation was attempting to implement it. For when the OECD produced a second report in 2000 entitled, *Towards Global Tax Co-operation,* it was revealed that the Organisation was treating its member states quite differently from the unilateralist and arbitrary stance taken with the targeted jurisdictions. First, while the targeted jurisdictions were quite categorically named as "tax havens", some OECD members, such as Switzerland, Belgium, Portugal, Luxembourg, Canada and the United States, were described only as having regimes that were "potentially harmful".[10] Second, the OECD carried out a unilateral evaluation of the jurisdictions they subsequently labelled as 'tax havens', but its own members each performed 'a self-review" to determine whether or not it had preferential tax regimes.[11]

WHY THE OECD HARMFUL TAX SCHEME?

So, what was behind the EU's interest in the OECD's 'harmful tax competition' scheme? And, why did the OECD launch it?

The EU members of the OECD have the highest taxes in the world. They also have the widest range of taxes. These include personal income tax, property tax, corporate tax, inheritance tax, capital gains tax, death duties and value-added taxes on almost all goods and services consumed within their States. People are quite literally taxed from the cradle to the grave and beyond.

Despite this wide range of high taxes, the Treasury Departments of several EU members of the OECD are finding it difficult to finance the activities of their governments. The cost of the military and their sophisticated weaponry is extremely high in many of these countries. In addition, the costs of social programmes are rising. For example, their populations are aging but living longer. At the same time, the work force's payments to social security are becoming proportionately smaller. Therefore, governments have to find more money to provide health care and pensions over a longer period.

But, it is difficult to raise additional money without imposing additional taxes. Given that the people of the European Union members of the OECD are already heavily taxed, only very imprudent governments would seek to tax them still further if they wished to be re-elected. Consequently, Treasury Departments began to look elsewhere for revenues to finance government programmes. Thus, many of them welcomed and endorsed the 'harmful tax competition' scheme first suggested by the representative of the UK Treasury.

The EU members of the OECD recognised that the international private banking market housed approximately sixteen trillion United States dollars, and they decided that much of this money came from their nationals or companies that were subject to tax in their countries. The leader of the private banking market, with a 33 percent share, was Switzerland – a non-EU member, but a member of the OECD. As a leading banking expert told the British Foreign and Commonwealth Office in London in June 1999, "Clearly Switzerland has to be party to any solution on harmful tax competition if a level playing field is to be created". However, Switzerland was not accommodating.

When the OECD produced its first report in 1998, Luxembourg and Switzerland, two of the OECD countries that are the biggest competitors with Caribbean jurisdictions for offshore banking services, both abstained from the vote on its passage in the OECD council. In a statement to the Council, Luxembourg declared that it "does not share the Report's implicit belief that bank secrecy is necessarily a source of harmful tax competition". Luxembourg's representatives also said that Luxembourg "cannot accept that an exchange of information that is circumscribed by the respect of international laws and respective national laws be considered a criterion to identify a harmful preferential tax regime and a tax haven". The representatives of Switzerland stated, "The Report presents the fact that tax rates are lower in one country than another as a criterion to identifying harmful preferential tax regimes. This results in unacceptable protection of countries with high levels of taxation, which is, moreover, contrary to the economic philosophy of the OECD".[12]

Switzerland then went on to make a telling statement. It said, "The selective and repressive approach that has been adopted does not give territories that make tax attraction a pillar of their economies an incentive to associate themselves with the regulation of the condition of competition and will therefore fail to combat effectively the harmful excesses of tax competition that develops outside of all the rules. On the contrary it could reinforce the attraction of offshore centres with all the consequences that this implies"[13]. In other words, Switzerland was not prepared to disadvantage itself by accepting OECD rules that were not equally binding on other territories regarded as offshore centres. Hence, the determination by the OECD – driven by European Union countries – to trap non-OECD countries in the net of its harmful tax competition initiative. Switzerland had to be assured that it would not lose its financial services business before it would conform to EU requirements, and the EU needed Switzerland's co-operation to establish a level playing field in Europe. This was an important factor, though not the only one, pushing the OECD's HTCI.

WHAT THE OECD SCHEME IS ALL ABOUT

Two things should be kept in mind as a backdrop to the OECD's HTCI. The first is that the OECD countries are in the forefront of pressurizing the world into globalisation and liberalisation of trade and services, because they want unrestricted access to markets around the world for their goods and services. Developing countries must erect no barriers to the importation of products from industrialised countries and should give no protection to their own farmers and manufacturers. If they do, the OECD countries will take them to the World Trade Organisation where the Disputes Settlement Tribunal will force them into compliance or impose sanctions against them. The WTO's own organisational ideology is based on the mantra of globalisation and liberalisation.

The second is that the OECD countries are the principal advocates of the virtues and merits of competition in the provision of goods and services globally. For them "competition" is the new panacea for the world's economic ills, because their industrial and agricultural capacity has reached the point where it needs unrestricted entry to global markets to continue to provide employment and profits to their people. Yet, while they promote competition in everything else, they decry it in taxation.

Their objection derives from the fact that, in a globalised world, the mobility of financial and other services, such as shipping and Internet gambling, provided an opportunity for small states and posed a threat to them. The low tax or no tax regimes of these small states coupled with literacy in English and good telecommunications gave them an advantage with which many OECD countries could not compete. Instead of trying to vie with small states by lowering their own taxes, the OECD responded by demanding that these small jurisdictions change their tax systems and structures or face damaging sanctions.

THE HTCI: WHAT IT IS

The OECD HTCI is not about offshore banks only. There is a popular belief that the offshore banks are the sole targets of the OECD's work, and the cause of their stance against the targeted jurisdictions. This is another impression fostered by the OECD through a poorly informed media, to make the domestic private sectors in the targeted jurisdictions believe that the scheme bore no relation to them. By fostering such an impression, the OECD hoped that opinion-makers within targeted jurisdictions would take the view that their businesses were being put at risk merely to protect offshore banks, and therefore, they would pressure governments into acquiescing to OECD demands.

In an OECD paper entitled: *Globalization: Impact on Tax Policy and Administration,* the Organisation revealed its thinking behind the 'harmful tax competition' scheme. It says:

"In this new global environment multinational enterprises will continue to move their manufacturing activities to low-cost countries... All countries will be forced to compete for this footloose investment: either by lowering regulatory standards or creating incentives, particularly tax incentives, to attract business to their jurisdictions."[14]

This analysis suggests a fear in the OECD countries that they will lose investment in a range of activities to developing countries that offer tax incentives to win investors. Hence, the HTCI said that a jurisdiction has harmful tax regimes if it has preferential tax regimes designed to lure investors. The OECD booklet on its Global Forum on Taxation specifically states, "As economic and financial barriers disappear, tax differentials can have a more significant impact on trade and investment. Bidding wars to attract foreign direct investment, for example, erode tax bases throughout the world while providing little economic compensation"[15]. Further, a paper by the Commonwealth Secretariat revealed that the OECD plans to target e-commerce activities from non-OECD countries. The paper says:

"One of the initiatives is to develop a new fiscal approach to indirect taxation of e-commerce. This will require non-OECD suppliers to register in each OECD country for indirect tax payments and to pay indirect taxation in each of the OECD countries to which they export goods and services through e-commerce. This is envisaged to create substantial hurdles for small developing country entrepreneurs seeking to use e-commerce to overcome market access barriers of distance and cost into major OECD markets. The European Union countries would not be subject to such taxes within the EU boundaries due to harmonisation of indirect taxes, hence it would mainly affect developing country e-commerce exporters".[16]

In addition, the 1998 OECD Report on 'Harmful Tax Competition' flagged that "tax incentives designed to attract investment in plant, building and equipment" including manufacturing would be addressed later.[17] Many Caribbean countries and other states give fiscal incentives and have special legal and fiscal regimes to attract investment to particular sectors such as hotels, export processing zones and manufacturing. The extension of the scope of the OECD initiative beyond geographically-mobile services would affect most if not all of these countries.

The OECD's concern is that its member states will lose investors who would otherwise be subject to their high taxation. Their purpose is to tax the profits and interest income of those investors wherever they may be. The consequence would be to deprive small developing countries from advancing their economic development through their tax structures and systems.

Of course, the OECD argument comes after many of its member states have reached a high level of industrial development precisely because of tax competition in which they lured foreign investment into their countries by tax breaks. In fact, many of them still do. In the United States, for instance, institutions, both banks and non-banks, held more than $1.8 trillion in deposits from foreign persons at the end of 2000.[18] That money is there because the US exempted the holders of those accounts from taxes on their interest income. The US banking system, particularly in Florida and New York, would face collapse if these trillions of dollars were to be withdrawn and taken elsewhere – a fact well known to the Governor of the State of Florida, J.E. Bush, who lobbied strongly against US exchange of information with tax authorities of other governments, including OECD ones. In June 2001, Governor Bush sent a letter to US Treasury Secretary Paul O'Neill arguing that regulation, contemplated by the Inland Revenue Service, to allow information to be passed to other countries about interest payments made to their nationals "would place US banks at a competitive disadvantage relative to banks in the Caribbean and Europe... and would seriously hamper the ability of US banks to continue to attract foreign depositors."[19] The United Kingdom also operates similar regimes designed to lure funds to its banks and bond markets from overseas. It is therefore very significant that in its 1998 report, the OECD declared that, "the tax treatment of interest on cross-border savings instruments, particularly bank deposits, is not considered in this first stage of the project".[20]

The OECD countries also make no distinction between tax avoidance and tax evasion. In their desire to get information on persons and companies, they equate these two concepts denying their legal definitions and differences.

WHAT THE HTCI IS NOT

The OECD HTCI is not about money laundering and financial crime. The OECD has deliberately allowed an ill-informed international media and legislatures in OECD countries to assume that the scheme is directed at curbing money laundering because this has won them support.

The Financial Action Task Force (FATF), along with the UN Commission on money laundering, are the entities concerned with money laundering. Indeed, in a June 2000 report entitled: *Towards Global Tax Co-operation*, the OECD itself acknowledges quite clearly that "other institutions, such as the FATF and the UN Commission on money laundering, are addressing serious international criminal activities and money laundering in particular".[21] Of the 41 countries that the OECD has targeted, very few are on the FATF's money laundering blacklist.

Few can argue with any credibility that, as the year 2002 began, the anti-money laundering regimes in all but a small number of countries were not entirely consistent with the highest international standards. Most of the Caribbean jurisdictions are in full compliance with the criteria set by the FATF, a group established by the G7 countries in parallel with the OECD.[22]

COMPLYING WITH THE FATF CRITERIA

The FATF criteria for judging the compliance of jurisdictions were tough. They required a comprehensive review of laws, regulations and practices to ensure adherence to international best practices including rules for reporting and investigating suspicious activities, the requirement to know beneficial owners of bank accounts and international business corporations, and to share information on criminal matters. In the case of Antigua and Barbuda, Prime Minister Lester Bird established a Working Group to study the country's arrangements against the FATF criteria and to recommend any changes required to the legal, supervisory and enforcement regime that might be necessary to ensure compliance. As a consequence of that work, Antigua and Barbuda overhauled many of its laws, strengthened its supervisory capacity and enhanced its investigative facilities. Subsequently, the country was found by the FATF to be a fully co-operative jurisdiction in the fight against money laundering and was never 'named and shamed' on its list. Countries that were listed also undertook the tough task of similarly overhauling their systems.

Undoubtedly, compliance with the FATF criteria has cost every Caribbean country dearly. Many financial institutions and international business corporations have left Caribbean jurisdictions because they did not like the new regimes, or they were struck from the registers for non-compliance with the new rules and regulations. Governments lost much-needed revenue from licence fees, and their economies also lost much-wanted jobs. In addition, governments have faced increased costs by strengthening supervisory, regulatory and investigative mechanisms. But, at the end of the day the countries that have complied with the FATF criteria have made themselves more reputable and reliable and therefore more attractive to legitimate business. And, in the long run, it is legitimate business that will sustain these economies, provide jobs and increase revenue.

HTCI: A SWORD OF DAMOCLES

However, like a sword of Damocles, a threat hung over the financial services sector of the Caribbean, because of the 'harmful tax competition initiative' of the OECD even though there was universal recognition and acknowledgement of the considerable strides that several jurisdictions have made in establishing regimes to effectively combat money laundering and other financial crime.

Caribbean government representatives did much, at several levels, to sensitise the international community, including the new Administration in the US, to the wrongness of the OECD's original initiative. Heads of Government raised the HTCI with French President Jacque Chirac in 2000 at a meeting in Guadeloupe. They strongly argued against the unacceptable nature of the OECD scheme even though they received a frosty reception from him. In 2001, Caribbean leaders also made it clear to Canada's Prime Minister Jean Chretien and the new US President George W. Bush in separate meetings that they considered the HTCI to be fatally flawed. Representatives of Caribbean and Pacific members of the Commonwealth also pushed the issue at several Conferences of Commonwealth Ministers. Indeed, the matter became so divisive within the Commonwealth that, in June 2001, a representative of Australia actually announced at a London meeting that Australia, an OECD member, did not support the OECD publishing a list 'naming and shaming' targeted jurisdictions.[23] Australia was due to host and Chair the next Commonwealth Heads of Government Conference and did not want the gathering dominated by a fight between the group of wealthiest Commonwealth countries, including itself, and the group of smallest states.

THE COMMONWEALTH ROLE

At a Commonwealth organised Global Conference on the Development Agenda for Small States in February 2000, the targeted jurisdictions confronted the OECD for the first time in a multilateral forum. In the course of the meeting, Frances Horner the Head of the harmful tax practices unit in the Organisation, admitted that the conference's focus on the problems of small states "had been a learning experience". She said that the OECD recognised that its approach to implementing the HTCI may have been flawed and expressed an interest in a more consultative approach.

The Conference was followed by a meeting of Commonwealth Finance Ministers in Malta which mandated the Commonwealth Secretariat to facilitate multilateral dialogue between the targeted jurisdictions and the OECD. Consequently, the Commonwealth Secretariat organised a High Level Consultation in Barbados in January 2001 in which the OECD participated. While there was pressure on the four large Commonwealth countries that were also OECD members from the Commonwealth targeted jurisdictions, the OECD hoped to secure agreement for the HTCI at the Barbados meeting. The OECD was keenly aware that representatives of the Republican Party had spoken out against the HTCI in US Presidential elections in November. While the result of the US elections were still being fought in the Courts, it was fairly obvious that George W. Bush would become President and this would mean the end of the strong Democratic administration support which the HTCI had enjoyed.

However, at the Barbados meeting with both sides waiting to see what the Bush administration would do, no agreement was reached on the HTCI. Instead, it was agreed to establish a Joint Working Group of the OECD and the targeted jurisdictions.[24] The work of the Group will be described later in this Chapter. Suffice to say that, in relation to the Commonwealth, the Secretariat did much to keep the issue of the HTCI alive and to try to persuade the OECD to drop its arbitrary stance and adopt a consultative and more constructive dialogue with the targeted jurisdictions.

WHAT CAUSED THE OECD TO MODIFY ITS STANCE

In the end, it was the new Republican administration of George W. Bush, which came to office in January 2001, that caused the OECD to review the HTCI which had been strongly supported by the previous Democratic Party government of Bill Clinton and particularly by his Treasury Secretary, Lawrence Summers. Much of the success with the Bush government was due to the collaboration of some Caribbean governments with the Center of Freedom and Prosperity (CFP) in Washington. The Center was established by a group opposed to tax harmonisation and information exchange on the basis of the damage that would be done to the US economy. The CFP worked hard to inform members of the US Congress and Senate and the new US Government of the serious flaws in the OECD initiative. As a consequence, the new US Secretary of the Treasury, Paul O'Neill, caused the OECD to amend its Initiative.[25] While there were other countries, such as Canada, that earlier saw the wisdom of such change, they lacked the strength to resist the domination of the OECD by the 15 EU countries who had been the driving force behind this scheme. In the event, the OECD modified the HTCI in November 2001, but only to refocus it on what O'Neill called its "core element", i.e., "the need for (OECD) countries to be able to obtain specific information from other countries upon request in order to prevent non-compliance with their tax laws".[26] The British Chairman of the OECD's Committee on Fiscal Affairs, Gabriel Makhlouf, played a significant role in negotiating the deal with the US Treasury.

THE TWO SIDES MEET

In the first quarter of 2002, Caribbean countries entered the final phase of an unfortunate confrontation between the OECD and the jurisdictions around the world that they targeted as so-called 'tax havens'. By November 2001, when the OECD Council issued its 2001 report, it had succeeded in wresting commitments from five more jurisdictions. These were: Aruba, Bahrain, the Isle of Man, the Netherlands Antilles and The Seychelles. Additionally, Tonga had agreed to make legislative changes to areas that the OECD had identified as harmful in its June 2000 report.

In its modified proposals, the OECD set 28 February 2002 as the date on which it would 'name and shame' the remaining 29 jurisdictions as practicing 'harmful tax competition' unless they publicly stated their agreement to eliminate aspects of their fiscal arrangements that the OECD has determined to be harmful. Originally, this 'naming and shaming' exercise should have taken place in November 2000 and sanctions imposed against them. But, in the wake of strong resistance from the targeted jurisdictions and the international campaign in which the matter was raised in almost every global forum, the OECD agreed to delay implementing "co-ordinated defensive measures" against anyone until 31 July 2001. Instead, in November 2000, it named 35 jurisdictions as 'tax havens' and declared that a further list "would be developed in the next 12 months" for the purpose of applying sanctions.[27] The report excluded the names of the six jurisdictions that also met OECD criteria as 'tax havens', but had made "advance commitments".

In the interim, a Joint Working Group of OECD and non-OECD countries was established in January 2001 under the co-Chairmanship of the Prime Minister of Barbados, Owen Arthur and the Australian Ambassador to the OECD, Tony Hinton. That Joint Working Group met twice – first in London in January and then in Paris in March 2001.

The point of the Joint Working Group was to try to seek ways in which confrontation could be avoided and the concerns of the OECD could be met in a mutually satisfactory manner.

The thirty-five targeted jurisdictions had no interest in the failure of the Joint Working Group. Attracting sanctions, however wrong they may be, from the world's wealthiest countries was a daunting prospect for these small jurisdictions whose economies would suffer, as would civil order and democracy which could not be sustained in conditions of economic decline. At the same time, the jurisdictions did not feel they could simply surrender to OECD demands. Nor could they accept that they should not compete through tax incentives for a share of global investment. To do so would be to cause their death by a thousand cuts.

Therefore, at the meeting of the Joint Working Group in Paris on 2 March 2001, the targeted jurisdictions unanimously offered the following three things to the OECD in writing:

(a) to sign a letter of commitment to the principles of non-discrimination, transparency and effective exchange of information as an entitlement to join the OECD's Global Tax Forum and its working groups so as to contribute to the development of principles and standards applicable to OECD and non-OECD jurisdictions,

(b) to complete a plan for implementing agreed principles by 31 July 2001, and

(c) to implement undertakings of an agreed plan by 31 December 2005. In return for these commitments, the targeted jurisdictions requested (i) no less favourable treatment in tax matters than is given to any OECD country, (ii) participation as equals in the decision-making process of an expanded Global Tax Forum that would include OECD and non-OECD jurisdictions, and (iii) the lifting of the threat of sanctions.

The OECD representatives on the Joint Working Group expressed 'discomfort' with some of the details of the proposal and asked to put forward new language 'in the course of the week'. Many of them, particularly the French representative Bruno Gilbert who was a Co-Chair of the OECD's Forum on Harmful Tax Practices, were adamant that their own, ironically named, 'Global Forum on Taxation' is the only forum in which the HTCI should be discussed. The only concession that they made to membership of the Forum was that targeted jurisdictions would be allowed to participate only after they blindly accepted the OECD's definition of the three broad principles and publicly declared such acceptance.

Amazingly to the non-OECD members of the Working Group, the new language that should have been submitted 'in the course of the week' took five months to be delivered along with answers to seventeen questions which were posed to the OECD in written form. On 17 July 2001, Ambassador Hinton, as Co-Chair of the Joint Working Group, wrote Prime Minister Arthur, as the other Co-Chair, forwarding a set of responses. The questions were designed to ascertain from the OECD whether or not its own member states would be bound by the same rules that were being applied to the targeted jurisdictions. The answers, none of which was plain and explicit, clouded the issues even more and gave rise to deeper suspicion about the motives behind the OECD's 'harmful tax competition' scheme.

WHAT THE OECD SOUGHT IN ITS 2001 REPORT

The OECD's modified proposal was contained in its document, *The OECD's Project on Harmful Tax Practices: The 2001 Progress Report* issued in November 2001. Effectively, the OECD decided to extend the deadline for 'naming and shaming' from 31 July 2001 to 28 February 2002 and to delay the imposition of sanctions to an unannounced date which, it said, would coincide with the applications of sanctions against their own defaulting members. Additionally, it had removed one of its criteria for naming a jurisdiction as a 'tax haven'. The criterion was: the existence of companies with 'no substantial activities' in the country. Such entities were regarded as 'ring fenced' if the tax regime it enjoyed was available only to non-resident investors or if its activities were limited to international transactions. It was well known by this time that the new United States government had insisted on the removal of this criterion as a condition of continued support for the HTCI, no doubt to protect the activities of places, such as Delaware and Montana, which were well known centres for registering companies with no substantial activities in those States and which enjoyed a "ring-fenced" regime.

According to the OECD's new proposals the HTCI would focus on only two things: 'transparency' and 'effective exchange of information'. These would be the only criteria to determine which jurisdictions were to be considered as un-co-operative tax havens".[28]

The document did not attempt to define what was meant by "effective exchange of information' saying only that appropriate safeguards would be implemented to ensure that information is used only for the purpose for which it is sought. It also did not define 'transparency', but US Treasury Secretary, Paul O'Neill provided details in a Statement to a US Senate Committee. He said, 'transparency means two things: (1) the absence of non-public tax practices, such as secret negotiation, or waiver, of public tax laws and tax administration rules; and (2) the absence of obstacles, such as strict bank secrecy or the use of bearer shares, to obtaining financial or beneficial ownership information within a jurisdiction'.[29]

The OECD Report indicated that jurisdictions that made commitments on 'transparency' and 'effective exchange of information' would have a year in which to develop plans to implement them. The Organisation wanted these commitments before 28 February 2002 when, as already noted, they planned to 'name and shame' jurisdictions by publishing a list that would declare them 'un-co-operative jurisdictions'. The Report also indicated that the OECD member-states would not apply sanctions against non-OECD countries any earlier than they would apply such sanctions against their own members who did not amend their harmful tax practices. While the OECD gave no date for the application of such sanctions, in his statement to the Senate Committee, the US Treasury Secretary indicated that this would not be 'until April 2003 at the earliest'.

Some of the things all the 41 jurisdictions were required to do were:

- provide information to tax authorities in OECD countries upon request and without the approval of the Courts for both criminal and civil tax matters with no regard to confidentiality laws. Information requested would not be limited to money laundering and tax evasion, and could be used to allow for other investigations.
- all resident companies, including domestic ones, would be required to keep financial accounts which are to be audited and filed with tax authorities.
- the beneficial owners of all bank accounts, companies, and trusts, both offshore and domestic must be known, and be capable of being revealed.

- there should be no negotiation with an investor over tax rates regardless of the size of the investment.

These small states, many of them former colonies of OECD countries, were being asked to take a leap of faith, one in which trust is placed in their former colonial masters not to take advantage of them once an advance binding commitment is given. It was not easy to take such a leap. After all, the historical experience was not one that bred trust; to the contrary it nurtured suspicion.

In sum, the OECD scheme appeared to be a dagger pointed at the heart of the capacity of small states to diversify and develop their economies and look after the welfare of their people. If the scheme were to be implemented, it would be another measure that helped to relegate them to the backwater of social and economic development and consign them to an existence on the margins of global life.

This point was acknowledged by the OECD when, in their several reports, they urged that the targeted jurisdictions dismantle their tax structure, accepting in its place aid and technical assistance. In other words, these small states should curb their ambition to compete for a place in the world, and accept instead the role of beggar living off the crumbs that fall from the table of the wealthy.

DOES THE OECD HAVE THE PROPER AUTHORITY?

In its communications, the OECD had indicated that jurisdictions that make a commitment would be invited to participate in the OECD's Global Forum Working Group that is addressing the two principles of "transparency" and "effective exchange of information".

But a fundamental difficulty still remained. It was one that had far-reaching implications and was by no means limited to this particular initiative of the OECD. Simply put, the difficulty was this. Should 41 jurisdictions around the world accept that the OECD has the right or authority to set itself up to make tax rulings which they expect non-members to follow? By doing this, would these 41 jurisdictions, targeted by the OECD as 'tax havens', not be opening the floodgates to a raft of other demands by an organisation with no international authority except the coercive power of its member states?

It should be recalled that the OECD is a multinational grouping of thirty countries. It is not an international organisation and it has no legal authority to speak for the world or to establish rules, norms or standards for any state except its own members. Nonetheless, it is now dictating terms on what, in short, could be described as cross-border tax matters.

It is significant that in the November 2001 modification to the HTCI, the OECD continued to assert that the modifications do not 'affect the application of the 1998 Report' whose factors for identifying tax havens 'remain unchanged'. This assertion is open to the interpretation that while the OECD had made a tactical withdrawal on one front, it had not abandoned the battlefield altogether and may have been merely postponing a further onslaught until after it had secured an opening into the camp of the affected jurisdictions and weakened their capacity for resistance.

Caribbean Governments could not disregard this important dimension of the problem. They had to take serious account of it in reaching a decision about whether or not to make a commitment to the OECD on the two remaining aspects of the HTCI. By the same token, they also had to consider carefully the consequences to their economies of the application of sanctions by those members of the OECD who are important partners to them in trade and financial services. The key players in this regard would have been the US, Canada and the UK.

PROPOSED OECD SANCTIONS

What are the sanctions that would be applied? The US Treasury Secretary told the US Senate Committee that the work in the OECD to refine the identification of appropriate sanctions is still at an early stage, but that some of the measures already identified have been part of the international tax policy of the US and other OECD countries for many years. They include enhanced audit and enforcement activities with respect to transactions and jurisdictions which may be used by their taxpayers to evade tax, and no tax treaties, such as double taxation agreements. Mr O'Neill also pointed out that the sanctions envisaged by the OECD would require legislation in the US and therefore would have to be approved by Congress.

The OECD 2001 Progress Report which contained its new proposals for the HTCI said that, in designing 'a framework of co-ordinated defensive measures', the OECD Committee on Fiscal Affairs would be guided by several considerations: (i) defensive measures should be proportionate and targeted at neutralizing the deleterious effects of harmful tax practices: (ii) the adoption of defensive measures is at the discretion of individual countries; and (iii) each country can choose to enforce defensive measures in a way that is proportionate and prioritised according to the extent of harm that a particular practice has the potential to inflict.[30]

In the event, it may well be that any 'defensive measures' or 'sanctions' that OECD countries impose on the targeted jurisdictions are challengeable under the dispute settlement provisions of the World Trade Organisation. Certainly, it is the opinion of reputable legal authorities in OECD countries that such a challenge could be successfully mounted. The targeted jurisdictions, acting together could yet request the establishment of a tribunal to test the legality of any sanctions imposed by OECD countries against targeted jurisdictions in the context of the HTCI. Sometime in the future, they might yet have to do so.

SEPTEMBER 11 ALTERS THE PICTURE

While Caribbean jurisdictions and others pondered how to deal with the pending OECD deadline for the naming of "un-co-operative jurisdictions", the atrocities of 11 September 2001 occurred. The terrorist attack on the World Trade Centre in New York and the Pentagon in Washington changed the thinking in the United States dramatically, including in the US Treasury.

Whereas prior to 11 September, Treasury Secretary Paul O'Neill and his staff opposed certain aspects of the HTCI and were lukewarm on the rest of it, the attitude changed in the wake of the atrocities. Evidence of the changed mood in the US was an executive order by President George W. Bush on 23 September 2001 requiring jurisdictions to establish a new counter-terrorism economic sanction and export control regime under the threat of more economic penalties. Further, the US introduced the Patriot Act imposing a series of extra-territorial measures targeting offshore financial institutions in the belief that they could be used to fund terrorist organisations. The belief that the terrorists and particularly the al-Qaeda organisation of Osama Bin Laden had used offshore financial centres to move money to finance their activities caused the US Treasury to temper its criticism of the OECD HTCI. In the first place, the US needed the other OECD member-states to help forge its coalition against terrorism, and in the second it was easy to believe that financial institutions in small jurisdictions might have unwittingly provided facilities for terrorist organisations through legitimate companies. It doesn't matter that, as it turns out, most of the terrorist bank accounts were actually in OECD countries including the US and the UK.

By November 2001, the United Kingdom government was advising its embassies in the targeted jurisdictions that the US commitment to the project (HTCI) in its modified form is firm. The word was that the events of 11 September had led the US to look more critically at offshore financial centres because of the potential risk of them being used by terrorists.

For their part, Caribbean governments realised that they could no longer rely on the new Republican administration in the US to continue to modify the OECD's HTCI.

As the deadline of 28 February 2002 approached, both Caribbean jurisdictions and the OECD eyed the date anxiously. The OECD Secretariat was desperate not to appear to have failed to get commitments from the small and relatively insignificant targeted jurisdictions. For their part, Caribbean jurisdictions were keen to maintain a solid front in any decision they made. If they continued to resist the OECD, they wanted to do so together, calculating that it would be unlikely that the OECD member states would apply sanctions against all the Caribbean jurisdictions. They also bargained that if the Caribbean, as a whole, were to give the OECD a commitment, not only would a level playing field be created in the region as a whole, but the terms of such a commitment could be jointly negotiated and, therefore, would be more advantageous than any conditions individual jurisdictions might secure.

ATTENTION FOCUSED ON BARBADOS

Barbados became a particular focus of attention by the United Kingdom Treasury whose officers were among the hardliners in the OECD. Gabriel Makhlouf was both the Head of the International Relations Department of the UK Treasury and Chairman of the OECD's Fiscal Affairs Committee. Diplomatic circles in London in late 2001 noted that the Barbados Prime Minister, Owen Arthur, wanted the threat of naming and shaming dropped but that the UK Treasury was insisting that this has been an essential part of the OECD's process without which there would be no need for the targeted jurisdictions to comply. In the event the decision was made by the OECD's Committee on Fiscal Affairs to focus efforts on persuading Barbados to commit to the HTCI. Gabriel Makhlouf was identified as a possibility to talk to the Barbados government.

Caribbean Heads of Government were due to meet in Belize, one of the targeted jurisdictions, on 4 February 2002, three weeks before the deadline set by the OECD for the "tax havens" to make a commitment to work with the OECD in establishing "transparency" and "effective exchange of information". It was generally felt that the current position with the OECD HTCI would be discussed in Belize and a joint position taken by the thirteen affected Caribbean jurisdictions.[31]

Nine of the Caribbean jurisdictions were meeting in Anguilla on 31 January 2002 as the Organisation of Eastern Caribbean States. The OECD matter was not on their agenda. However, during the course of their meeting, it was drawn to their attention that the OECD and Barbados had issued a joint statement that morning announcing that "Barbados will not appear on the forthcoming list of un-co-operative tax havens. Discussions have shown that Barbados has transparent tax and regulatory systems and has in place a mechanism that enables it to engage in effective exchange of information". The joint press release went on to say, "Barbados is also willing to enter into tax information exchange arrangements with those OECD member countries with which it currently does not have such arrangements".

The Anguilla meeting received the news with surprise and

bewilderment particularly as many of the Heads of Government had left the lead role on dealing with the OECD to Prime Minister Arthur and they expected that, if there were a change in Barbados' circumstances, they would have been informed prior to any public announcement. The Heads of government formally noted that the removal of Barbados by the OECD from its blacklist "could have implications" for them.[32] However, privately many expressed great disappointment over this development, calculating that their resistance of the OECD would be greatly weakened. As it turned out, when all the Heads of Government of the Caribbean Community and Common Market (CARICOM) met in Belize a few days later on 4 February, no one raised the issue even though it had been on the agenda of every meeting over the preceding two years.

Subsequently, criticisms of Barbados appeared in the region and international press accusing it of weakening the position of the targeted OECD jurisdictions.[33] This caused Prime Minister Arthur to make a robust defence of his government at a press conference on 5 March 2002. He stated that, "the OECD had in its deliberate judgement decided to take Barbados off the list". A report of the press conference circulated by the Barbados Ministry of Economic Development on 6 March 2002, said:

"When the OECD took a decision to reform the initiative, it decided that the issue of discriminatory taxation would no longer be part of the initiative. In the circumstances, Barbados took the position that it had no issue to face with the OECD, because the country had already been compliant as regards transparency and exchange of information. The OECD agreed".

Significantly, Prime Minister Arthur insisted that "there were still outstanding issues" and he went on to explain these as the absence in the international community of "evolved international norms or agreements to deal with cross-border tax matters". He said, "Since that was the case, these issues would continue to be of concern especially for small states."

TARGETED JURISDICTIONS GIVE CONDITIONAL COMMITMENTS

Several Caribbean countries, led by Antigua and Barbuda, then took the decision to make a commitment to work with the OECD on the principles of "transparency" and "effective exchange of information". The Prime Minister of Antigua and Barbuda, Lester Bird, in a statement on 20 February, made it clear that his government was doing so not only because the "OECD has considerably modified those aspects of its original harmful tax competition initiative which cause us great concern", but also because "Antigua and Barbuda will participate as an equal partner with OECD countries in the Global Forum so that we can protect our interests and ensure a level playing field in financial services".

Representatives of the Antigua and Barbuda government had met on 18 and 19 January 2002 in Antigua with a team from the OECD to hammer out an agreement. At the end of the meeting, government representatives said, "great progress has been made in the discussions, however no decision has yet been made about whether or not Antigua and Barbuda will make a commitment. Prime Minister Bird will consult with our Caribbean partners at the forthcoming CARICOM Heads of government conference in Belize in early February".[34] During those discussions, the Antigua and Barbuda team had insisted on a level playing field for all countries – OECD non-members and OECD members alike – as a precondition to making a commitment to the OECD. The government argued that if the OECD failed to apply the same standards of transparency and effective exchange of information to all of Antigua and Barbuda's potential competitors including OECD members, this would be ground for abandoning the commitment. The OECD team accepted this position.

The insistence on a level playing field became a condition precedent to any commitment to the OECD by all Caribbean countries. By early March, all the Caribbean jurisdictions and many others had decided to work with the OECD but only on the condition that a level playing field be established among all OECD members countries and those non-member jurisdictions with which there is material competition in the provision of cross border financial services. Their position was summarised by the Minister of Finance of The Bahamas, Sir William Allen, who said in a statement on 15 March;

> "The success of this OECD initiative rests on the adherence to the principle of parity in the obligations assumed by all jurisdictions, OECD and non-OECD member counties in relation to standards and timelines in the move to greater transparency and information exchange. Clearly, if this principle is not observed financial services business will migrate from one financial service centre to another and the stated objective of the OECD initiative will, therefore, be defeated".

This position found support among Commonwealth Heads of Government when they met in Australia from 2 to 5 March for a meeting that had been postponed from October 2001 in the aftermath of the atrocities in the United States on 11 September. Among the governments that agreed the Communiqué were four OECD member-states, Australia, Britain, Canada and New Zealand. They reiterated that, "the standards and timelines for non-OECD jurisdictions should be no more onerous than those for OECD members."[35]

It is left to be seen whether the OECD will honour its commitment to a level playing field for all, particularly as this will mean applying sanctions against their own member states such as Switzerland and Luxembourg who have, so far, shown no inclination to accept the principles set out in the HTCI. A level playing field also means that countries such as the US and UK may also have to change existing regimes in financial services that compete with many of the targeted jurisdictions. Before this test, however, the OECD countries will have to convince the targeted jurisdictions that their participation in the Global Forum is meaningful and that their views will carry equal weight in the definition and application of the concepts of transparency and effective exchange of information.

The entire initiative may yet collapse if there is any evidence of bad faith. What is certain is that none of the targeted jurisdictions – not even the five who gave an early commitment – did so willingly. A great deal of bitterness and anger surrounded their acquiescence to the OECD's coercion. Each of them knew that simply appearing on and OECD blacklist was in itself a sanction, staining the reputation of their financial services sector. They had little choice, and it galled them.

THE FUTURE OF FINANCIAL
SERVICES FOR SMALL STATES

Essentially, from the OECD standpoint, the HTCI is about pursuing their nationals who, they believe, may be evading the payment of their taxes. There is no proof that their premise is correct. For instance, US Treasury Secretary, Paul O'Neill himself told the US Senate Committee that 'it is impossible to quantify precisely the extent to which US tax payers are using offshore entities to evade their US tax obligations'. The information, he said, is 'anecdotal', but he believes that the 'potential' is significant.[36]

Therefore, small jurisdictions are being expected by the OECD to institute measures and practices to facilitate a hunch that some of their taxpayers may be evading taxes. However, these measures may have the effect of causing perfectly legitimate activities to leave – or to not come – to these jurisdictions simply because they want to maintain the privacy of their business. In other words, the financial services sector and economies of small states could suffer real hardship because of the desire by OECD countries to seek out possible tax evaders rather than known tax evaders.

MOST OFFSHORE FINANCIAL SERVICES
ARE IN OECD COUNTRIES

The truth is that 80 percent of the total offshore financial services industry is located in the OECD countries, excluding their colonies. The remaining 20 percent is in the non-OECD countries, with even this segment dominated by a few large centres such as Hong Kong and Singapore which, conveniently, the OECD had not named as 'tax havens'. This means that approximately less than ten percent of offshore business in the world is done in the targeted jurisdictions. The law of averages suggests, therefore, that very little tax-evasion money may be in the Caribbean and other small states at all. Much of it may well be in the OECD countries themselves. It is noteworthy that on the money laundering side, while much publicity always surrounds illegal activity that is uncovered in the Caribbean, the actual incidents and sums involved are a very tiny fraction of the numerous incidents and vast sums of money that are unearthed in the OECD countries.

Account should also be taken of the fact that searches of banks throughout the world for money used to finance terrorism in the wake of the atrocities of 11 September 2001 in New York and Washington, revealed that most of the hundreds of millions of dollars of the al-Qaeda organisation and other terrorist groups was found in the banks of OECD countries. Only US$20 million was discovered in The Bahamas after a search by that country's authorities, and even then it was in a branch of a bank headquartered in an OECD country.

THE RIGHT TO COMPETE IGNORED

Caribbean countries and other small jurisdictions have the same right as others to compete in the global financial services sector. Their well-educated populations, their high propensity for computer literacy, the relatively lower costs of business in comparison with others, their first class telecommunications and low tax levels give them international competitiveness. During the years 1999 to 2000, they moved rapidly to a better-supervised financial system, onshore and offshore. Most of the Caribbean countries now meet international standards that compare favourably with the best practices.

Seen as weak and powerless jurisdictions, small states in the Caribbean and the Pacific have been victims of the worst form of bullying by big, strong and powerful nations that the world has witnessed since the 19th Century.

Indeed, the 21st Century dawned with ominous signs that there were those who yearned for a return to a world ruled not by principles of justice and fairness, but by power and force. And, while Caribbean countries and other small jurisdictions made a brave fight against considerable odds in taking on the OECD and delaying its programme of fiscal colonialism, it was unlikely that the Organisation and its powerful member-states would accept defeat.

The HTCI may well come to be regarded as a failure by the world's wealthiest nations to grasp an opportunity for international co-operation, opting instead to enforce their will by a raw display of power. This display struck a massive blow against the principle of multilateralism and the rule of international law. It was more massive because its victims were small and powerless.

But, its success is pregnant with dangers for more than just small and powerless states. As a Commonwealth paper pointed out, "Many countries give fiscal incentives and have special legal and fiscal regimes to attract investment to particular sectors, (such as export processing zones in the manufacturing and service sectors, and the development of petroleum and mining sectors). It is likely that these countries, by an extension of the scope of the OECD HTCI beyond geographically mobile services, could be considered as engaging in potentially harmful tax practices with regimes that could be categorised as preferential regimes".[37]

The OECD's enforcement of the HTCI by crude power policies and practices could set undesirable precedents not only for the future of international tax setting and compliance, but for internationalism itself. The small are the bully's first victims; they are seldom the last.

NOTES & REFERENCES

1   The Organisation for Economic Co-operation and Development (OECD) comprises 30 of the world's richest countries including its founder members, Austria, Belgium, Canada, Denmark, France, Germany, Iceland, Italy, Luxembourg, Portugal, Sweden, Switzerland, Turkey, the United States and the United Kingdom. Japan joined in 1964.

2   Gaffney, Mason in Racheter, Donald P, and Richard E Wagner (eds), *Federalist Government in Principle and Practice*, Boston, Kluwer Academic Publishers, 2000.

3   Persaud, Prof. Bishnodat, 'OECD Curbs on Offshore Financial Centres: A major issue for small states', *The Round Table: The Commonwealth Journal of International Affairs*, number 359, April 2001, London.

4   The independent Commonwealth Member states were: (Caribbean) Antigua and Barbuda, The Bahamas, Barbados, Belize, Dominica, Grenada, St Lucia, St Vincent and the Grenadines, St Kitts-Nevis, (Africa) The Seychelles, Mauritius, (Pacific/Asia) Nauru, Samoa, Tonga, Vanuatu, (Mediterranean) Cyprus, Malta. The UK Overseas Territories or colonies were: (Caribbean) Anguilla, British Virgin Islands, Montserrat, and Turks and Caicos, (Europe) Isle of Man, Jersey, Guernsey, Gibraltar. The New Zealand Overseas Territories were: (Pacific) Cook Islands and Niue.

5   *Harmful Tax Competition: An Emerging Global Issue*, OECD, Paris, 1998.

6   *Op. Cit.*, Note v, p. 27.

7   Circular letter to Heads of Income Tax Departments of 41 jurisdictions dated 15 February 1999 and signed by Bruno Gilbert (France) and Phil West (USA), Co-Chairs of the OECD Forum on Harmful tax practices.

8   See, UK Treasury Press Release 71/1998 of 9 May 1998.

9   See, Explanatory Memorandum in *Proposal for a Council Directive to ensure a minimum of effective taxation on savings income in the form of interest payments within the Community,* Commission of the European Communities Document COM (1998) 295 of 20 May 1998.

10 *Towards Global Tax Co-operation: Report to the 2000 Ministerial Council Meeting and Recommendations by the Committee on Fiscal Affairs*, OECD, Paris, 2000, p. 12, para 10.

11 *Ibid., p. 9, para 5.*

12 *Op. Cit., Note v, pp 73-77.*

13 *Ibid., p. 78.*

14 presented to a Ministerial Conference hosted by the Government of Barbados in association with the Commonwealth Secretariat and the Global Forum on International Taxation of the OECD, 8-9 January 2001.

15 *Global Forum on Taxation*, OECD, Paris, 2000.

16 *Current Status of OECD's Harmful Tax Competition Initiative*, Paper CGSS 10(01)4, Commonwealth Secretariat, London, prepared for Tenth Meeting of Commonwealth Consultative Group on Small States on 28 August 2001.

17 Op. Cit., Note v, p. 8, para 6.

18 King, Harlan W, 'The International Investment position of the United States at Yearend 2000', *Survey of Current Business*, US Department of Commerce, July 2001

19 Cited in 'US Treasury to review proposed information exchange rules', by Mike Godfrey, in *Tax-News.com* on 3 July 2001, *www.tax-news.com.*

20 *Op. Cit.* Note v, p. 9, para 12.

21 *Towards Global Tax Co-operation: Report to the 2000 Ministerial Council Meeting and Recommendations by the Committee on Fiscal Affairs*, OECD, Paris, 2000.

22 In January 2002, of the twelve Independent Commonwealth Caribbean countries, only four Dominica, St Vincent and The Grenadines, St Kitts-Nevis and Grenada were still on

the FATF black list as "non-co-operative" jurisdictions is relation to money laundering. The Bahamas was taken off in September 2001. None of the non-independent Caribbean territories were on the list; the Cayman Islands which was originally on the list was also taken off in September 2001.

23 Commonwealth Secretariat Resource Week meeting at Marlborough House, London, 25 June 2001.

24 The Joint Working Group was Co-Chaired by Australia and Barbados and included Antigua and Barbuda, the British Virgin Islands, the Cook Islands, France, Ireland, Japan, Malaysia, Malta, The Netherlands, the United Kingdom and Vanuatu.

25 See, Statement of Paul H. O'Neill before the Senate Committee on Governmental Affairs Permanent Subcommittee on Investigations, OECD Harmful Tax Practices Initiative, 18 July 2001.

26 *Ibid.*

27 *Op. Cit.*, Note x, p. 17. The 35 jurisdictions were: (Europe) Andorra, Isle of Man, Jersey, Gibraltar, Guernsey, Liechtenstein, Monaco (Africa) Liberia, Seychelles, (Caribbean) Antigua and Barbuda, Anguilla, Aruba, Bahamas, Barbados, British Virgin Islands, Belize, Dominica, Grenada, Montserrat, Netherland Antilles, Panama, St Kitts and Nevis, St Lucia, St Vincent and The Grenadines, Turks and Caicos, US Virgin Islands (Asia'Pacific) Cook Islands, Marshall Islands, Maldives, Nauru, Niue, Samoa, Tonga, Vanuatu, (Middle East) Bahrain.

28 *The OECD's Project on Harmful Tax Practices: The 2001 Progress Report,* OECD, Paris, 2001, p. 10, para. 28, and detailed in paras 37 and 38.

29 *Op. Cit.,* Note xxv.

30 *Op. Cit.,* Note xxviii, p. 13.

31 These were the independent states of Antigua and Barbuda, The Bahamas, Barbados, Belize, Dominica, Grenada, St Kitts-Nevis, St Lucia, St Vincent & The Grenadines; and the three British overseas territories of Anguilla, British Virgin Islands and Turks and Caicos.

32 Summary of decisions of The Thirty-Fifth Meeting of the Authority of the Organisation of Eastern Caribbean States in Anguilla, 31 January-1 February 2002.

33 See, for example, *The Financial Times*, 5 March 2002.

34 See, press release, "Antigua and Barbuda team and OECD conclude two-day discussions", St John's, 18 January 2002.

35 Communiqué of the Commonwealth Heads of Government Meeting in Coolum, Australia, 5 March 2002.

36 *Op. Cit.*, note xxv.

37 *Op. Cit.*, Note xvi, p. 4, para 14.

CHAPTER THIRTEEN

Crime in the Caribbean: An Overwhelming Phenomenon[1]

If "transnational crimes" were defined as drug trafficking, international gunrunning, money laundering, cross border fraud, theft of intellectual property, terrorism and terrorism financing, and facilitation of tax evasion, we would find that several of them either do not exist in the Caribbean or they are at a level that poses no significant threat to the international community.

Certainly, this observation is true of theft of intellectual property, the facilitation of tax evasion, cross border fraud, international gunrunning, and terrorism and terrorism financing.

It is also arguable that, today, the instances and volume of money laundering are not a significant threat either to the Caribbean or the international community.

Drug trafficking is the principal transnational crime in the Caribbean. But let us consider those which are not.

TERRORISM FINANCING

To deal with terrorism financing first, in the aftermath of September 11th, it was discovered that financial transactions for terrorist groups occurred regularly in eleven of the thirty OECD countries including the US, the UK, Switzerland, Germany and Austria. By comparison only six non-OECD countries were found to have handled terrorist accounts and only three were Caribbean jurisdictions.

The sums unearthed by the three Caribbean jurisdictions were *de minimis* in comparison with the huge amounts found elsewhere.

In the event, Caribbean countries were among the first to sign-up to UN Security Council Resolution 1373 on Terrorism and Terrorism Financing, and Caribbean jurisdictions were also among the lead countries to pass counter terrorism financing legislation. Included in that legislation is provision for immediate freezing of assets leading to forfeiture, and severe penalties including jail sentences for terrorists associated with financial transactions and the financial institutions that facilitate them.

TAX EVASION AND EXCHANGE OF INFORMATION AGREEMENTS

With respect to the facilitation of tax evasion, it is instructive that 80 percent of the world's financial services centres are located in OECD countries, excluding their colonies. The remaining 20 percent is in the non-OECD countries, with even this segment dominated by a few large centres such as Hong Kong. This means that less than ten percent of the world's financial services business is conducted from the 41 jurisdictions targeted by the OECD as "tax havens". Of those 41 jurisdictions, less than half are Caribbean.

The law of averages suggests, therefore, that apart from anecdotal information, there is little evidence to support the claim that tax-evasion money is swimming around in Caribbean banks.

Nonetheless, all the Commonwealth Caribbean jurisdictions have signed Tax Information Exchange Agreements with the United States, and several have such agreements with other countries.

In any event, tax evasion is a crime in the majority of Caribbean countries, and many of them have Mutual Legal Assistance Treaties with the United States and other countries.

The point is that, through these Mutual Legal Assistance Treaties and Tax Information Exchange Agreements, Caribbean countries have demonstrated a willingness to exchange information with other countries on tax evasion cases and to co-operate in the prosecution of offenders.

THE OECD AND EXCHANGE OF INFORMATION

The Caribbean had a different problem with the OECD and its "harmful tax competition initiative" which sought to address exchange of information on 'civil' as distinct from 'criminal matters', and which equated tax 'avoidance' with tax 'evasion', the latter being a crime in most Caribbean jurisdictions and the former being perfectly acceptable in most countries in the world including many in the OECD.

The Region's problem with the OECD stemmed from what could be called in short, the "usurpation of global governance".

The OECD is not an international organisation. It has no legal authority to set and impose standards and practices on any jurisdictions except its own membership.

Yet, in attempting to enforce its 'harmful tax competition initiative' upon 41 small jurisdictions mostly in the Caribbean and the Pacific, that is precisely what it was attempting to do. It was arrogating to itself the authority of an international law enforcement body to dictate global governance of cross-border tax matters.

What is more, it created a blacklist of jurisdictions and threatened them with sanctions if they did not comply.

Any such sanctions would probably have been open to challenge at the World Trade Organisation. One day, they still may be.

For the time being, however, the targeted jurisdictions agreed to participate with the OECD in a so-called "Global Forum" to explore the OECD's requirements for exchange of information related to tax matters provided that a level playing field was established for all. In other words, the expectation was that rules would be agreed by all and applied equally to all.

Then in January 2003, the European Union countries, many of whom are OECD members, decided to exclude three of their member states from requirements for exchange of information and extended the exclusion to two other OECD members, Switzerland and the United States, on what amounts to an open-ended arrangement.

Meanwhile the targeted jurisdictions, including those in the Caribbean, are required to comply with the exchange of information requirements by 2005.

Naturally some of the affected governments have called a halt to this process. Antigua and Barbuda, for one, has demanded a meeting of the Global Forum to decide whether there is any merit left in the OECD initiative.[2] Caribbean Community Heads of Government have endorsed Antigua and Barbuda's position on this matter. The Secretary-General of the OECD, Mr Don Johnston, has agreed to a meeting of the Global Forum but the OECD members are experiencing some difficulty in setting a date.[3]

The OECD is mentioned at such length because often the 'harmful tax competition initiative' is paraded as if it is related to crime. It is not. Its focus is cross-border tax matters of a civil nature.

Even more serious is that the way the "initiative" was handled demonstrates a readiness by the big and powerful to bully the small and weak.

MONEY LAUNDERING

The Caribbean experience with the global governance of money laundering issues was not dissimilar to its experience with the OECD on harmful tax.

The Financial Action Task Force (FATF) was the creation of a handful of rich nations which took it upon themselves to produce 40 Recommendations to counter money laundering and to impose them on selected areas of the world using the threat of sanctions to force compliance.

In this case, while there was every virtue in the objective that the FATF identified: to curb money laundering and financial crime, it was the manner in which the matter was handled that galled jurisdictions worldwide. It appeared to many to be nothing short of a usurpation of global governance by rich nations with the clout to do so.

What is noteworthy is that while much adverse publicity surrounded the few illegal activities that were uncovered in the Caribbean, the actual incidents and sums involved were a very tiny fraction of the numerous incidents and vast sums of money that were unearthed, and continued to be discovered, in many of the FATF countries.

Indeed, to date, no study has been produced to show that the number and volume of transactions in the Caribbean connected to money laundering and financing of terrorism undermine the global financial system. Caribbean jurisdictions, under the umbrella of the Caribbean Financial Action Task Force (CFATF) have decided to commission such a study to be undertaken by a legal firm in the United States.

Nonetheless, over the past four years, the Caribbean has readily adopted the FATF's 40 Recommendations on money laundering and its more recent eight recommendations on terrorism financing.

Throughout the region, Governments have established legislative, regulatory, supervisory and enforcement machinery to implement the FATF's recommendations, and, in some cases, to go beyond them.

With only one exception, every Caribbean country that was included in the FATF's blacklist of non-co-operative countries and territories has now been removed.[4] This process was not easy. Governments had to make very hard choices by moving scarce resources previously allocated to health, education, and much needed physical infrastructure to comply with the requirements of the FATF.

The significant anti money laundering legislation that has been instituted in the Caribbean Region has resulted in the virtual collapse of the offshore sector in one jurisdiction. In all of them, there has been a significant reduction in the number of businesses, revenue and employment.

In the case of one country, The Bahamas, US$36 million were spent setting-up machinery demanded by the FATF. Every other country spent amounts that, in relation to their Budgets, were similar in size to The Bahamas.

In Antigua and Barbuda, for instance, where the register for offshore banks numbered over 50 in 1998, there were only 15 banks in March 2003.

This is due not only to strict compliance with FATF requirements but also to adherence to the US Patriot Act and the recommendations of the Basle Committee which require that these banks have a physical presence in the jurisdiction including not only books and records but 'mind and management' as well. Many of these institutions could not afford to lay-out even more capital to fulfil these new obligations.

All this is taking place during a period that the President of the Caribbean Development Bank, Professor Compton Bourne, describes in this way:

"In terms of the standard measures of economic performance, Caribbean states are wobbly. Economic growth rates which averaged between two percent and four percent per annum during the 1990s have fallen, some into the negative zone. Unemployment rates have increased in some countries, while not decreasing significantly in others. Vulnerability to external economic shocks and to natural disasters has not lessened. Caribbean countries lack economic resilience.

The main industries, except petroleum and natural gas in Trinidad and Tobago, face formidable challenges. WTO rulings on EU banana trade have dealt this industry a crippling blow. The filing of WTO complaints by Australia and Brazil on 27 September 2002 in respect of the EU sugar protocol threatens similar damage. Tourism, a mature industry, displays the characteristics of the economically aged, i.e. outmoded products, production inflexibility, high cost-returns ratios and vulnerability to newcomers."[5]

At the bottom line, in an international milieu that is unhelpful to their economic growth and development, Caribbean jurisdictions now operate and enforce standards and practices to curb money laundering that are higher, tougher and more stringent than obtain in many FATF countries.

Money laundering in the Caribbean has not disappeared, and it probably never will, but the instances of it, which were relatively small to begin with, have been dramatically reduced, and the opportunities for it have been strangled to a far greater extent than in many OECD and FATF countries.

What is more the machinery for international co-operation in anti-money laundering and counter terrorism financing, including information exchange on criminal matters, is well established and is working.

Through mutual evaluations of each other's jurisdictions under the umbrella of the Caribbean Financial Action Task Force, Caribbean states are also monitoring their own performance regularly and remedying deficiencies in their systems.

In connection with all this, governments in the region need all the help they can get in order to ensure that the anti-money laundering and counter terrorism financing frameworks that continue to be constructed are supported and adequately maintained. They are, after all, small economies with limited resources that are being thinly spread to meet developmental needs as well as the demands for increased security and anti-money laundering and counter terrorism financing measures. Their resources are simply insufficient to satisfy all the demands.

The international community – especially those countries of the

FATF that make the greatest demands – must be willing to help. Failing this, criminal organisations will resume their activities using their significant wealth to corrupt officials of both the public and private sectors and so channel their illegal funds into the financial system.

IMF/WORLD BANK SUBSTITUTE FOR FATF

In the midst of all this, a new and worrying development has taken place.

Claiming that they were responding to criticisms of their lack of legitimacy in setting and imposing international standards and practices to curb money laundering, the FATF decided in October 2003 to allow the International Monetary Fund and the World Bank, on a 12-month pilot project, to jointly undertake assessments of jurisdictions for anti-money laundering and counter terrorism financing.

On the face of it, this might appear to be a good development, one which internationalises the governance of the money laundering issue. Such an assumption would be misleading.

Caribbean countries were not consulted directly about the transfer of this matter to the IMF/World Bank or on the content and scope of the methodology that would be applied.

Caribbean Ministers have taken the most strenuous objection to the procedures followed in relation to the purported 'transfer' and the methodology contemplated by the IMF in furtherance of it. These concerns were conveyed directly to the staff of the Fund at a Ministerial Meeting of the CFATF in The Bahamas on 17 October 2002 and again, more recently, and more vigorously, at a similar encounter with IMF representatives in Barbados on 15 January 2003.

The Caribbean has taken the view that the fight against money laundering and terrorism financing is firmly rooted in the criminal justice system of all countries based on the original requirements of the Vienna Convention. They consider that the current IMF/World Bank initiative goes beyond the mandate of the bank and Fund and should be a matter for full discussion at the annual meeting of the IMF/World Bank group later in the year when all member countries are present.

In that context they called for a truly global forum on money laundering convened under the auspices of the United Nations with a view to concluding an international convention that would set agreed standards to be applied equally to all jurisdictions.[6]

INTERNATIONAL GUNRUNNING

With regard to international gunrunning, there have been few such instances associated with the Caribbean. In the best-known cases, the Caribbean was used as a transhipment point; none of the material originated in the Region.

These incidents were illegal in the jurisdictions in which they occurred, and actions have been taken to guard against their recurrence.

FIREARMS TRAFFICKING INTO THE CARIBBEAN

Trafficking in firearms into the Caribbean is a different story.

This pernicious activity is linked to the drug trade. Narcotics traffickers use weapons for protecting shipments, intimidating customers or competitors and executing informants. Dependent drug users tend also to commit crimes to obtain money to fund their drug purchases and may use firearms that are illegally obtained to perpetrate violent crimes.[7]

The increased number of murders in some countries in the Region, particularly of Police and other law enforcement officers, is directly linked to the trafficking in drugs and the associated trafficking in firearms.

Trafficking in firearms in the Caribbean, therefore, poses a far greater threat to the security and stability of the Region than it does to the rest of the world.

As a Caribbean Community Task Force on Crime and Security observed recently:

"The seemingly uncontrollable rise in armed crime and violence as evidenced by the unusually high murder rates in some member states has not only threatened legitimate governments but has become very serious threats to the basic fabric of our societies".[8]

There is a popular belief that the increase in sophisticated crime is, in part, attributable to the deportation of criminals by the United States and Canada to the Caribbean countries of their origin, sometimes tenuously ascribed. Some statistics indicate that a percentage of these deportees are charged with crimes in the countries to which they are returned, but it is doubtful that the statistics are a sound indicator since many who plan and organise and commit crimes may not be caught.

In addition, there is now some evidence of a network of criminals throughout the Caribbean who were known to each other in Canada and the United States. Through this network a criminal could be imported from one Caribbean country to carry out a criminal activity in another where he has no Police record or profile.

Concern over this matter of the impact of deportees on the escalating rate of crime sufficiently exercised Caribbean Community Heads of Government at a Conference in February 2003 that they agreed that the existing "Association of Caribbean Commissioners of Police must be recognised and institutionalised as an agency of the Community, reporting to a Joint Committee of Attorneys-General and Ministers Responsible for National security".[9] The point of this is to design more effective tracking, monitoring and control of high-risk deportees (and other high risk criminals) including sharing information on their profiles and their movements between one Caribbean country and another.

KIDNAPPING – A GROWING INDUSTRY?

Kidnapping in Guyana and Trinidad and Tobago is now part and parcel of the crime scene with deleterious effects for investment and economic and social development in these countries. Although the governments of the two countries are yet to calculate the effect of these kidnappings on domestic and foreign investment, they have become so bad that one Caribbean criminologist has described them as an "industry".[10] Anecdotal evidence suggests that investment and tourism have been badly affected, and even social life curtailed. People are shunning restaurants and public places for fear of being kidnapped.

Up to 20 April, Guyana with a population of approximately 700,000 had experienced 20 kidnappings for the first four months of 2003;

Trinidad and Tobago with 1.5 million people had 65 abductions. According to the Police Commissioner in Trinidad more than US$3.3 million had been demanded in ransoms and just over US$1 million had been paid out.[11] The figure in Guyana had not been quantified but it is well known that the ransom asked for the most publicised case, that of Regional Security Officer at the US Embassy, Stephen Lesinak, the sum of US$300,000 was demanded although, in the end, his girlfriend was reported to have paid US$15,000.[12]

Kidnapping in the English-speaking Caribbean started in Jamaica, as part of the armoury of drug traffickers. Persons who were potential witnesses in drug cases before the courts or police informants were kidnapped and murdered. Seldom was any ransom sought.

In Guyana and Trinidad and Tobago, while kidnapping has emerged from a growing culture of crime linked to drug trafficking, it is focused on the payment of ransoms.

What is significant about the phenomenon of kidnapping in both countries, as is also the case in Jamaica, is that the police seem powerless to stop it. A leading Trinidadian criminologist has suggested that there may even be police collusion, part of the web of corruption that is the underlay to the carpet of crime in the Region.[13]

Police collusion or not, kidnapping is now a huge problem in Guyana and Trinidad and Tobago, and given the copycat mentality that has been evident in other forms of aberrant behaviour in the Caribbean, it may not be too long before it spreads into other parts of the Region.

DRUG TRAFFICKING

In 1992, in what turned out to be a prescient observation, a Commission established by Caribbean Community Heads of Government to chart a course for the Caribbean into the 21st Century, said this:

"Nothing poses greater threats to the civil society in the Caribbean Community countries than the drug problem; and nothing exemplifies the powerlessness of the regional governments more".[14]

Over the last decade the problem has simply worsened.

Individual Caribbean countries do not have the resources to match the vast capacity of the drug traffickers. A recent report reveals that, "the Caribbean is emerging as a major supplier of drugs to Europe as the total income generated from the illicit drug industry in the region last year totalled more than three billion US dollars".[15] With regard to the United States, the Report also stated that while cocaine use in that country decreased, cocaine exports transhipped through the Caribbean to the US market rose from 29 percent in 1990 to 48 percent in 2001".[16]

None of this means that Regional governments have not tried. Again, scarce resources were diverted from social and economic programmes to fight drug trafficking. Evidence of these efforts is the increase in both the number of arrests of traffickers and the seizure of drugs. The majority of prisoners in the now over crowded jails of the Caribbean are drug offenders.

Despite the best efforts of governments, the Caribbean, because of its geographical location between the supplier and market nations, remains a significant corridor for illicit drugs.

Yet, we are witnessing now a marked withdrawal of resources from the Caribbean by the international community to address this problem at a time when the range of criminal activity that it spawns is threatening the economic, social and political stability of the Region.

THE CRIME SITUATION IN THE REGION

The types of crimes that are now prevalent directly affect good governance through the corruption of law enforcement agencies, but they threaten governance itself through violent crimes such as murders – including killings of police officers, witnesses, and competitors.

In 2002, there were 1,040 murders in Jamaica (amongst the highest per capita in the world), 171 in Trinidad and Tobago and 152 in Guyana of which 16 were policemen. Dominica witnessed an increase of 17 percent in major crimes between 2001 and 2002.[17]

Up to 5 May 2003, nine policemen had already been gunned down for the year in the Guyana streets, and up to 1 May 2003, the number of murders in Trinidad and Tobago had reached 71 for the year.

The situation in Guyana was so alarming in March 2003 that the

241

Secretary-General of the Caribbean Community and his staff issued a public statement in which they said:

> "No issue has concerned us more than the rising crime wave which threatens to envelop the Region. And in this regard, no situation has disturbed us more than that in Guyana, the Headquarters of the Community, and the Member State wherein we and our families have made our home, however temporarily.
>
> The sudden and persistent violent loss of life which marks a dramatic departure from the Guyana we had come to know, and now risks becoming part of the social culture, is one which is having tremendous negative effect on the Guyanese Community, including the staff of our Organisation, some of whom have been directly affected.[18]

This upsurge in crime, linked to drug trafficking, has been facilitated by the economic downturn in Caribbean countries occasioned by loss of markets for their primary products, a reduction in aid, a decline in foreign investment, a decline in tourism and a hostile onslaught on their financial services sector.

Nonetheless, Caribbean countries have been committing scarce resources to fighting transnational crimes that are less of a threat to the Caribbean than it is to other countries in the international community.

REDUCTION OF SUPPORT FROM INTERNATIONAL COMMUNITY

In this extremely troubling situation, the international community has been less than forthcoming in supporting the efforts of Caribbean governments to tackle the problems.

Instead, there has been an obvious reduction in support to Caribbean drug law enforcement. The European Commission Drug Control Office, which operated from 1999 to 2001, was closed; the post of a Caribbean-based UK police adviser was removed to be replaced by an adviser based in London; the Caribbean United Nations Office on Drugs and Crime was significantly scaled down; the US Caribbean Drugs Control Co-ordinator was recalled; and a Regional

Maritime Co-operation Project ended – this project was the mechanism for collaboration among Caribbean States in the restriction of drug trafficking by maritime means.

When the Guyana government appealed to the United States for help in coping with the spiralling crime situation, they were directed to a private agency whose bill would have to be met by a country considered to be amongst the poorest in the Region.

It is significant that when the international community was providing assistance, the entire focus was on restricting the supply of drugs with little or no attention to the problems that transhipment was creating for Caribbean countries themselves. Thus, a British Foreign Office Minister, Mike O'Brien, while estimating that 65 percent of cocaine going to Europe originates in the Caribbean, hailed as "an excellent example of international co-operation in the fight against drugs", the seizure by the Grenada coast guard in March 2003 of 150 kilos of cocaine with a street value of US$13.76 million. The UK government provided US$427,305 for the financial year 2002/2003 to train East Caribbean Coast Guards in operational skills needed to intercept drugs.

POLICY OPTIONS

Caribbean countries have already instituted policies to address the transnational crimes that are a problem in the region.

These have been most successful in the areas of curbing money laundering and countering terrorism financing.

Drug trafficking, however, has become the pillar of transnational criminal activity in the Caribbean resulting in an exponential increase in corruption and violent crime. In Guyana and Trinidad and Tobago, kidnapping purely for ransom has also emerged as a major destabilizing phenomenon both economically and socially.

Regional governments are considering how best to institute several measures to try to meet the overwhelming phenomenon of crime and security against the background of studies undertaken by a Task Force on Crime established in July 2001.

They have also instructed that a Regional Plan for a co-ordinated response to crime be completed to provide a framework for regional collaboration.

ACTION BY REGIONAL GOVERNMENTS

Some analysts of the Regional scene, especially the noted West Indian journalist Rickey Singh, have shown dissatisfaction with the slow pace of regional governments in implementing regional machinery for dealing aggressively with crime.[19]

At least one Caribbean Head of Government is also unhappy that there has been too much study of the problem and not enough action. Antigua and Barbuda's Prime Minister Lester Bird has been calling since February 2001 for regional mechanisms that would deal immediately with the problem of crime.

He has argued for the establishment of a Regional Authority to effectively formulate and implement an anti-narcotics strategy and also for the creation of a Regional Rapid Response Unit dealing with drug-related and serious crimes throughout the Caribbean Community countries.

According to Bird, the proposed Regional Authority would be a Caribbean Drug Control and Crime Prevention Office (CDCPP) – working to a Council of Ministers of National Security.

He envisaged that the Office "would be charged with the responsibility of devising and approving a regional anti-narcotics and crime prevention strategy; managing the policy including supervising the drug enforcement units; drafting common anti-narcotics legislation; negotiating co-operation treaties with other countries; executing an educational programme against drugs, and mounting a diplomatic *démarche* on behalf of all Caribbean states".

In justifying the importance of a Regional Authority, Prime Minister Bird argued, "It is inconceivable to me that we, in CARICOM, could be moving as rapidly as we are toward a Caribbean Single Market and Economy (CSME) with all the unrestricted movement of goods, and the increased freer movement of people, without an attendant mechanism for addressing the problems of increased drug trafficking that is bound to flow from it".

The Antigua and Barbuda Prime Minister also argued for the early establishment of a single well-trained, well-equipped, Rapid Response Unit dealing with drug-related and serious crimes throughout the Caribbean Community countries.

He elaborated that the Rapid Response Unit should ideally fall under a Committee of Commissioners of Police who would themselves be an institution of the CDCCP. As he saw it, through a series of Memoranda of Understanding, the Unit would be deployed into each member country to conduct investigations and make the necessary arrests.

Mr Bird justified the need for the Unit on the reality facing local police forces. He said:

"To expect ill-equipped, ill-trained national police forces to successfully fight the sophisticated trafficking of illegal narcotics is almost an impossibility. Many of our countries do not now have the resources to equip and train our police forces individually. It is unlikely that even in the medium-term we will separately have the resources for such an undertaking.

Therefore, we have to pool our resources to select the best officers from all our national forces to form the special response unit. They can then be trained and properly equipped to gather intelligence, investigate crimes, and make arrests. Financing for the unit would come from each government on a formula similar to contributions to the CARICOM Secretariat.

The fact that this will be a regional response unit with its members having no particular ties to the communities in individual States would provide it with an objectivity that would be advantageous to its work."[20]

Had such a Unit been created, it would have undoubtedly been of immense assistance to Guyana and Trinidad and Tobago in curbing the spate of kidnappings that they have experienced. Thus far, however, Caribbean governments have taken no action on either of Prime Minister Bird's proposals, though the Regional Task Force on Crime and Security has considered both ideas.

ACTION BY THE INTERNATIONAL COMMUNITY

The Regional Plan formulated by the Task Force as well as Prime Minister Bird's proposals could form the agenda for a limited International Conference that considers the problem of violent crime, drug trafficking and illegal arms in the Caribbean in the context of a "development" agenda.

For, if the problem continues to escalate it will suck scarce government resources away from education, health and poverty alleviation. It will also scare away investment and curtail economic growth. Quite soon, the relatively stable Caribbean could slip into social and economic deprivation and political instability, rendering it vulnerable to the adventures of those external terrorist organisations now targeting the interests of US and other industrialised nations.

With the best will in the world, Caribbean countries will not win the battle against drug trafficking and all its pernicious consequences, unless they receive meaningful support from the international community, particularly those countries whose demand for illegal narcotics sustains and enlarges the traffic.

There is an urgent need for the international community to address the problem of violent crime in the Caribbean that has resulted from drug trafficking and illegal arms.

Caribbean governments should work for the early convening of an international conference on Crime in the Caribbean. In addition to the Caribbean countries themselves, participation should include the relevant United Nations agencies, the Commonwealth Secretariat, the Organisation of American States (OAS), the European Commission, the IMF, World Bank and the Inter-American Development Bank, as well as interested countries such as The United States, the United Kingdom, Canada, Spain, France and The Netherlands. The latter two countries are included because of their overseas territories in the Caribbean, and Spain because of its ties to the Dominican Republic in the Caribbean and to neighbouring countries in the Caribbean Sea.

The Commonwealth Secretariat, which already has a mandate to tackle issues of importance to Small States, should be approached to work with the United Nations Office on Drugs and Crime (UNODC) in Vienna in organising and convening the Conference which should be held at the highest level.

Such a conference should treat the problem in "developmental" terms and not simply as crime. The CARICOM Task Force on Crime and Security underscored the urgency of this when they observed in their Summary Report:

"The negative impact of crime and violence on the sustainable development of most member states compels us to see a clear link between crime prevention and development strategies. Foreign investment, which is an essential requirement in the development process, is impeded by the social instability which exists in several member states. Social stability, on the other hand, can only be achieved if there is specific investment in the communities. This 'chicken and egg' situation, in the view of the Task Force, necessitates an urgent shift in emphasis from that which approaches crime as "security issue" to one that tackles crime as a "developmental and social issue".[21]

An important item on the agenda of such a Conference should be 'demand reduction in the narcotics importing States', for the problem of narcotics cultivation and trafficking will never be adequately and comprehensively addressed until the issue of demand is tackled comprehensively.

If the Caribbean is not provided urgent assistance to confront the overwhelming problem of crime, this idyllic Region – playground of holiday makers from Europe and North America and a haven of democracy and economic and social stability – may very well become an area shunned by tourists and investors with all the disastrous consequences both domestically and internationally that such an unfortunate development would cause, including the possible creation of a base for international terrorism and financial crime.

NOTES & REFERENCES

1   This chapter is an expanded version of a Keynote Speech delivered in Ottawa, Canada at a Conference on "Crime in the Caribbean Basin: Options on Transnational Crime", organised by the Canadian Foundation for the Americas on Monday, 3 March 2003. It was first published by Hansib Publications in May 2003 and then in *The Round Table: The Commonwealth Journal of International Affairs*, London, July 2003.

2   See, letter from Sir Ronald Sanders to Donald Johnston, Secretary-General of the OECD, dated 27 January 2003 on website: www.antigua-barbuda.com

3   Letter dated 17 February 2003 from Donald Johnston, Secretary-General of the OECD to Sir Ronald Sanders.

4   The exception is St Vincent & The Grenadines and the expectation is that the FATF will remove it from the list in mid 2003.

5   "Small States in the context of Global Change", Professor Compton Bourne OE, President of the Caribbean Development Bank, at 4th Annual Conference of Sir Arthur Lewis Institute of Social Studies, University of the West Indies, 15 January 2003, Sherbourne Conference Centre, Barbados.

6   Communiqué of Special Ministerial Meeting of the Caribbean Financial Action Task Force (CFATF) with IMF representatives in Barbados on 15 January 2003.

7   Final Report of the CARICOM Regional Task Force on Crime and Security, presented to CARICOM Heads of Government Conference in Guyana in July 2002.

8   Summary Report of the Seventh Meeting of CARICOM Task Force on Crime and Security: Priority Proposals on Crime Prevention, Paper for the consideration of the Inter-Sessional Meeting of Heads of Government, Trinidad, 14-15 February 2003.

9   Communiqué of the 14th Inter-Sessional Meeting of the Caribbean Community (CARICOM) Heads of Government Conference held in Trinidad, 14-15 February, 2003.

10 Professor Ramesh Deosaran, independent legislator speaking in the Senate of Trinidad and Tobago, and reported by CMC on 20 April 2003.

11 Police Commissioner Hilton Guy, reported by CMC on 20 April 2003.

12 *Caribbean Insight*, Vol. 26, No. 13, 11 April 2003, London.

13 Professor Ramesh Deosaran, Op Cit, note 1.

14 *Time for Action – Report of the West Indian Commission*, June 1992.

15 Report of Caribbean Regional Office of the United Nations Office on Drugs and Crime, cited in the CMC news report, 26 February 2003.

16 *Ibid.*

17 Statement by Acting Prime Minister Osborne Reviere at the opening of a legal aid clinic in Dominica on Friday, 25 April, reported by CMC.

18 Statement issued by Edwin Carrington, the Secretary-General of CARICOM and his staff, CARICOM Secretariat, Georgetown, 8 March 2003.

19 See, for instance, 'Caricom's Crime Spree', by Rickey Singh, Guyana Chronicle, 5 January 2003.

20 A Concept Paper on dealing with drug-related crime, presented by Lester Bird, Prime Minister of Antigua and Barbuda, to 22nd Conference of CARICOM Heads of Government, in Nassau, Bahamas on 5 July 2001.

21 Op. Cit., Note 7.

INDEX

249